Animals, politics and morality

Published in our
centenary year
 2004
MANCHESTER
UNIVERSITY
PRESS

Issues in Environmental Politics

series editors Mikael Skou Andersen and Duncan Liefferink

At the start of the twenty-first century, the environment has come to stay as a central concern of global politics. This series takes key problems for environmental policy and examines the politics behind their cause and possible resolution. Accessible and eloquent, the books make available for a non-specialist readership some of the best research and most provocative thinking on humanity's relationship with the planet.

already published in the series

Animals, politics and morality

Second edition

Robert Garner

Manchester University Press

Manchester and New York

distributed exclusively in the USA by Palgrave

Copyright © Robert Garner 1993, 2004

The right of Robert Garner to be identified as the author of this work has been
asserted by him in accordance with the Copyright, Designs and Patents Act
1988.

First edition published 1993 by Manchester University Press
Reprinted 1994

This edition published 2004 by
Manchester University Press
Oxford Road, Manchester M13 9NR, UK
and Room 400, 175 Fifth Avenue, New York, NY 10010, USA
www.manchesteruniversitypress.co.uk

Distributed exclusively in the USA by
Palgrave, 175 Fifth Avenue, New York,
NY 10010, USA

Distributed exclusively in Canada by
UBC Press, University of British Columbia, 2029 West Mall,
Vancouver, BC, Canada V6T 1Z2

British Library Cataloguing-in-Publication Data
A catalogue record for this book is available from the British Library

Library of Congress Cataloging-in-Publication Data applied for

ISBN   0 7190 6620 4   *hardback*
EAN   978 0 7190 6620 7
ISBN   0 7190 6621 2   *paperback*
EAN   978 0 7190 6621 4

This edition first published 2004

13 12 11 10 09 08 07 06 05 04   10 9 8 7 6 5 4 3 2 1

Typeset in Sabon
by Action Publishing Technology L
Printed in Great Britain
by Bell & Bain Ltd, Glasgow

Contents

Tables

Preface

It is over ten years now since the first edition of this book was published in 1993. Since then, there have been significant developments which more than justify, I believe, this substantially revised and updated second edition. We have witnessed major campaigns and public controversy over the export of live animals, and the use of animals in research. Major campaigns have been mounted against companies such as Shamrock and Huntingdon Life Sciences. The impact of genetic engineering on the welfare of animals has also emerged as an important area of concern. In addition, the controversy over hunting has become even more pronounced, primarily because of the election, in 1997, of the first Labour government for almost twenty years, and the launch of the pro-hunting Countryside Alliance. This government has been generally more proactive on a whole range of animal issues, and legislative and regulatory initiatives at the national and supranational levels have moved on apace. Finally, the welfare of animals has also been an important factor in the BSE and foot and mouth crises visited upon successive British governments.

Partly as a response to the increasing political saliency of animal protection, in Britain and elsewhere, a considerable amount of academic scholarship on the issue, both theoretical and empirical, has been published in the last decade. Of particular importance has been the emergence of a second generation of animal ethics literature, widening and deepening the debate. The fact that this literature includes a critique of the major arguments of the first edition of this book is further justification for taking the time to respond. Finally, my own research on the issue has developed since the early 1990s and this second edition provides an opportunity to review the directions it has taken.

The chapter structure has remained the same but there has been a considerable amount of tinkering, including the renaming of two chapters. Some of the material in the original Chapter 7 on the animal protection movement has been moved to Chapter 2. Chapter 1, on animal ethics, has been expanded, and there is a great deal more information on the role of the EU in Chapter 7 and elsewhere. I have come to think that some of the arguments in Chapter 6 of the first edition, on wild animals, were flawed, and so this chapter has been comprehensively rewritten. Finally, there is a more concerted attempt to engage in a comparative approach, with particular emphasis on developments within the United States.

I would like to repeat what I said in the first edition and point out how fortunate I have been to have had the opportunity to write a book which enables me to combine my professional knowledge as a student of politics with my long-standing interest in, and concern for, the plight of animals and our moral obligations towards them. It still remains the case that the specialised nature of the academic world militates against interdisciplinary projects such as this. I do not hold to the view that academics should avoid pronouncing on controversial social and political issues. To do so is a product of the debilitating trend in liberal theory and practice towards neutrality and an acceptance of moral pluralism. Having said that, this book is not a polemic. But I do hope I manage to persuade at least some that there really is a strong case for fundamental changes in the way we think about, and behave towards, the other species with whom we share the planet.

I wish to thank Tony Mason and Lucy Nicholson at MUP for helping to make the task of preparing the manuscript as painless as possible. I am also grateful to all those organisations who, over the years, have interrupted their busy schedules to answer my pleas for information, to two anonymous referees who provided helpful advice and to my institution, the University of Leicester, for providing study leave to enable me to finish writing the book. The book is dedicated to my gorgeous son Keir, and to his mother Kate.

Abbreviations

AHA	American Humane Association
ALF	Animal Liberation Front
APC	Animal Procedures Committee
ASPCA	American Society for the Prevention of Cruelty to Animals
BALE	Brightlingsea Against Live Exports
BFSS	British Field Sports Society
BSE	Bovine Spongiform Encephalopathy
BUAV	British Union for the Abolition of Vivisection
BVA	British Veterinary Association
CA	Countryside Alliance
CAP	Common Agricultural Policy
CAPS	Captive Animals Protection Society
CBD	Convention on Biological Diversity
CITES	Convention on International Trade in Endangered Species of Wild Fauna and Flora
CJD	Creutzfeldt Jakob Disease
CIWF	Compassion In World Farming
CRAE	Committee for the Reform of Animal Experimentation
DEFRA	Department of the Environment, Food and Rural Affairs
EU	European Union
FARM	Farm Animal Reform Movement
FAWC	Farm Animal Welfare Council
FoE	Friends of the Earth
FRAME	Fund for the Replacement of Animals in Medical Experiments

GECCAP	General Election Co-ordinating Committee for Animal Protection
HLS	Huntingdon Life Sciences
HSA	Hunt Saboteurs Association
HSUS	Humane Society of the United States
ICBP	International Council for Bird Preservation
ICRW	International Convention for the Regulation of Whaling
IFAW	International Fund for Animal Welfare
IUCN	International Union for Conservation of Nature and Natural Resources
IWC	International Whaling Commission
LACS	League Against Cruel Sports
NAVS	National Anti-Vivisection Society
NCDL	National Canine Defence League (now Dogs Trust)
NFU	National Farmers' Union
NIH	National Institutes of Health
PDSA	People's Dispensary for Sick Animals
PETA	People for the Ethical Treatment of Animals
RDS	Research Defence Society
RSNC	Royal Society for Nature Conservation
RSPB	Royal Society for the Protection of Birds
RSPCA	Royal Society for the Prevention of Cruelty to Animals
SHAC	Stop Huntingdon Animal Cruelty
UFAW	Universities Federation for Animal Welfare
UNCED	United Nations Conference on Environment and Development
UNESCO	United Nations Educational, Scientific and Cultural Organization
WSPA	World Society for the Protection of Animals
WTO	World Trade Organisation
WWF	World Wide Fund for Nature

Introduction

Our treatment of, and attitudes towards, animals varies to quite an extraordinary degree – from concern, respect, devotion and even love at one end of the spectrum to fear, neglect, cruelty and torture at the other. Acts of violence towards animals (often sanctioned by the law) are countered by acts of violence on behalf of animals. This book is about these apparently contradictory responses. It seeks to examine moral theories that endeavour to tell us how we ought to treat animals, as well as how individuals and the law actually do treat them. That there is a political dimension here is precisely because increasing numbers of people feel there is a gap between what morality prescribes and the law allows.

Of course, the relationship between animals and humans has long been subject to philosophical, scientific and political debate.[1] Over the past three decades or so, however, there has been a major upsurge in public interest and activity which has put the issue firmly on to the political agenda. The long-standing animal protection lobby has been revitalised and a plethora of new groups has emerged to campaign for radical change. As a result, countervailing forces, seeking to defend the traditional use of animals for human benefit, have had to mobilise in order to challenge this threat to the status quo. Both as a cause and effect of this expansion of pressure group activity, public opinion has become much more willing to accept the view that at least some harms done to animals need to be alleviated. Central to this explosion of concern has been the philosophical input. Since the 1970s, those concerned about the treatment of animals have had the benefit of a sustained attempt by academic philosophers to change radically the status afforded to animals in moral thinking. This has had profound implications both for the movement which seeks to protect animals and for the way in which the debate about their treatment has been conducted.

The moral status of animals

Philosophic debate about the moral status of animals is not new. Many illustrious thinkers, from Aristotle to Descartes to Bentham in the nineteenth century, have considered this issue (see Clarke and Linzey, 1990 and Regan and Singer, 1976). The contemporary debate, however, differs in two principal ways. In the first place, the volume of literature available has increased dramatically. Thus, in his extensive bibliography, Charles Magel (1989: 13–25) allocates ten pages for philosophical material on animals up to 1970 and no less than thirteen pages for material published after that date. Since the late 1980s, this literature has mushroomed even further. Our treatment of animals is now taken seriously as a mainstream branch of applied ethics to be examined along with other moral questions, such as abortion and euthanasia, in degree level philosophy courses and is increasingly a topic for discussion in schools. As one commentator noted, in 1969 the Philosopher's Index did not even recognise the heading 'animals', whereas in 1980 alone forty articles specifically related to the issue were listed (Nelson, 1985: 13). Likewise, Peter Singer (1990: 241), writing in the second edition of his ground-breaking critique of the moral orthodoxy, could state that, in the early 1970s, 'I had to search hard to find a handful of references by academic philosophers on the issue of the status of animals; today I could have filled this entire book with an account of what has been written on this topic during the past fifteen years.'

Secondly, much of this recent literature has challenged the widespread assumption that animals have an inferior moral status to humans. Since the nineteenth century, most legislation affecting animals has assumed that, whilst humans have an obligation to avoid inflicting unnecessary suffering on animals, we are entitled to use them for our benefit. This itself was progress, since before then there was a widespread belief, influenced by the Christian tradition of Man's dominion over non-human nature, that animals existed for the use of humans and that we had no moral obligations towards them. Such a view sanctioned what we would now regard as unbelievable acts of cruelty. Gradually, through the influence of the work of intellectuals such as Bentham and Darwin, humanitarian activists and a general change in the social climate, some of the worst excesses of animal abuse were ended. Indeed, by the early part of the twentieth century, the framework of modern animal welfare legislation was in place, at least in Britain. The animal protection movement remained active but, with few exceptions, the debate was largely constrained within the framework provided by the moral orthodoxy. That is, there was no sustained challenge to the view that only unnecessary suffering should be avoided; only occasional disputes as to what constituted animal suffering.

Since the 1960s, however, there has been a radical change in the debate. Two works in the 1960s – Brigid Brophy's article for the *Sunday Times* (1965) and Ruth Harrison's *Animal Machines* (1964), a thorough-going critique of factory farming – set the scene for a major explosion of intellectual challenges to the moral orthodoxy from 1970 onwards. The Oxford connection here was marked. In 1972, three Oxford philosophers – Roslind and Stanley Godlovitch and John Harris – edited a set of articles collectively published as *Animals, Men and Morals*, with contributions by Brophy, Harrison and Richard Ryder, among others. In 1973 this volume was reviewed by Peter Singer (an Oxford-educated Australian university teacher) in the *New York Review of Books*. Encouraged by the response, Singer proceeded to write *Animal Liberation* (published in America in 1975 and in Britain a year later) which, in an impressive mix of philosophical arguments and empirical evidence, provided a radical critique of our treatment of animals and the moral orthodoxy on which it was based (further references to Singer's book relate to the second edition published in 1990).

Singer bases his case, as we shall see, on utilitarian grounds. Others sought to articulate a case for treating animals, along with humans, as beings who are holders of rights. The initial attempts were provided by Andrew Linzey (1976; 1987), from a Christian perspective, and Stephen Clark (1984). To complete the Oxford connection (both Linzey and Clark have Oxford backgrounds) mention should also be made of Richard Ryder (whose book

Victims of Science, published in 1975, was an influential – animal rights-based – attack on the use of animals for experimental purposes) and Mary Midgley (1979; 1983) who has also written extensively on the moral case for treating animals with greater respect. Meanwhile, on the other side of the Atlantic, the philosopher Tom Regan began to develop, in a series of articles (1982), a rights-based critique of the moral orthodoxy culminating in *The Case for Animal Rights* (1984), a lengthy and sophisticated work which has earned him a formidable reputation within the animal protection movement and, indeed, beyond.

This first wave of intellectual challenges to the orthodox position has been supplemented since by a second generation of substantial texts, partly responding to the philosophical backlash against the idea of animal rights provided by authors such as Carruthers (1992), Leahy (1991) and Scruton (2000), and partly taking the debate in new and interesting directions. The result is that there is now a considerable body of diverse work upon which the animal protection movement can call. These ideological challenges also provide us with a framework within which to consider the contemporary debate about animals. It reminds us of the crucial point that how we treat animals depends upon our moral assessment of their worth. Thus, if we are to grant them an inferior moral status or, indeed, no moral status whatsoever, a justification is required – and such a justification must spell out why it is that we are entitled to treat them differently from ourselves and what it is that their moral status entitles us to do to them. The impact of the 'new' morality here is, of course, central. For the language it uses towards animals is not structured around charity but is about justice; not, that is, exclusively about the sentimentalism of showing mercy in our treatment of animals but of treating them well because we have duties and obligations to treat them with respect. It is not even necessary to like them. Indeed, for the modern animal rights activist, to be called an 'animal lover', as the media persist in doing, is to belittle the deadly seriousness of the cause. Just as my decision whether or not to harm another human being should be independent of whether I like that person or not, my decision whether or not to harm a member of any other species should be based on the same criteria (Brophy, 1979: 65).

Animals, objectivity and the scope of this book

The contemporary debate about animals, then, has been structured around competing moral theories. As a reflection of their importance, Chapter 1 is devoted to a consideration of the considerable bulk of philosophical literature on the moral status of animals that has appeared in recent years. What has made this philosophical debate so important, of course, has been its impact on the realm of practical politics.

In Chapter 2, the re-emergence of the animal protection movement is documented, an attempt is made at a classification of its key characteristics, and a number of explanations for its development are explored. What is revealed is that the growing influence of the 'new' morality emphasising animal liberation and rights has revitalised the movement by successfully challenging the prevailing ideological orthodoxy of a passive welfarism. This, however, has been achieved at the cost of internal dissension.

With the rise of a movement to expound the radical philosophy, the debate about the treatment of animals has also fundamentally changed and Chapters 3 to 6 seek to examine the nature of this debate by relating competing moral theories to the variety of uses to which humans put animals. By so doing we can assess more effectively the extent to which these uses and the law related to them are justified. Before we can pass judgement on any specific use of animals, though, two further tasks are necessary (Dawkins, 1980: 128).

Firstly, it is obviously crucial to know what is done to animals – how they are kept, how many are involved and so on – and, secondly, an assessment of the level of suffering is required. This, of course, necessitates an analysis of the impact of a particular practice on an animal's welfare. Welfare in this sense is an objective term referring to 'its state as regards its attempts to cope with its environment'. It is thus possible to measure, utilising a variety of devices, an animal's welfare in a particular environment and locate it on a continuum from good to poor (Fraser and Broom, 1990: 41). This assessment of suffering is obviously related to moral questions since the level of suffering involved will affect our ethical judgement. Indeed, the development of the science of animal welfare has itself altered moral positions by demonstrating the complexity and sophistication of animal behaviour and the capacity of animals to suffer, which can go beyond merely experiencing pain (259).

How we ought to treat animals, however, remains a question that is distinct from the extent to which they suffer. Purely objective assessments of animal welfare do not by themselves tell us whether the infliction of suffering is justified without some prior moral theory. In addition, it is arguably the case that welfare judgements only apply whilst an animal is alive and, if so, they have nothing to say on the crucial moral question of whether it is right to kill animals where no suffering (pain or fear or whatever) is involved. Nevertheless, it is obviously crucial to describe accurately what happens to animals in human hands, whether this be in the home, the circus or the zoo (the subject of Chapter 3), on the farm (the subject of Chapter 4), in the laboratory (the subject of Chapter 5) or in the wild (the subject of Chapter 6).

A central aim of the animal protection movement, of course, is to achieve political change. As Chapters 7 and 8 reveal, there are a variety of arenas within which the animals issue can be debated and decisions taken, and a variety of strategies have been adopted by the animal protection movement (and its opponents) to try to influence decision makers. It will become apparent that the debate about tactics has been deeply affected by the radical challenge to animal welfarism. Not surprisingly, the radical conviction that much more is wrong with our treatment of animals than had previously been recognised has led to a greater campaigning zeal. In turn, however, this has provoked perennial disputes about the direction the newly invigorated movement should follow.

Two major dimensions have become apparent. In the first place, there is the question, examined in Chapter 7, of whether animal protection groups should, on the one hand, seek to engage in a regular dialogue with government, accepting the need for compromises inherent in a pluralistic decision-making structure or, on the other, whether moral purity should be retained in the form of mass campaigns to alter the social climate through influencing consumers and voters. Secondly, there is the issue of direct action. It is the willingness of some elements in the animal protection movement to take direct action that has provoked the greatest publicity for the cause of animal protection in recent years. In Chapter 8, therefore, we explore the wide variety of forms this direct action has taken and look at reactions to it from inside and outside the movement, before considering its moral and political justifications. In Chapters 7 and 8 attention is devoted to the nature of modern pressure group politics and, in particular, it is asked, with the help of various theoretical approaches, to what extent the political system provides for fair competition between the animal protection movement and those with a vested interest in continuing to exploit animals.

This book, then, is about the growing political relevance of animals. It is focused on Britain, although extensive reference is made to other countries and particularly the United States. The issues covered are complex and contentious, and I am conscious that justice is not done to some (perhaps even many) of them here. A detailed coverage was not, in any case, the intention. Rather, the more limited aim is to identify key themes, controversies and players in the debate. In particular, the relationship between moral theory and practice is examined in order to show how central the former is both in terms of the way in which we, as individuals, treat animals and in terms of how the political battle has been, and continues to be, fought out.

Although this is primarily a work of political science in the sense that it is as much *about* the movement for change as *for* it, as much of the available literature is, it is not claimed that this is a detached or impartial account. I must admit to a sneaking admiration for Stephen Clark's (1984: 3) admission that he is 'not engaged in any pretence of standing above the fray: I am a committed crank and zoophile, and my hope is to convert my audience'. Such an approach has the advantage of a clearly stated position which is the best means of furthering any subsequent debate. In addition, by seeking to convert minds and thereby behaviour, it promotes a much-neglected aspect of academic discourse. Of course, whether one can attain objectivity in social science is in any case debatable and this is particularly the case with an issue which is connected inextricably with moral principles – hardly the stuff of cast-iron certainties! In this context – of both the validity, and perhaps inevitability, of presenting a case imbued with the values of its author – it will be argued that the widely accepted assumption of human moral superiority lies on surprisingly shaky foundations and that justice requires that animals are owed more than we feel able, at present, to give them.

Personal prescriptions count for little, however, in the context of harsh political realities where human interests remain paramount. The animal protection movement may have been reinvigorated by philosophical radicalism, but it is probably fair to claim that it has achieved most in recent years when it has sought to challenge the importance (and sometimes the very existence) of the benefits it is claimed humans derive from making animals suffer rather than from the ethically-based denial that humans have a right to benefit from such suffering. In the pages that follow, then, it is suggested that even if we have a fairly low opinion of their moral worth – inferior to humans but having interests which should not be sacrificed unnecessarily – the concept of unnecessary suffering is sufficiently flexible for there to be a great deal that could be done, and is beginning to be done, to improve the lot of animals.

Note

1 For the sake of simplicity, the terms *humans* and *animals* will be used throughout this book. This is not to imply, of course, that there is a great gulf between the two. It is recognised that the term *animals* can equally be applied to humans who can then be contrasted with non-human animals.

1
Animal ethics

Philosophers throughout the ages have considered the moral status of animals, and those who have in the past sought to improve the ways in which they are treated have done so primarily because they perceived a moral wrong that needed correcting. More than at any time in the past, however, the contemporary debate about animals has been nurtured by moral philosophy, and much of it seeks to challenge the orthodox way in which we think about, and behave towards, animals. Because this new radical philosophy has had a profound influence on the development of the modern animal protection movement, and hence the content of the social and political debate about animals, this first chapter is devoted to an assessment of its claims.

To cut a very long story short, determining the moral status of animals or, to put it another way, deciding how we ought to treat them, depends largely on identifying morally relevant differences between humans and animals. If we decide there are not any then there is nothing to prevent us from regarding animals and humans as morally equal. In this scenario, we would not be morally entitled to treat animals any differently from humans, so if we do not eat humans or experiment on them in laboratories then we are not entitled to use animals in this way either. Of course, we all know that animals differ from humans in a large variety of ways, but these differences need to be *morally* relevant to have any impact on the moral worth of animals and humans. There is a widespread acceptance now, for instance, that the race or gender of a human has no bearing upon his/her moral status, and to say otherwise is to invite a charge of racism or sexism. The question for us is whether species is a morally relevant difference, or whether those who insist that humans are morally more worthy than animals should be accused of being speciesist, a term first coined by Ryder (1975: 16).

Citing species membership alone as a justification for unequal treatment, without any accompanying reasons, is invalid. In order to illustrate this, philosophers have increasingly come to use the principle of the equal consideration of interests to define how to determine the moral worth of animals (see DeGrazia, 2002; Francione, 2000; Rowlands, 2002; Singer, 1990). This principle is generally used by those thinkers who advocate a much higher moral status for animals than the moral orthodoxy would permit, not surprisingly because by promoting the interests of animals it offers the prospect of demoting the moral importance of the human species. However, the equal consideration of interests should not, as it sometimes is, be confused with greater moral equality between humans and animals. All it does is to suggest that we ought to consider interests equally. We still, however, have to identify what those interests are, and it could be that we decide that animals either have no morally relevant interests at all or have interests which are inferior to those of humans.

The nature of animals and the 'continuum of recognition'

From the substantial literature on the moral status of animals, it is possible to identify a continuum of views graduated in order of the moral recognition which the major exponents consider we ought to accord to animals.

1 Completely lacking moral status. Only indirect duties owed to animals as
   (a) animals lack sentiency (Descartes, Carruthers);
   (b) animals are sentient but lack any morally significant interests (Kant, Frey).
2 Moral orthodoxy/Animal welfare/Humane treatment – some moral status but inferior to humans.
   (a) Animals have an interest in not suffering but this can be overridden to promote the greater good of humans who are autonomous agents (common view held by many contemporary moral and political philosophers).

  (b) Even if moral orthodox is accepted there are few uses of
      animals which are necessary (Francione).
3 Challenges to the moral orthodoxy.
  (a) Animals have rights
      (i) based on animals having inherent value (Regan);
      (ii) based on sentiency (Rollin, Ryder).
  (b) Utilitarianism (Singer).
  (c) Contractarianism (Rowlands).

Animals as machines

The view that animals are thoughtless brutes – automata or
machines – was held, most importantly, by the seventeenth-
century philosopher René Descartes (1912). Since animals are not
conscious, Descartes held that we have no moral obligations
towards them and can therefore treat them as mere objects. The
growing use of live animals in experiments at this time (without
anaesthetics which were not yet available) could in this way be
justified. Carruthers (1992) provides a contemporary version of
this theory suggesting that beings that cannot use language
cannot think about their experiences or be conscious of them. As
a consequence, animals, for Carruthers, cannot feel pain.

  Although there is a substantial literature seeking to argue that
moral worth can be attached to non-sentient parts of nature,
whether living or inanimate (for a review see Dobson, 2000: ch.
2), it is easy to see why it might be argued that moral worth is
really only applicable to sentient beings. We can certainly harm
non-sentient objects, but in what sense could it be said that we
can wrong them if they cannot feel what is being done to them?
Happily, we do not need to get bogged down in that debate
because virtually no one today disputes that animals are sentient.[1]
Behavioural, physiological and evolutionary evidence is put
forward to suggest that animals can experience pain (see
DeGrazia, 2002: 41–5; Regan, 1984: ch. 1; Rowlands, 2002: 5–9;
Singer, 1990: 10–15). Humans and animals have similar physiological reactions to painful stimuli, in the form for instance of the
production of endogenous opiates, sweating, increased respira-
tion rate, and secretion of adrenal hormones. Moreover,
awareness of pain is functional for survival since animals can take
steps to avoid it. It makes evolutionary sense, therefore, to impute

sentiency to human and non-human animals, whereas it does not for plants who do not have the capacity to escape from harm.

Some philosophers want to deny moral worth to animals even when their sentiency is accepted. Traditionally, this was often based on an 'appeal to God', that all humans were made in his likeness, or have immortal souls or are his preferred creatures. This type of argument is not really available for philosophers now because, as Frey (2002: 20), points out, 'Precisely what is in doubt, in our more secular age ... is this preferred status.' Descartes based a great deal of his case on the claim that humans, unlike animals, have immortal souls. Obviously, such an assertion cannot be proven and, in any case, it is not clear why it might be morally significant. If anything, it would seem to lead us to the opposite conclusion – that we are obliged to treat animals well since they, unlike humans, do not have the prospect of an after-life.

For Kant, and, more recently, Narveson, among others, only moral agents – those capable of recognising right from wrong – can be directly morally wronged. In Narveson's account (1987) only moral agents are subject to moral rules because only they can enter into a contract whereby everyone recognises it is in their interests to agree to uphold a set of moral rules. Frey (1980) too argues that we should not exaggerate the claims that follow from granting that animals are sentient. In particular, he wants to deny that sentiency is an adequate grounding for the possession of interests. He begins by distinguishing between something being in someone's interests and someone being interested in something. The former corresponds to having an interest as a need. In this sense animals do have interests since it is quite acceptable to say that, for instance, it is in Fido the dog's interests to be fed since Fido needs food to stay alive. But, for Frey, this is a rather mean-ingless argument since it also applies to inanimate objects – water, for instance, is in a car radiator's interests since it needs it to do its job properly (Frey, 1980: ch. VII). Only humans, Frey contin-ues, possess interests in the second sense of being interested in something. This is so because to be interested in something requires the existence of desires which in turn presuppose beliefs. Thus, the desire for food must (if it is not to be regarded as mere instinct) be accompanied by the belief that food will have the effect of satisfying hunger. Since, for Frey, animals cannot have

beliefs, they cannot have desires and therefore cannot have interests. This claim is based upon the inability of animals to use a
language, since without language it is impossible for animals to
believe that any particular statement (e.g. that the purpose of
food is to satisfy hunger) is true or false.

In my view, Frey clearly undervalues the importance of
sentiency, and exaggerates the importance of language. While the
use of language undoubtedly enriches existence, it is surely churl-
ish to deny that animals have an interest in not suffering pain
whether or not they believe, and can express, that a certain action
will lead to the experience of pain. And, since animals (as Frey
himself accepts) are sentient, then clearly not all interests which
do not require beliefs apply to inanimate objects. In this sense,
then, Bentham (1948: 311) was right when he wrote that the key
question regarding animals is not 'Can they reason? nor Can they
talk? but, Can they suffer?'.

Even if we regarded animals as mere things, it would not necessarily give us *carte blanche* to do what we liked with them. A
number of thinkers have argued that we may not have any direct
duties to animals but we still have *indirect* duties. Thus, it is not
wrong to kick an animal because we wrong the animal itself, but
because we wrong another sentient being in the process – the
animal, for instance, may have been owned by that being. In the
same way, it would be wrong to damage that person's house. A
similar view, held by Locke, Aquinas, Kant and others, rules out
cruelty to animals on the grounds that those who engage in such
behaviour are likely to be inclined to treat humans in the same
way.

I am not convinced by any version of indirect duty views. The
first type requires us to deny that animals are sentient, a view
which, as we saw, is not taken seriously these days. The second,
by the very act of recognising sentiency, rules out the possibility
that animals cannot be harmed, in the sense of being made to feel
pain. It follows, then, that we harm them *directly,* irrespective of
the harm done to anyone else involved. If we maintain that only
moral agents can be morally worthy then it follows that children
or the mentally deranged do not fit into this category, and therefore we cannot owe direct duties to them either. A discussion of a
related aspect of this problem follows below. For now, it should
be noted that our moral intuition suggests that this is not how we

regard such humans and it is certainly the case that this is not, on the whole, how society treats them in practice.

The moral orthodoxy

Assuming, as I think we must, that animals are sentient, it needs to be asked: what moral significance does the capacity to experience pleasure and pain have? For many of the pro-animal philosophers a great deal follows from this. Peter Singer, for instance, bases his case for the equal consideration of human and animal interests on the grounds that the latter, like the former, are sentient. Likewise, Tom Regan (1975: 181–214), at least in his early writings, accords rights to animals on the same basis.

Superficially, at least, there seems no reason to conclude that by granting sentiency to animals we ought necessarily to consider animal and human interests equally, let alone regard them as moral equals (the latter requiring us to accept the more stringent proposition that, because humans and animals have the same interests, what we ought not to do to humans we ought not to do to animals). The recognition that animals can suffer pain surely places some constraints on our behaviour towards them. In addition, few would dispute that animals can suffer in other ways which are not equivalent to pain but which nevertheless represent an interest which should be taken into account. Suffering here refers to a 'wide range of unpleasant emotional states' that may include fear, frustration, exhaustion, stress and loss of social companions as well as physical pain. Modern animal welfare science has devised effective ways – mortality, productivity, physiological changes, abnormal behaviour – of measuring such suffering (see Dawkins, 1980). The problem with this, though, is that it leaves out of account those other characteristics – such as rationality, a language capability, free will, self-consciousness and so on – which, it might be argued, are morally significant and are possessed exclusively by humans.

Obviously, these terms are very difficult to define. For the sake of simplicity it is useful to adopt the generic label 'autonomy' to describe the mental characteristics that we might assume are possessed by normal adult humans but not by animals. Autonomy provides the benchmark for personhood (not to be confused with the label 'human being' since this is to assume that only humans are autonomous which, as we shall see later, is disputed). It requires a being to be self-governing; to have beliefs and preferences and to be able to act according to them, changing behaviour when the evidence suggests that beliefs can no longer be supported (see, in particular, McCloskey, 1979: 23–54 and Townsend, 1976: 85–93).

Such an autonomous being – with thoughts, intentions and beliefs – can be held morally responsible for her actions and can recognise when a wrong is inflicted on her. In particular, she can recognise that a harm might be inflicted when she is prevented from fulfilling her wants or, to put it in a grandiose fashion, her life plan. A being lacking autonomy, on the other hand, would not be aware of itself as a distinct being with wants, desires and preferences and consequently cannot have a concept of life or death and a preference to continue living. Following Rachels (1983: 280–2), clarification of this distinction between autonomy and mere sentiency is provided by distinguishing between an individual being alive and having a life. The former refers to a 'functioning biological organism' whilst the latter is about a notion of biography rather than biology – about, that is, an individual's attitudes, beliefs, actions and relationships. In this way, we can talk quite sensibly of a life (in the biological sense) not worth living (in the biographical sense) in the case, say, of a seriously retarded human.

What follows then from granting that animals are sentient but not autonomous? Townsend's (1976) argument is typical. He argues that it allows us to distinguish between two sorts of moral considerations. The first, applicable to animals, is based on welfare and requires us to act so as to do what is conducive to the living of a pain-free happy life. The second, applicable to humans only, is based on a respect for autonomy – for what an individual wants or values. Thus, our approach to other humans should be based upon the presumption that they should be allowed to pursue their lives with as little interference as possible, and that the duty to help others is subordinate to our duty not to harm others, even if the consequence of helping others results in less harm than would otherwise have occurred. This approach is only applicable, Townsend argues, to autonomous beings, since only beings with beliefs, thoughts and intentions can be harmed by interference which does not involve the infliction of pain. Because animals are only sentient, however, they have an inferior moral status and the interests of autonomous beings take precedence. Thus, we are entitled to sacrifice the interests of animals to further human interests, whereas we are not entitled to treat humans in the same way – as part of a cost–benefit analysis.

Attempts have been made to refine this position. Robert Nozick (1974: 35–42), for instance, identifies a position which he describes as 'utilitarianism for animals, Kantianism for people'. Thus, since animals are sentient and therefore can suffer, we should establish that inflicting suffering on them is justified (in terms of the extent to which it produces an outcome in which the benefits, to humans and animals, is greater than the suffering inflicted and where no viable alternative to the infliction of suffering is available) and attempt as far as possible to minimise it once we have established it is necessary. What is not permitted, however, is to treat humans in the same way. That is, it is not permissible to sacrifice the significant interests of humans in order to achieve a greater aggregate good for animals or other humans. This position amounts closely, I think, to the moral orthodoxy, at least in the developed world. Thus, it is morally permissible to inflict suffering on animals if by so doing a human interest in not suffering (pain or even death) is upheld or even if a human autonomous interest is threatened by not so doing.

As Townsend (1976: 92) points out: 'The orthodox morality thus assigns only an intermediate status to the other animals; from a moral point of view they count for more than mere things but less than persons'. This rules out inflicting unwarranted suffering on animals; suffering, that is, which does not result in any significant human benefit. It could be argued, as Francione (2000) insists, that, in reality, virtually all animal suffering at the hands of humans is unnecessary, either because it does not produce the benefits claimed for it, or because these benefits can be achieved by some other means.[2] This claim, of course, is, partly at least, a matter of empirical examination and subsequent chapters will seek to assess its validity. For now, it should be noted that, whatever the outcome, the moral orthodoxy does recognise that an animal's interest in not suffering counts for something.

Sentiency and the argument from marginal cases

There are at least three main responses to the moral orthodoxy. Firstly, we can deny that every human possesses autonomy. This approach is adopted in the so-called 'argument from marginal cases'. The second is to accept that humans alone possess autonomy but to claim that the use of sentiency on its own is enough to challenge effectively the moral orthodoxy regarding animals. The third is to accept that autonomy is morally significant but deny that all animals lack the capacity to be autonomous.

The argument from marginal cases, a term coined by a critic of the approach (Narveson, 1977: 161–78), is probably the most debated issue in the literature (see, in particular, Pluhar, 1995). It is not difficult to see why it is regularly utilised by the philosophical defenders of animals. As indicated, if we were to ask why it is that humans should have a superior moral status to animals then it would be necessary to identify a morally-relevant characteristic possessed by humans and not by animals. One such characteristic is autonomy which, it is claimed, humans possess while animals do not. The problem with this is that it is possible to point to humans who are not autonomous. These marginal cases would include human infants and so-called 'human defectives' such as the severely mentally retarded. It is important to note two versions of the argument from marginal cases (Pluhar, 1995: 63–4). In the 'categorical' version, *because* 'marginal' humans have maximum moral significance then so do at least some animals. In the 'biconditional' version, *if* marginal humans are regarded as having maximum moral significance, then so do at least some animals. The second version is, of course, weaker, because it could, and has, been used to exclude both marginal humans and animals from maximum moral significance.

There have been a number of responses to the argument from marginal cases, a debate we can only sketch in brief here. The first is the argument that young children have the potentiality to become rational adults and therefore should not be treated any differently. This is not entirely satisfactory. It is not clear why 'potentiality' is morally important given that the aim of distinguishing full-personhood or autonomy is to demonstrate that those with that characteristic at that point in time are capable of greater suffering than those without it. Even if we accept this argument, it still leaves the, for want of a better phrase, human mental defectives, those who will never become normal healthy adult humans. Some resort to a justification of a partial speciesism. As Townsend (1976: 93) points out: 'There will be pragmatic and sentimental reasons for not viewing the interests of incapacitated persons in a strictly utilitarian manner.' A more common response is to stress that what matters are not the exceptions but the commonly held characteristics of a species (Benson, 1978). Surely, though, this is not good enough. Resorting to sentiment or dealing in tendencies is hardly the stuff of rational argument and does not answer the speciesist charge that defective humans are being granted a privileged moral status merely on the grounds that they are humans.

By far the most consistent retort is to deny that all humans should be treated in the same way, thus allowing us to lump together animals and marginal humans as a group possessing less moral status than normal adult humans. This is the approach adopted by Frey, and is an example of the use of the biconditional version of the argument from marginal cases (Frey, 1987; 2002). Of course, he is then open to the charge that this is counter to our moral intuition, that we would not dream of treating defective humans in the same way that we treat animals. Frey is right, of course, to say that doctors do have to make decisions concerning the value of life every day, particularly when it is a matter of utilising scarce resources. There is a great difference, though, between letting a seriously defective human being die peacefully through not administering expensive medical treatment and deliberately inflicting pain on an animal in a laboratory experiment. Frey (1983: 114–15) does accept, though, that it might be justified to use in such experiments those humans with a lower quality of life than healthy animals (see Chapter 5). But then we must ask what kind of morality is it that allows some humans to be treated in this way? Would we really want to live in a society where this took place?

Sentiency, life and death

If we do not accept the argument from marginal cases, the task of the pro-animal philosophers is much greater, since we are no longer prevented from considering other characteristics, incorporated within the term autonomy, which normal adult humans may possess but animals may not. This leads us to our second response, outlined above, which is the suggestion that sentiency alone can justify a considerable moral status for animals. Here, we should start by emphasising that identifying characteristics which humans possess and animals do not is only relevant in this context if they are morally significant. Thus, it needs to be demonstrated why it is that the possession of autonomy entitles us to distinguish between moral rules which apply to animals and those which apply to humans. The possession of autonomy alone does seem to justify differential treatment. Put simply, a being with wants and desires can be harmed if he is prevented from furthering those wants and desires. The ultimate sanction, of course, is to take the life of such a being. By contrast, the death of a being without autonomy, is arguably not a wrong since it is not depriving that individual of the freedom to pursue his life plan (given that beings without autonomy do not have such a life plan). This is, of course, why we regard the untimely death of a human at an early age as particularly unfortunate since the individual has not had the opportunity to develop his life according to a set of beliefs and preferences. We do not feel quite so intensely about a person dying at a great age because that person has had, in his 'long innings', the opportunity to fulfil his hopes and aspirations (Rachels, 1983: 282).

According to this view, then, it would seem justified to kill an animal, for whatever reason, provided (and this is the key point) that it is killed painlessly. It should be noted that there is a significant difference between the view that killing an animal painlessly is not morally wrong and the view that killing a human painlessly is a *greater* wrong than killing an animal. The latter view is more promising (although its implications for practical decision making are more complex) since the former denies that animals have any interest in life. As Johnson (1983: 123–33) points out, although it might be argued that humans, because of their greater mental complexity, have a greater interest in life (although he denies even this), it is a dubious assertion that animals have no interest in continuing their lives since life offers the possibility (although the animal might not be aware of this) of benefiting from the opportunities to satisfy their desires (for food, fresh air or whatever). Singer (1990: 21) himself accepts that it might be justified, in

theory, to regard the killing of humans as a greater wrong than
the killing of animals (notwithstanding the argument from
marginal cases). As he points out:

> to take the life of a being who has been hoping, planning and
> working for some future goal is to deprive that being of the fulfil-
> ment of all those efforts; to take the life of a being with a mental
> capacity below the level needed to grasp that one is a being with a
> future – much less make plans for the future – cannot involve this
> particular kind of loss.

But, though Singer has his doubts about the painless killing of
animals, his reliance on sentiency alone forces him to accept that
it is not clear why killing an animal without inflicting pain is a
wrong, as long as this death is made good by the creation of a new
animal which will lead an equally pleasant life (1979). Clearly,
having an interest in avoiding pain is not enough to have an interest in living. Indeed, dying may be a preferable option to someone
whose life is dominated by unbearable pain. The problem, it
seems, is that Singer (1990: 228–9) is not prepared to limit
animals to sentiency alone. The need to argue the case for animals
having greater mental complexity is not attempted, however, on
the grounds that, in practice, modern farming and experimentation techniques do not and cannot kill without the imposition of
pain (Singer, 1990: 210, 229–30).

   I agree with Singer though in the sense that it is not clear why,
as the moral orthodoxy suggests, it is a greater wrong to inflict
pain on a human rather than an animal. For surely, if we assume
that animals have an interest in not suffering (because they can
experience pain) then this capacity, in the absence of any reasons
to the contrary, is as great as a human's capacity to suffer pain
and should be treated equally. I can see no reason why we should
not regard the infliction of pain on humans as equivalent to the
infliction of pain on sentient animals. Not to hold this position
would seem to be speciesist, in the sense that the reason why the
pain inflicted on humans is a greater wrong than the pain inflicted
on animals is simply because they belong to a different species.
We could, of course, adopt a utilitarian position which allows a
moral cost–benefit analysis and, as we shall see later, Singer is a
utilitarian. However, if we are to adopt such a position, and we
accept (as I think we must) that the pain inflicted on animals is

equivalent to the pain inflicted on humans, then we must also include animal and human pain equally in the utilitarian calculation (as Singer does). But this, of course, is precisely what the moral orthodoxy is not prepared to allow.

The failure to see that the identification of one characteristic that humans possess and animals do not is not sufficient for the claim that *all* human interests are morally superior to *all* animal interests is, I believe, a common mistake. As Rachels (1983: 275–8) rightly points out in the context of rights: 'That is far less plausible than to think that the characteristics one must have in order to have a right vary with the rights themselves.' Thus, to have the right to freedom of worship it is necessary to possess the characteristics – the ability to understand religious beliefs – required for worship to have some meaning. To have a right not to be tortured, on the other hand, is justified on the grounds that it hurts: 'It is the capacity for suffering', then, 'and not the possession of sophisticated concepts, that underlies the wrongness of torture' (Rachels, 1983).

If we accept the view that animals possess interests which ought to be treated equally with like human interests, then radical implications follow. For it enables us to challenge the moral orthodoxy in fundamental ways without having to prove anything more than that animals are sentient, which, as we have seen, is widely accepted. The implications of holding this position will be considered in the chapters that follow.

The mental complexity of animals

We move on now to consider the third of the responses to the moral orthodoxy outlined earlier. This is the view that we underestimate the mental capabilities of animals and that it is wrong to assume that anything other than sentiency is beyond them. An examination of this view is necessary because by establishing that at least some animals are autonomous, we remove completely the barrier towards granting these animals equal moral status with humans. In particular, autonomy, unlike sentiency alone, provides the basis for a right to life. Without such a principle a number of common practices involving animals may still be morally sanctioned. Thus, if animal autonomy can be established, the arguments of the previous two sections become largely redundant since there are no significant differences between the mental capacities of animals and humans whose significance we need to debate.

Examining the mental complexity of humans (let alone non-human animals) is extraordinarily difficult, although this has not prevented a sizeable literature on this subject emerging in recent years (see Rowlands, 2002: 1–23 for a useful review of the evidence). We should note firstly that the assumption that a being is either autonomous (having a full range of mental powers) or simply sentient is obviously simplistic. Clearly, some non-human animal species are more sophisticated mentally than others and it would therefore be wrong to claim that any moral imperatives that flow from the possession of autonomy apply either to all animals or none. It might be useful here to grade animals in three (admittedly fairly crude) categories; those, such as single cell animals, who probably are not sentient, those who are sentient and those who are mentally more sophisticated. The arguments in this section apply to the last category alone. It is fairly safe to limit the discussion this way since even Regan (1984: 76–8), one of the foremost advocates of animal rights, wants only to claim that mammals, one year of age or over, have mental capacities which can be compared favourably with humans.

It should be said that this is a somewhat arbitrary dividing line. Some birds, for instance, appear to have a greater ability to learn than mammals. Leaving that aside, there is the further problem that the moral obligations we owe to the mammals identified by Regan are not the same as those owed to animals who are less endowed mentally. Regan himself certainly does not want to claim that all animals have what he describes as inherent value. He excludes, for example, chickens and turkeys (1984: 349). Nevertheless, he claims that our knowledge is so limited that we should give some animals the benefit of the doubt. This is something of a weak argument particularly if the use of the animal in, say, a scientific experiment can produce immense human benefit. Because of this Regan (1984: 367–8) introduces another argument to the effect that allowing the use of less complex animals may encourage the view that all animals can be used in this way. Like the indirect-duty view of Kant and others (that those who are cruel to animals are likely to develop behaviour patterns which will lead them to behave in the same way towards other humans), this is surely a matter of empirical observation and is not a central part of Regan's moral theory which applies to a limited number of species.

A useful way into the debate about the mental complexity of animals is the argument presented by Frey which we outlined earlier. Frey, you will remember, claims that an autonomous being has beliefs which in turn require desires which presuppose a language capability. Since animals do not possess a language they cannot have desires or beliefs. This denial is crucially important since rationality, intelligence, or whatever one may define it as, depends upon the ability to develop beliefs which, when converted into action, consistently produce meaningful behaviour. Frey, of course, denies that animals act in this way.

Regan (1984: 10–17) disputes Frey's assertion that animals lack beliefs. In the first place, as tests have shown, it is by no means certain that at least some animals – non-human primates – do not have a linguistic capability. The problem with this response is that it leaves unchallenged Frey's assertion that language is a requirement for beliefs. Attributing linguistic competence to some animals remains an extremely contentious issue and thus provides a shaky foundation for an effective critique of Frey. In addition, it would, in any case, lead to the conclusion that, since the vast majority of animals show no linguistic ability, only those animals that do can be considered for the possession of beliefs. Better then to challenge Frey's assertion, that a language is necessary for the possession of a belief system, head on.

Language, as we pointed out earlier, is clearly an important way of expressing beliefs, but it is surely not the only way. Beliefs can also be expressed through a variety of non-linguistic behaviour. Thus, Regan (1984: 38–49) points to the case of a small child who throws his toy snake in front of a person who possesses no language ability whatsoever. The startled and frightened reaction of the individual demonstrates, for Regan, that beliefs (in this case the belief that the snake is real and might be dangerous) are not always dependent upon a language. All that is required in this case is the belief that snakes can be harmful – which can have been gained from observing snakes in the past. Moreover, Regan points out that for children themselves to learn a language, a set of pre-verbal beliefs is necessary otherwise they would not be able to associate certain objects with the words used to describe them. Thus, if humans can have non-linguistic beliefs, then so can animals.

There is a weaker version of the language requirement. This is to say that because animals lack a language we cannot say whether or not and to what extent animals have beliefs since, quite simply, they cannot tell us. One response to this is to say that this does not prove they do not have beliefs. A second, much stronger, response is to claim that we do have reason to believe, through observation, that animals do have beliefs. Thus, we can assume, for example, that Fido the dog chooses to head for his bone since he desires it, on the grounds that past experience has taught him to believe that it will prove to be tasty. And if Fido can behave in this way, then why not other mammals as well (Regan, 1984: 59)?

It is important to recognise the context of Regan's critique of Frey. Regan's early work (1975) was reliant on the argument from marginal cases. If, he argued, rights are granted to 'marginal' humans, then they ought to be granted to many animals as well since there are no morally relevant differences between them. This approach (pioneered by earlier writers such as Singer, Linzey and Clark), as we have seen, requires nothing more than showing that animals are sentient. In his later work, Regan wants to claim far more for animals. By accepting that animals are aware, have beliefs and act intentionally 'a good deal more follows concerning the cognitive powers they must have'. We must recognise them as having a memory, being self conscious and capable of having an emotional life (Regan, 1984: 73, 75). The latter, in particular, is – if valid – of great significance. For it means that animals can be angry, be afraid of what might happen to them, feel loss and so on. This clearly does follow from grant-ing belief systems to animals. If an animal believes, for instance, that a knife can hurt, it will fear it.

Regan, of course, does draw far-reaching conclusions from his analysis of the mental complexity of animals. Because they have beliefs and preferences, animals have a welfare which is capable of being harmed by both inflictions of pain and deprivations. The ultimate deprivation is death since it forecloses all possibilities of finding satisfaction in life (Regan, 1984: 94–9). It follows that normal, adult humans (described as moral agents) and retarded humans, children and mammals one year of age or over (described as moral patients) are 'subjects-of-a-life'. That is, they have inherent value since beings whose lives are characterised by beliefs and desires and who are thus capable of acting intentionally to satisfy their preferences have lives worth living – lives that can be harmed by pain, suffering, frustration and death.

Responses to Regan's arguments from fellow philosophers have tended to dismiss rapidly his claims before putting forward an alternative theory based upon, in their eyes, a more realistic interpretation of the capabilities of animals. Narveson (1987: 31), for instance, comments simply that Regan's claims are, for most of us, 'seriously overstated'. A more weighty response has been provided by Frey (1987). By challenging the internal consistency of Regan's case he argues, in particular, that the assertion that moral patients and moral agents have equal inherent value does not follow from the type of autonomy identified by Regan.

Frey begins by explaining why the concept of autonomy is crucially important in imputing value to lives. Autonomy matters, he argues, because of what it enables us to make of our lives. The crucial idea here is *control*. Thus, it involves individuals themselves choosing what they want to achieve and organising their lives in pursuit of this goal. We will not be autonomous to the extent that we allow ourselves to be coerced by others and to the extent that we allow our life plan to become subservient to our 'first-order' desires – eating, drinking, drugs and so on. Frey then denies that this conception of autonomy as control can be applied to animals. What is more, he also claims that Regan himself realises this and, in order to incorporate moral patients within a theory of autonomy, develops a weaker sense of the term (preference autonomy). This weaker sense of the term only requires that beings be able to have desires, or preferences, and have the ability to initiate actions with a view to satisfying them.

For Frey, however, Regan's preference autonomy is an 'impoverished' form of the concept, lacking all of the features of his 'control' sense of the term. The latter involves a much higher quality of life involving a rational assessment of desires and a willingness to shed or moderate some, particularly first-order, desires if they are not consistent with an individual's conception of the good life. At most, animals are only capable of dealing with a very basic set of first-order desires which denies them 'means to

that rich full life of self-fulfilment and achievement' which is
'quite apart from any satisfaction and fulfilment that comes
through the satisfaction of our appetites'. Frey (1987: 61) also
appears to be saying, and here I disagree, that Regan is prepared
to sanction including as autonomous beings those who have irrational preferences, the pursuit of which can be damaging to the
individuals concerned. This is not, it seems to me, what Regan is
suggesting. Indeed, he goes to great lengths, as we have seen, to
show that animals do have beliefs which are rationally related
to the achievement of their desires, however basic these desires
may be.

Regan, of course, is well aware that the mental capabilities of
humans are greater than animals and that, without an additional
argument, it would be difficult to conclude that they possessed
equal inherent value. Recognising this, he invokes the argument
from marginal cases. Thus, if autonomy as control does not apply
to animals then neither does it apply to marginal humans. But this
only applies if one is not prepared to admit that some *human* lives
are less valuable than others. The problem is that Frey, as we have
seen, is prepared to concede this. Indeed, he is prepared to go as
far as to say that some human life has no value at all (Frey, 1987:
59). 'A life wholly and irreversibly in the grip of senile dementia',
he writes, for instance, 'is a life not worth living'. Once this is
admitted, of course, there is nothing to stop us from concluding
that moral agents have greater inherent value than moral patients
and therefore should be treated differently. As a final point here
though, even if we accept this to be the case, there is a significant
difference between saying that animals have *no* inherent value
and saying that animals have *some* inherent value. Accepting the
latter position would seem to question the morality of, even painlessly, killing animals. Certainly, the work of the increasing
number of scientists operating in the field of animal intelligence
has added weight to the philosophical claims made for animals
and this should, at the very least, make us feel uneasy about some
of the things we allow to be done to them in our name.

Animal liberation, animal rights and contractarianism

Our discussion so far has been incomplete. We have been mainly
concerned with a consideration of differences between animals

and humans that might be morally significant, but this does not, by itself, provide us with a moral guide to our actions. That is, we have to ask what follows from granting that animals have inter-ests which ought to be considered equally with humans or that animals, like humans, are subjects-of-a-life. Answers to this ques-tion have traditionally revolved around the advocacy of utilitarianism on the one hand, and rights on the other. More recently, other approaches have emerged to challenge this domi-nance. In this section, the validity of the contractarian approach is, relatively briefly, assessed, and in the final section of this chapter we move on to outline the competing claims of feminism and socialism to be the correct ideological location for animal protection.[3]

It still remains the case that Singer's utilitarian emphasis on the equal consideration of interests and Regan's assertion that at least some animals are possessors of rights, are the approaches, rightly or wrongly, which have been subject to most scrutiny by their academic peers. I have avoided focusing on the term animal rights until now because its use tends to lead to confusion. What should be made clear is that both the utilitarianism of Singer's animal liberation and the animal rights view put forward by others chal-lenge the moral orthodoxy outlined above. There are two key differences, however, which have led to a great deal of debate between the two camps. Firstly, Regan imputes to animals a far greater degree of mental ability than Singer. As we saw, Singer bases his case on the sentiency of animals and argues that there-fore animal suffering ought to be considered equally with human suffering. Regan, on the other hand, wants to claim that the capa-bilities of at least some animals are such that we should, in all essentials, treat them as if they were humans, in particular grant-ing them a right to life. Secondly, Singer and Regan are exponents of two very different ethical theories – utilitarianism and rights respectively – which they hold apply to our treatment of both animals and humans.

This section is concerned with a consideration of the latter difference. Thus, it is assumed that both Singer and Regan have satisfactorily incorporated animals into their moral theories in the way they intended and that the debate is exclusively concerned with finding the correct moral theory which can be applied across the board – that is, to both humans and animals. Thus, the distinction between levels of mental complexity should not be confused with the distinction between utilitarianism and rights. That is, it would be possible, at this stage, for us to contemplate Singer as holding that animals have a right not to have pain inflicted upon them (which he does not) just as much as it would be possible to contemplate Regan as holding that animals have the even more fundamental right to life (which he does). Interestingly, Richard Ryder (1989: 325–6) – who, incidentally, was offered by Singer the co-authorship of *Animal Liberation* – adopts Singer's emphasis on suffering as the 'bedrock of morality' whilst tending to 'agree with Regan that it is *wrong to aggregate across individual sentients'*, thus leading him to a rejection of Singer's utilitarianism.

The distinction between Singer's and Regan's work has not always been appreciated by their critics, not surprisingly given that Singer has been prone to using the word 'rights' particularly in his earlier writings. At times, Singer does talk (particularly in *Animal Liberation*) as if the killing of animals for food and their use for experimental purposes should be morally condemned *per se* because the infliction of pain means that they lead miserable lives. Such a view could be taken to mean that he thinks they have a right not to have pain inflicted on them. Singer is clear, though, that he is not an advocate of rights, although he has not helped matters by agreeing to the assertion of animal rights as 'handy political slogans'. Thus, he writes (1990: 8) that:

> The language of rights is convenient political shorthand. It is even more valuable in the era of thirty-second TV news clips than it was in Bentham's day; but in the argument for a radical change in our attitude to animals, it is in no way necessary.

In addition to the confusion caused, the use of this rhetorical device by Singer arouses suspicion that he is an ideologue for animals rather than someone who sees the claims of animals emerging from a more or less neutral and general ethical theory. This is unfortunate not least because he has a strong case without resorting to this sleight of hand.

The debate between utilitarianism and rights is a constant theme in moral philosophy. Although the advocacy of rights is an age-old device of philosophers, until recently rights have had something of a bad press. Traditionally, they were linked to the existence of God, as things granted by an all-powerful being. As the theological emphasis declined, however, it was common for thinkers to deny their existence. Chief amongst these have been the so-called legal positivists (of whom Bentham was a leading exponent) who argue that the only rights that exist are those acquired through statutes formulated by legislatures or by a person's voluntary act. More recently, however, the idea of natural (or unacquired) rights – those belonging to individuals as a consequence of the type of beings they are – has made something of a comeback, particularly in the United States (see Dworkin, 1977).

Clearly, rights are a useful device since, as Rollin (1983: 106) states, they are:

> moral notions that grow out of respect for the individual. They build protective fences around the individual. They establish areas where the individual is entitled to be protected against the state and the majority *even where a price is paid by the general welfare.*

Thus as Rachels (1983: 279) has noted, at least three important consequences follow if we grant rights to individuals as opposed to simply making them objects of moral concern. In the first place, it only makes sense to say that someone has a right not to be treated in a particular way (in the sense of a claim on someone) if that duty is owed directly. Thus, if we accept the rights view, it rules out the possibility that we have no direct duties to animals. Secondly, rights-bearers can strongly insist that their rights are upheld and complain and feel resentment if they are not. It therefore places a compulsion on others which does not exist where the infringement of rights is not at stake. Finally, with obvious implications for the protection of animal rights, third parties are entitled (or even required) to intervene and compel an individual to cease violating the rights of another.

Utilitarianism is very different from the rights view in that it is a consequentialist theory. For the utilitarian, an action is deemed to be right or wrong according to the consequences that flow from that action. There are several different types of utilitarianism, each with a different version of the good to be pursued. Thus Bentham (1948), the main nineteenth-century exponent of utilitarianism, was a hedonist in the sense that an action was good in so far as it maximised the pleasure and wrong in so far as it

maximised the pain of the others affected by the act. As many
have pointed out, Bentham's assumption that men do pursue
pleasure and avoid pain is either an inaccurate psychological
theory (since it is easy to show that, if we try to provide a content
to pleasure and pain, then it is not true that all men act in this
way) or an empty theory (since, without providing a content to
pleasure and pain, it boils down to the truism that men want what
they want). To rescue it, later utilitarians, including Singer, have
argued that the good to be pursued is the maximisation of preferences or interest satisfaction. Thus, we act morally if our actions
maximise the preferences of others and immorally if they do not.

Equality of consideration, and not of treatment, is the key
feature of utilitarianism. No individual is to be worth more than
another. Singer is very much in this tradition. For him, of course,
the interests of animals are to be included in the utilitarian calculation. If we adopt this approach, Singer argues, then our
treatment of animals in many areas (in particular, the raising and
killing of animals for food and their use in scientific experiments)
becomes indefensible. However, Singer has been criticised
heavily, particularly by Regan, for allegedly putting forward a
theory which does not provide a watertight justification for the
radical alteration in our current practices he seeks. Utilitarianism
requires, as we have seen, an analysis of the consequences of our
actions. So, the moral condemnation of our treatment of animals
requires this analysis to show that the use of animals for, say,
scientific experiments is not conducive to the maximisation of
interest satisfaction or pain over pleasure. Singer (1990: 9) clearly
thinks that this is the case. As he points out:

> the overwhelming majority of humans take an active part in, acqui-
> esce in, and allow their taxes to pay for, practices that require the
> sacrifice of the most important interests of members of other
> species in order to promote the most trivial interests of our own
> species.

Leaving aside the problem of how interests or pleasures and pains
are to be measured (which is a perennial problem for utilitarians),
one can agree with Regan that it is by no means certain that
such an analysis would support the case for abolition. Such a
conclusion would depend upon empirical examination. Thus, if it
could be demonstrated that experiments on animals produced

enormous benefits for other humans *and* animals – by, say, discovering a cure for a disease which caused immense suffering to and/or killed millions – then it would be clearly justified on utilitarian grounds. For a utilitarian, then, each case would have to be judged on its merits. Some uses of animals may be justified, others may not. Furthermore, if it were established that, at present, no animal experiments were justified, this still leaves open the possibility that at some point in the future they may be. The problem is, in general terms, that utilitarianism can justify as right actions which our moral intuition would find abhorrent. This, of course, is because it would seem to allow the sacrificing of an individual's vital interests (whether human or animal) in order to promote the well-being of others.

Singer himself appears to respond in three ways to this criticism. In the first place, he claims that present practices do conclusively support a utilitarian case for radical reform. Thus, meat is eaten for 'trivial' reasons despite the immense suffering of the animals raised for this purpose, and most animal experiments, whilst involving the infliction of great pain, provide few beneficial results. Such conclusions are, as later chapters will attempt to show, debatable to say the least. Secondly, Singer points to the flexibility of his approach as compared to the rights view, since it would not rule out some harm being inflicted if great benefits were to accrue (this is a valid response which will be considered in more detail below).

Thirdly, and most importantly, is the response that a utilitarian calculation of present practices is not required anyway since *all* of these present practices are speciesist. This is because, of course, the interests of animals are not considered equally. If this were the case, why is the debate about whether we should farm or experiment upon animals? Why do we never consider whether humans should be eaten as food or experimented on? That is, present practices have an in-built assumption that non-trivial human interests are not to be counted as part of the utilitarian calculation, but merely defended *whatever* the cost to animals. This, of course, is the key difference between Singer's utilitarianism and the moral orthodoxy. So, until it is recognised that, as a result of a cost–benefit analysis, humans might be harmed in the way that animals are, Singer has no criticism to answer. And, of course, if humans did face the prospect of being eaten or experimented on, then we would surely make it our business to establish that there were very good reasons for these practices to cease. Nevertheless, the fact remains that, even with this proviso, utilitarianism does sanction harming individuals for a greater aggregate good.

Moral theories based upon rights, though, are not without their problems. In the first place, some claim that only moral agents – those who can recognise right from wrong and are able to act accordingly – can be the recipients of rights since only they can claim what they are due (McCloskey, 1979). This, of course, would rule out animals as holders of rights. In my view, this is mistaken. Clearly, animals cannot have acquired rights since they cannot enter into the kind of agreement required for them to be meaningful. For example, animals cannot be expected to understand what it is to keep a promise or understand when a promise made to them has been broken. However, the same does not apply to unacquired rights. The inability of animals to claim such rights may make it more likely that their rights will be infringed, but this does not prevent others – moral agents – claiming them on behalf of animals. This, of course, is what the animal rights movement is all about.

For his part, Singer (1985: 49) recognises the attractions of a rights-based view. 'Regan,' he points out, 'does not have to get involved in the awkward predictions and calculations that so bedevil utilitarians and others who judge actions by their consequences.' But this is to assume that unacquired rights actually exist. Holders of a rights view may be correct to say that their approach protects animal (and human) interests from being sacrificed for the greater good. But that is quite different from an argument *in support* of this approach – that is, the validity of the rights view itself. The aim of a moral theory should be to enable us to distinguish between right and wrong but Regan, and other rights advocates, leave themselves open to the charge that they adopt exactly the opposite approach. Thus, instead of developing a theory which provides arguments for the validity of animal rights and against utilitarianism, they start with an antipathy towards utilitarian conclusions (because, in Regan's case, it might in certain cases provide a justification for eating meat or experimenting on animals) and justify the rights view on the grounds that it does not produce, possibly repugnant, utilitarian conclusions. But this is to prejudge the issue for it is to ignore the case for those very utilitarian conclusions (see Frey, 1983: ch. 8).

Regan himself relies upon our moral intuition which, he says, rules out utilitarian conclusions, but intuition is a dubious method of choosing between moral principles simply because competing intuitions are held. As was intimated above, Singer criticises the inflexibility of a rights-based view. What if, he asks, the death of one animal (or human, for that matter) in an experiment was enough to enable us to find a cure for cancer? Singer would be willing to sanction this but Regan's assertion of inherent value would prevent us. Is not Singer's view more in line with our intuitions than Regan's, despite the latter's reliance on intuition? Indeed, Singer claims that if a choice was made available, between a society organised along the lines of his principles and one adopting Regan's, most people would opt for the former (Singer, 1984: 11).

Regan recognises this problem of inflexibility in *The Case for Animal Rights* and attempts to deal with it head on (287–96). The right not to be harmed can be overridden, he suggests, on the following grounds. Firstly, in the event of self-defence; secondly, to punish those who are guilty of harming others; and thirdly, in the case of someone being used as an innocent shield, the harming of whom is necessary to prevent harm being done to others by someone using the shield. It is when he gets to the case of what to do when it is necessary to choose between sacrificing the equivalent rights of two or more people that the particular problems faced by the advocates of rights becomes apparent. Most important in the context of the present discussion is what to do if one or more of those involved is an animal. Regan (1984: 324–5) deals with this by adopting the so-called 'lifeboat' example. Here, he argues that in the event of an overcrowded lifeboat containing four men and a dog and a situation where there was no hope of survival for any of the five unless one was thrown overboard, the dog should go because the death of the dog 'though a harm, is not comparable to the harm that death would be for any of the humans'. The problems here for Regan are obvious. By trying to force his theory into line with our moral intuition he comes close to undermining his whole argument. For, as Singer (1985: 49) points out:

can a theory that tells us that all subjects-of-a-life (including dogs)
have equal inherent value be reconciled with the intuition that it is
the dog that must be sacrificed?

The answer must be no! But why should intuition always be right?
The aim of animal rights theories is to challenge orthodox morality, so why should we accept the 'normal' response to this kind of
problem? Regan, I think, was forced into this corner by an over-
reliance on appeals to intuition. In this case, however, he risks
inconsistency with his practical conclusions. For, as we shall see in
a later chapter, the lifeboat case might be used as a basis to justify
animal experiments if the result were the discovery of a cure for a
fatal disease, since it is a similar situation of 'them or us'. Yet,
unlike Singer, Regan refuses to countenance such experiments.
The problem is, of course, that without a further justification for
rights other than intuition, Regan is forced to adopt it in this case.

Of course, it should be said here that the advocacy of rights
remains very important for it has, as Frey (1983: 73) points out,
the effect of directing 'attention away from the task of working
out principles of rightness and justification of treatment' and by
placing 'one's opponents on the defensive' it shifts 'the burden of
argument on to those who will not otherwise cede what one
wants'. As we shall see, the granting of rights to animals has been
used in exactly this way to provide an easily grasped frame of
reference for activists.

Rights and utilitarian approaches have been challenged in
recent years by a sustained attempt, provided by Rowlands
(1998), to justify a, for want of a better word, contractarian
approach to animal ethics. This approach is concerned with
adapting the social contract theory of John Rawls to include
animals. Rawls' (1972) theory of justice, widely regarded as one
of, if not the, most important works of political philosophy since
1945, uses an imaginary pre-social 'original position' in which
individuals meet to decide upon principles of justice. To avoid
self-interest, the individuals in the original position are subject to
a 'veil of ignorance' behind which they have no knowledge of
their actual position in society. Rawls concludes that from such a
position individuals would choose to live in a society which
pursues, amongst other things, a policy of distributive justice in
which – the so-called 'difference principle' – social and economic

inequalities are to be arranged so that they are to the greatest benefit of the least advantaged.

Rawls does not think that a theory of justice applies to animals (see below), but Rowlands and others have suggested that there is no reason why they should not be beneficiaries of Rawls' theory of justice. Just as age, race, gender and class are hidden behind the veil of ignorance, Rowlands and others have suggested that species ought to be too. As a result of this, the contracting parties would have to take into account the possibility that they might turn out to be beings who have a lower level of mental complexity than normal humans, and this could be either 'defective' humans or animals. Rawls' difference principle, then, would now benefit all sentient beings, including animals.

In the competition between rights and utilitarianism, Rawls' theory of justice is seen as an eloquent statement of the former against the latter. Rowlands (1998: 3) sees Rawls' theory of justice as the 'greatest ally' of animal rights because the status of animals as rights holders emerges from a more or less objective process. So, there is no need to engage, as we have done in this chapter, with contentious justifications for granting animals a high moral status because it is chosen as one of the principles of justice deriving from universal assent by those participating in the original position.

If this objective derivation of principles of justice from a social contract is correct, then the stakes are high for being able to show that animals should be included. But, whilst there would seem to be a good case for incorporating animals as beneficiaries of Rawls' theory of justice, it is not clear that Rawls' theory does the work required by Rowlands. In particular, Rawls (1972: 20) himself admits that radically different principles of justice might derive from the adoption of a contractarian approach, and to justify his principles he tests them, in a process he describes as 'reflective equilibrium' against our moral intuitions, adjusting them when it is necessary. Because of this, the advantage Rowlands claims for this approach is devalued since the conclusions deriving from the original position, including those relating to animals, are dependent on, or at the very least influenced by, pre-existing values. Therefore, the task of seeking to justify according animals a higher moral status independently of a contract remains essential.

New directions in animal ethics

In recent years, academic discourse about the moral status of animals has moved in a number of new and interesting directions. Constraints of space permit only a perfunctory glance at these here (see Garner, forthcoming). The starting point for this review should be the recognition that the philosophical attempts to challenge the moral orthodoxy have been derived predominantly from within the liberal tradition, hence the focus on rights, utilitarian and contractarian approaches above. This is hardly surprising given the dominance of liberal thought in Western liberal democracies. The question asked increasingly, however, is how far is the liberal tradition the most appropriate ideological location for animal protection?

A number of problems have been identified. In the first place, it should be asked whether the granting of rights to animals is ever likely to occur, particularly given the benefits humans gain from exploiting animals. A cause which seeks to defend non-human species even when there is a human cost requires a level of altruism which may not be forthcoming. If this is the case, we have to ask further what animal welfare really amounts to in liberal societies. Arguably the answer is not very much.

One potential problem is the importance attached to the status of animals as property. The sanctity of private property is a central pillar of liberal theory and practice, and a number of legal scholars have argued that whilst remaining the property of humans there is little prospect of the welfare of animals being advanced (Francione, 1995, 1996; Wise, 2000). In reality, it is suggested, animals become little more than inanimate objects in the eyes of the law and their owners are allowed to do pretty much as they please with them. Only when animals are liberated from their present status as property will they receive adequate protection. This argument has been used by Francione, among others, as evidence that only an abolitionist animal rights strategy, that removes the property status of animals, will succeed in protecting their interests.

I have argued elsewhere that the emphasis placed by Francione and others on the property status of animals is misplaced (Garner, 2003). For one thing, it is not clear that abolishing the property status of animals will produce the animal rights Garden of Eden sometimes claimed. One only has to look, for instance, at the lack of protection afforded to many wild animals, despite not being owned by a private individual or concern. Conversely, one should also bear in mind the possible benefits to animals of being private property. Compare, for instance, the loved companion animal with the life of a stray, or the wild fox threatened by the hunt against the fox protected on land owned by an animal protection organisation. More importantly, whilst there is some element of truth in the assertion that the welfare of animals is constrained by their property status, particularly in the United States, it is wrong to assume that because they are owned by humans, animals are regarded, in the law and in wider society, as inanimate objects. The law has on numerous occasions intervened to protect animals against their owners, and a viable programme of animal welfare is not inconsistent with their property status.

There is an additional problem with animal welfare in liberal societies (see Garner, 2003a). It is noticeable how animals are excluded as beneficiaries of justice by major liberal political theorists such as Rawls (1972) and Barry (1995). Whilst it is not the intention of either to deny that we have moral obligations to animals, the effect of depriving them of the protection afforded by rights is to make them vulnerable to the consequences of moral pluralism. That is, for Rawls in particular, if the treatment of animals ceases to be a matter of justice, it enters the realm of morality, and a central feature of most modern liberal political thought is the belief that the state and society should refrain from intervening in favour of one set of moral beliefs over another, provided that they do not impact on the physical integrity of other *humans*. As a result, what is done to animals then depends on individual moral preferences rather than collectively observed and enforced moral principles enshrined in laws and customs. Existing as a principle in abstract political theory is one thing, but, as we shall see in the course of this book, there is also evidence that the issue of moral pluralism has an impact on the way at least some animal issues, not least hunting and ritual slaughter, are configured

If liberalism has its weaknesses from an animal protection perspective, is there an alternative, and more appropriate, ideological location? Two such locations, socialism and feminism, have received most attention in the literature. There is empirical

and theoretical support for socialism being the most appropriate
ideological home for animal protection. Research suggests that
left of centre legislators, in Britain and the United States, are more
likely to support animal issues (Garner, 1999). There are historical links, too, between the labour and socialist movements and
the animal protection movement. Many late nineteenth-century
socialists, for instance, endorsed anti-vivisection and vegetarianism, and actively supported the Humanitarian League founded by
the animal rights thinker and activist Henry Salt (Keane, 1998:
132–4). More recently, there has also been some left-wing
support for animal issues particularly in the 1980s, and, of
course, hunting has always been seen as a Labour issue (see
Chapter 7).

We can speculate that this support for animal issues from
socialists has been partly to do with animals been perceived as
another exploited group requiring defending against, if not capitalist, then certainly major corporate interests. Attempts to
theorise a socialist dimension to animal protection have come
primarily from the work of the British social theorist Ted Benton
(1993). Benton adopts a Marxist theory of justice based on needs,
a theory that can easily incorporate animals as beneficiaries,
unlike theories based on desert or entitlements. He also suggests
that liberal rights language is a not the most appropriate way of
protecting animals. This is partly because it is difficult to identify
who is responsible for infringing the rights of animals in an institutional system of exploitation, and partly because there is a
world of difference between the formal proclamation of rights
and the upholding of them in reality. What is required then, is a
genuine transformation of attitudes towards animals, the end
result being that formal rights would no longer be necessary.

There are limits to the ideological compatibility between
socialism and animal protection. Accompanying the support of
some socialists has been indifference, and even hostility, from
others. For some socialists, animal protection has been seen as a
middle-class fad, an irrelevance to the interests of the working
class. Moreover, whilst Labour party programmes have contained
some animal welfare commitments, these, with the exception of
hunting, have usually been no more radical than the other parties'
(see Chapter 7). Traditional socialist thought has reflected the
prime concern of socialist and labour movements and has been

irredeemably anthropocentric. Anthropocentric values, then, are not a characteristic limited to capitalist societies any more than socialist or communist societies would be happy to forgo cheap food, safe products or scientific advance. Indeed, socialism's historic roots lie in the same set of materialist and anthropocentric values as liberal capitalism and it therefore has no greater claim to be considered as an ideology that can incorporate animal protection in particular or environmentalism in general.

Benton's valiant attempt to rescue socialism for animals, whilst ingenious, is problematic. His need-based principle leads to reformist rather than abolitionist principles, and is therefore hardly likely to satisfy advocates of a higher moral status for animals. In addition, the Marxist insight that relationships between humans can be improved by a change in the economic system is not readily transferable to animals. The ending of animal exploitation will require human attitudes to change, and this can only come about through the dominance of ideas, a perception that sits uneasily with the Marxist emphasis on the primary of material forces. In other words, maybe liberals were right all along.

Feminist arguments for animal protection, part of a broader eco-feminist literature, have emerged in recent years (see Donovan and Adams, 1996). Two major strands are employed. In the so-called 'oppression' strand, particularly associated with Carol Adams (1990, 1994), it is suggested that sexism and speciesism are but one side of the same coin, and that women are more able than men to empathise with the exploitation of animals. The second, 'values' strand, draws on the work of Gilligan (1982), and rejects rights theory, which it perceives to be based on masculine language – such as rationalism, universality and fairness – in favour of an ethic of care, which invokes feminine values – such as compassion, empathy, sympathy, and context.

Whatever the validity of these approaches, the gender dimension is worth exploring because an interesting facet of the animal protection movement is the important role played by women. One American study estimated that 70 per cent of the animal protection movement consisted of women (Rowan, 1989: 99–100), and the situation is much the same in Britain, with one survey in the late 1980s revealing that women are twice as likely to be vegetarians as men (Porritt and Winner, 1988: 197), and data provided by the International Fund for Animal Welfare a decade later revealing that no less than 72 per cent of its members are female (*Daily Telegraph*, 10 July 1997).

In terms of the oppression strand, it is true that women are the regular victims of male-induced violence, and that the patriarchal language sometimes used to describe women – as 'meat', 'cow', 'bitch' and so on – is animalistic and exploitative. However, this parallel is of limited utility, not least because the law in most societies prohibits violence against women, as well as sexist action in general, whereas it positively encourages violence against animals. It is also true that, despite predominating in the animal protection movement, the vast majority of women do eat meat and are not animal protection activists.

The values strand is based on the assumptions that the values associated with rights theory are in fact masculine and that they are unhelpful in securing the protection of animals. Both assumptions can be challenged. Rights theory, by emphasising respect for individuals and seeking to prevent harm to them, cannot be said to be entirely devoid of the values – of care, sympathy and compassion – that eco-feminists applaud. Moreover, an ethic of care does not provide us with much of a guide to action. Does it for instance preclude the eating of meat or does the care only continue until the point of slaughter? Further, how do we reconcile caring for animals with caring for humans who might benefit, say, from the exploitation of animals in the process of developing a cure for a fatal illness? Rights theory can offer us more clear-cut answers to these questions and at the very least it seems hasty to abandon it without first considering whether the two approaches might be combined in some way.

The arguments reviewed in this chapter, although complex and contentious, provide us with the necessary framework within which we can consider the specific issues that involve our treatment of animals and the activities of pressure groups who have been contributors to and influenced by this debate. Thus, in the pages that follow, the implications for holding the positions identified in this chapter will be explored. That is not to say that I am adopting a pluralist position as regards the moral theories presented in this chapter. Certainly, problems arise due to the intractability of moral theory itself rather than the particular case of animals. Nevertheless, whilst not convinced by all of the claims made on behalf of animals by Tom Regan, I do think that the moral orthodoxy is seriously flawed and, in particular, that it seriously underestimates, for the reasons indicated above, the importance of the interest that animals have in not suffering. In addition, I am more convinced by the protection afforded to both humans and animals by rights than I am by utilitarianism, with the difficulties of measurement and its unpredictable results.

Whatever the validity of the challenges to the moral orthodoxy it is important to recognise that they have played, as the next chapter will show, a key role in the development of the animal protection movement in recent years. Likewise, whatever the flaws in the moral orthodoxy, mainstream debate concerning animals is structured around it, and is likely to continue to be structured around it for the foreseeable future. That is not to say that the 'new' morality has not had an impact or that this impact will not increase. What will be emphasised, however, is that even if we accept only the minimalist position represented by the moral orthodoxy there is still a great deal of scope for reform. Since it is agreed that, at the very least, animals should not be outside our moral concern and, as a consequence, we have some duties towards them, the evidence provided in Chapters 3 to 6 should make the reader somewhat uncomfortable.

Notes

1 Even Carruthers recognises the widespread academic and public acceptance of the capacity of animals to suffer, and devotes most of his book-length study to the development of an argument, similar to Frey, against the moral standing of animals despite their ability to suffer.

2 It is somewhat ironic that Francione adopts this approach after criticising my advocacy of it in the first edition of this book (see Francione, 1996: 136–9).

3 It is not being claimed that this chapter provides a comprehensive account of all of the varied attempts to justify according to animals a higher moral status. Mention here should also be made of Stephen Clark (1984: 186) who, in an effective demolition of the arguments utilised to demonstrate man's dominion over animals, does not himself offer 'any consistent moral system in the course of my explorations' and indeed doubts 'if there is any set of rules, any clear and

compendious system that does full justice to the vagaries and unformalizable sensitivities of our moral experience'. Similarly, Andrew Linzey (1976, 1987) has provided the most sustained attempt to justify the greater protection of animals from within the Christian tradition. Both Ryder (1975) and Rollin (1981, 1989) argue for rights by invoking the sentiency of animals, rather than their inherent value. Last, but not least, Mary Midgley (1979, 1983) in seeking to rescue a moderate reformist approach from absolutist animal rightists, asserts that even if one concludes that human interests take precedence over those of animals, we should not assume that by upholding the interests of animals we necessarily have to sacrifice the interests of humans – a perceptive observation that has, as we shall see, great relevance in a discussion of the arguments for vegetarianism, the reduction, or even abolition, of the use of animals in scientific experiments and the protection of wildlife.

2

Radicalism and revival: the animal protection movement since the 1970s

We have seen that the philosophical challenge to the way in which animals are treated has been both sophisticated and persuasive and that moral theory in general provides the key to understanding the modern debate about animals. Philosophical ideas, however sophisticated and persuasive, though, only become socially and politically important when they strike a public chord. This chapter, then, seeks to explore the movement which has grown up to protect animals. This movement has its origins in the nineteenth century, but since the 1970s has been revitalised. This revitalisation, moreover, has coincided with, and is no doubt partly explained by, the emergence of an increasingly influential number of groups and individuals who seek to campaign for the radical demands warranted by the granting to animals of a higher moral status. This resurgence, and the character it has taken, is documented and an attempt is made to explain the growing political importance of animal protection.

History and growth

The cause of animal protection is far from new. In both Britain (and, indeed, in most northern European countries) and America, the origins of the movement date back to the nineteenth century. The first national animal welfare society in the world was the Society for the Prevention of Cruelty to Animals (SPCA; the Royal prefix was added in 1840) founded in London in 1824, fifteen years after the formation of the oldest known group in the world, the Liverpool Society for Preventing Wanton Cruelty to Brute

Animals, which later became a branch of the SPCA. This was followed, later in the century, by the creation of a number of other societies mainly concerned with the specific issue of vivisection. In America, the first animal welfare society – the American Society for the Prevention of Cruelty to Animals (ASPCA) – was set up by Henry Bergh in 1866. By the 1890s three further national animal protection societies and numerous local humane societies and SPCAs, had been formed, mainly in the north east. In 1877, these local societies were united in the federal organisation of the American Humane Association (Rowan, 1989: 97; Ryder, 1989: 171–3).

It is interesting to note the links between animal protection and other social reform movements. Most suffragettes tended also to be in the forefront of campaigns against vivisection. Likewise, William Wilberforce and Fowell Buxton, two founding figures of the RSPCA, were also leading lights in the fight against slavery. Lord Shaftesbury, similarly, was not only a campaigner against cruelty to animals but also author of the Factory Acts and instrumental in the setting up of the National Society for the Prevention of Cruelty to Children. The idea for a society devoted to protecting children had come from Henry Bergh's ASPCA which had prosecuted a child cruelty case (by using statutes designed to protect animals!) and had been involved in the creation of the New York Society for the Prevention of Cruelty to Children, which began life from a corner of the ASPCA office (Turner, 1964: 129; Singer, 1990: 221–2).

For much of the twentieth century, in marked contrast to the Victorian era, the animal protection movement failed to make much of an impact. Since the 1970s (and a decade later in the United States), however, there has been a marked revitalisation and this upsurge has coincided with a growing radicalism, both in terms of objectives and methods. In Britain, as we shall see, a number of new animal rights groups were formed and there was a shift in emphasis towards grass-roots campaigning. Moreover, the older anti-vivisection societies were reinvigorated.

In the United States, there were two streams to the development of the animal rights movement. One centred on New York and Henry Spira's well-documented campaigns against laboratory animal exploitation (see Finsen and Finsen, 1994: 58–60; Jasper and Nelkin, 1992: 26–9; Singer, 1998). The other centred on the creation of People for the Ethical Treatment of Animals (PETA). Here, an important role was played by Alex Hershaft who, in the 1970s, organised a series of vegetarian conferences at which he and others agitated for the inclusion of an animal rights agenda. These initiatives led, in 1981, to the creation of a number of animal rights organisations, most notably PETA, Hershaft's own Farm Animal Reform Movement (FARM) and Trans-Species Unlimited (Jasper and Nelkin, 1992: 29–31).

There are a number of ways of measuring the revitalisation of the animal protection movement. Firstly, there has been a marked increase in the number of groups existing. Calculating numbers is really dependent upon the criteria for inclusion and such a bewildering variety of groups exists that it is possible to develop a number of different lists. The figure for Britain is arrived at by adopting very loose criteria: firstly, all those groups with a national focus (or international provided that a branch exists in Britain), and, secondly, those who have a significant concern for the protection of animals. Taking this set of conditions, it is possible to identify about 150 groups. A better guide is to consider the major groups – defined here as those with either a large membership or considerable wealth or a high public profile. Such a distinction is somewhat arbitrary but serves the purpose of making our analysis a little more manageable. The result, as shown in table 2.1, is a list of thirty-five organisations.

It will be seen that the growth of the movement has been uneven. Eight were created in the nineteenth century, and a further eight between 1902 and 1944. There then followed a gap between the end of the Second World War and 1960 when only one new group was formed. Since 1960, however, another period of expansion has taken place with eighteen substantial new groups emerging, six in the 1960s, five in the 1970s, three in the 1980s, and four in the 1990s. A similar pattern has occurred in the United States. As table 2.2 shows, from 1890 to 1950, very few national organisations emerged to add to the initial flourish between the 1860s and the 1880s. By contrast, in the forty years between 1950 and 1990, a further thirty-one organisations were formed, the bulk (twenty-two) in the 1970s and 1980s.

The number of new groups created does not tell us the whole story and might even underestimate the growth of the animal protection movement since the 1970s. For a more accurate

Table 2.1 *Major animal protection organisations in Britain with formation dates*

Advocates for Animals (1902)[a]	LACS (1924)
ALF (1976)	Lynx (1985)[e]
Animal Aid (1977)	NAVS (1875)
Animal Concern (1876)[b]	PDSA (1917)
Blue Cross (1897)	PETA (1995)
BUAV (1898)	Respect for Animals (1992)
BVA (1881)	RSNC (1912)
CAPS (1957)	RSPB (1889)
Cats Protection (1927)[c]	RSPCA (1824)
CIWF (1967)	SHAC (1999)
Dogs Trust (1891)[d]	UFAW (1926)
FoE (1970)	Uncaged Campaigns (1994)
FRAME (1969)	Vegan Society (1944)
Greenpeace (1977)	Vegetarian Society (1969)[f]
HSA (1964)	Viva (1994)
International Donkey Protection Trust (1968)	Whale and Dolphin Conservation Society (1987)
International League for the Protection of Horses (1927)	WWF (1961) Zoo Check (1984)

Notes
[a] Formerly the Scottish Society for the Prevention of Vivisection.
[b] Formerly the Scottish Anti-Vivisection Society.
[c] Formerly the Cats Protection League.
[d] Formerly the NCDL.
[e] Lynx went out of business in 1992 and was replaced by Respect for Animals
[f] The modern Vegetarian Society was set up in 1969, although the word 'vegetarian' was first coined in 1842 and the original Vegetarian Society was founded in 1847.

picture we also have to look at the membership figures of both the new and the old groups. It is difficult to estimate the total number of those involved. Clive Hollands (1985: 171), a leading animal rights campaigner in the 1970s and 1980s, estimated in 1985 that the paid-up membership of all the animal protection groups in Britain was fewer than 500,000, less than 1 per cent of the total population. Although not confirmed, this figure almost certainly excludes those groups – such as the Royal Society for Nature Conservation (RSNC) – concerned with

Table 2.2 *Founding of national animal
protection organisations in the
United States by decade*

1860	2
1870	1
1880	2
1890	0
1900	0
1910	0
1920	1
1930	0
1940	0
1950	5
1960	4
1970	11
1980	11

Source: Rowan (1989: 97–100).

wildlife habitats. As a calculation for the membership of 'pure' animal protection groups it certainly exaggerates, as Hollands recognised, the total numbers involved since there is little to stop individuals from being members of more than one group. Only the RSPCA has regularly sought to expel people on the grounds that their views are incompatible with membership and, even then, the expulsions have involved a minuscule number of activists. Given this, there is little doubt that considerable overlap does occur. In 1977, for instance, a survey of Hunt Saboteurs Association (HSA) members revealed that 25 per cent also belonged to the RSPCA, 40 per cent to the League Against Cruel Sports (LACS), 20 per cent to Friends of the Earth (FoE), 12 per cent to vegetarian organisations and 18 per cent to anti-vivisection groups (Thomas, 1983: 161).

This, of course, affects the overall numbers involved but, by itself, does not stop us from making valid comparisons with the total numbers involved in the past, if we had the figures to hand, since there is no reason to think that overlapping membership did not also occur in the past. What does make this exercise futile is that there are now far more groups to join, therefore further potentially multiplying the overlap. Given this, the best guide is the membership increases within individual groups. Not surprisingly perhaps, the biggest increases have occurred in those organisations concerned with wider environmental and/or conservation issues. Thus, the Royal Society for the Protection of Birds (RSPB) had a membership of 890,000 in 1995 compared to 561,000 in 1987, 300,000 in 1983, 98,000 in 1971 and around 4,000 in the 1930s (Garner, 2000: 121). Similarly, the World Wide Fund for Nature (WWF) increased its membership from 12,000 in 1971 to 220,000 in 1995, FoE from 1,000 to 110,000 and the RSNC from 64,000 to 250,000 in the same period. Lowe and Goyder (1983: 1) have estimated that, in the early 1980s, one in ten British adults belonged to an environmental group. This gives a total of nearly three million people – a figure which had quadrupled since the 1960s.

Membership increases in the 'pure' animal protection groups have usually been less dramatic but still significant. Kim Stallwood, a leading British animal rights activist in the 1980s, for instance, reflected on the 'appallingly archaic and Dickensian' nature of the British Union for the Abolition of Vivisection (BUAV) when he first joined in 1978 (Windeatt, 1985). Within seven years, he claimed, a paper membership of 4,000 had been transformed into an active force of 16,000, although a member of the executive committee suggested that the figures were 8,000 in 1986 and 12,000 in 1989 (personal communication from Taggert King, BUAV executive member, 21 September 1989). Animal Aid, likewise, began life in Jean Pink's home but had to move to proper offices two years later in 1979 as the membership began to expand. By 1983, even bigger office space was necessary as the membership topped 10,000, and it now stands at around 16,000. In a similar vein, the LACS increased its membership from around 6,000 in 1950 to 12,000 in 1982, around 15,000 in 1989 and 20,000 by the end of the twentieth century; membership of the Vegetarian Society rose by 20 per cent between 1988 and 1989, and finally, the British branch of PETA, founded in 1995, and SHAC, founded in 1999, claim memberships of 4,000 and 14,000 respectively (*Guardian*, 6 November 2001). More spectacular increases have been recorded in the United States. PETA, for instance, has a membership of about 250,000, whilst the Humane Society of the United States (HSUS) increased its membership from around 35,000 in 1978 to 520,000 in 1988, and by the late

1990s claimed a membership of subscribers and supporters of over two million (Garner, 1998: 98; Rowan, 1989: 98).

With increased membership and general interest in the activities of animal protection organisations comes increased wealth. Again, the wildlife conservation groups have the highest incomes. For example, in the United States for the year 1996, The Nature Conservancy had a budget of $312m, the National Wildlife Federation $100m, the Wildlife Conservation Society $66m, the World Wildlife Fund $63m, the Sierra Club $44m, and the National Audubon Society $42m (Garner, 1998: 99). In Britain, similarly, the income of the WWF rose from £9 million in 1988 to £22 million in 1990, and the RSPB received a total income of £22.4 million in 1990 thereby displacing the RSPCA as the wealthiest animal protection group in Britain (*WWF News*, January 1992: 30; *Birds Magazine*, Autumn 1989: 8).

The wealth of the mainstream animal protection organisations is less substantial but still considerable. In the United States in 1996, the HSUS had a budget of $31m (and employed over 100 full-time staff), the ASPCA $18m, PETA $13.4m, and the AHA $6m (Garner, 1998: 99). In Britain, the income available to the RSPCA dwarfs all of the others, although it should be remembered that this has to finance a range of secondary activities as well as campaigning, as do the incomes of the ASPCA and AHA (see below). Drawn mostly from legacies and donations, as opposed to membership subscriptions, the RSPCA's total income in 1990 was £21.7 million, and this had risen to £66m by 2002 (although this represented a decline from the late 1990s, plunging the Society into some financial difficulty – see below) (RSPCA Accounts 1990: 2–4). The income of other animal protection organisations in Britain is much smaller. In 2002, for instance, the income of NAVS was £1.4 million, 67 per cent of which came from legacies and only 13 per cent from membership subscriptions and donations (NAVS Annual Report, 2002).

It is appropriate at this point to examine the relationship between the national leadership of the animal protection groups and the membership. Although animal protection groups do have national memberships, they do not tend to have separate branches at the local level. Rather, local groups have emerged in a voluntary fashion and remain largely independent of particular national organisations, although paid employees are appointed by many national groups to assist with the creation and campaigning of local groups. Sometimes, in addition, national groups provide funds for specific campaigns run in a particular locality. Again, the exception to this general pattern is the RSPCA which has a strong local and regional structure, reflecting its longevity and its independence from the emergence of the more radical movement. Most local groups, though, consist of people who may be members of a variety of national organisations (or none at all). The main link is through a system of contacts, whereby a partic-ular member of a local group becomes the appointed representative of a national organisation. This remains an infor-mal arrangement, however, and certainly involves no real obligations on either side except where a national organisation provides a grant to aid a local group.

The reason for focusing on local groups here is that another dimension of growth, and radicalism, is the emergence of active local groups since the 1970s, which has been startling. According to the computerised list compiled by a co-ordinating organisation based in Nottingham, there are over 600 animal rights groups in England, some college-based, some branches of national organi-sations, and others independent (the Animal Contacts Directory can be found at www.veggies.org.uk). By contrast, the size and diversity of the United States, and its concomitantly decentralised political system, means that local or state-wide groups are extremely important. Indeed, it may be that focusing on national groups underestimates the rapid development of autonomous groups operating at a lower level. Very little information exists on this. One commentator suggested that by 1990 some 7,000 animal protection organisations existed in the United States with a total membership (again bearing in mind the problem of overlap) of over ten million. Another report has suggested that between the mid-1970s and mid-1980s five- to tenfold increases in membership were common in many of them (Rosenberger, 1990; Rowan, 1990: 16).

The final indication of growth in the animal protection move-ment involves the idea of what Lowe and Goyder call the 'attentive public', those who are not members of any groups but who share, to a greater or lesser extent, their aims (Lowe and Goyder, 1983: 9). In the first place, this manifests itself in the gap between public opinion and the state of the law. This particularly applies to hunting where, although the membership of anti-hunting groups remains relatively small, opinion polls have indicated considerable opposition to hunting for many years, and this has continued despite the emergence of the Countryside Alliance (CA) in the late 1990s. Thus, a Gallup poll taken in the aftermath of the CA's first national demonstration in 1998 revealed that opposition to hunting was just as strong with 78 per cent disapproving of it (*Daily Telegraph*, 7 March 1998).

It is clear that the young in particular are concerned about the treatment of animals. A remarkable poll conducted for Sky Magazine in 1989, for instance, showed that one in five of those polled between the ages of sixteen and twenty-five (and one in four of those aged between sixteen and nineteen) supported the Animal Liberation Front's (ALF) 'terrorist' campaigns and 45 per cent agreed with the group's aims but not its methods. Furthermore, 40 per cent said they did not approve of animal experiments under any circumstances (*Sunday Times*, 10 September 1989).

As we shall see in a future chapter, one of the key strategies of animal protection groups has been to influence the consumer. Here there have been significant shifts in recent years with the decline of the fur industry in Britain and the increasing popularity of 'cruelty-free' products, sold by general supermarkets as well as specialist retailers such as Beauty Without Cruelty and the Body Shop. There has also been a substantial increase of people declaring themselves to be vegetarians. As late as the early 1970s, being a vegetarian was regarded as distinctly odd. Now, it is verging on the commonplace. By 1997, a survey revealed that 6 per cent were now vegetarian, and 14 per cent did not eat red meat (*The Times*, 20 May 1997), about double the number of a decade previously. Of course, one can abstain from meat for a variety of reasons but disquiet about animal welfare has been an important factor in the dietary revolution.

Characterising the animal protection movement

In order to develop a greater understanding of the animal protection movement it is useful to identify key classificatory dimensions. Much of the rest of this chapter will be concerned with exploring these dimensions. These are:

1 Cause/sectional
2 Primary/secondary functions
3 Scope
4 Animal rights/welfare
5 New social movement?

Before we begin this exploration, it is worth mentioning that there is a sixth important classificatory dimension, that of strategy, but since this will be covered comprehensively in Chapters 7 and 8, it will not be touched upon in this chapter.

Cause/sectional

The most popular distinction in the pressure group literature is between sectional or interest groups, on the one hand, and promotional or cause groups on the other. The former exist to defend the interests of a particular section of the community (such as a particular occupation or type of business) and membership is usually restricted to those who belong to that section. These groups are not exclusively, or even mainly, concerned with putting pressure on public authorities but also engage in providing various services – such as pensions and legal advice – to their members. The latter seek to promote a particular idea or belief and membership is open to all those who share the same view. A noted feature of pressure group politics has been that since 1945, and particularly since the 1960s, there has been a rapid expansion of cause groups.

Of course, one of the causes which has been revitalised is that of animal protection. All animal protection groups seek to promote the cause of animals and anyone who is concerned about vivisection, hunting, the fur trade, factory farming or whatever can find an organisation to belong to. Not all, though, are exclusively promotional. Thus, the Vegetarian and Vegan societies in Britain and elsewhere all campaign to end animal cruelty (which, for them, involves the end of the meat industry), but at the same time seek to defend the interests of their members – advising on diet and encouraging the food industry to cater for their needs. Similarly, the British Veterinary Association (BVA) seeks to promote the cause of animal welfare but also represents vets in all aspects of their work. Various trading companies too – most notably Beauty Without Cruelty – are sectional organisations with a vested economic interest in the move away from the use of animals in the production of cosmetics and toiletries.

One of the key questions asked by interest group and social movement scholars is why do individuals become involved in voluntary group activity? One seminal answer provided by Olson (1965) was that individuals only participate when there are what he calls 'selective incentives' to be gained from doing so. Joining a group because of the collective objectives that a group pursues is not sufficient justification for Olson's rational choice approach because, he calculates, individuals will take a 'free ride', enjoying the benefits of the goals without participating in their achievement. Only if benefits are exclusively available to members, then, will there be an incentive to join. If correct, this interpretation has profound implications for the nature of pressure group politics since only sectional groups can provide significant selective incentives in the form, for instance, of cheaper insurance policies or legal advice. Cause groups, who first and foremost are concerned with achieving collective goals, will then, according to Olson, be severely disadvantaged.

Cause groups such as those concerned with animal protection have, as we have seen, prospered particularly since the 1960s. Where does this leave Olson? Well, it can either be argued that Olson was wrong, and that individuals do join cause groups because they value the achievement of collective goals, or that cause groups compensate for the absence of selective incentives in some other way. One example of the latter is that cause groups make up for lack of members by the existence of entrepreneurs, who pay the costs of setting up organisations in return for an income from them once established. This might have some relevance in the animal protection movement where there have been many examples of individuals almost single-handedly getting an organisation started – Jean Pink in the case of Animal Aid, and Christine Stevens in the case of the Animal Welfare Institute in the United States being two prime examples (see Garner, 1998: 73–5 for other examples).

The animal protection movement has become a mass movement, however, and this would seem difficult to explain in Olsonian terms. Moreover, the achievement of collective animal rights-inspired goals would seem to be the major reason why individuals join the animal protection movement (Garner, 1998: 76–8). One possible speculative explanation which is closer to a rational choice position is that individuals join the animal protection movement for the solidaristic benefits of so doing, that joining a movement containing like-minded people meets deep-seated psychological needs. It may well be, therefore, that the distinct identity offered by membership of the animal rights movement is functional for organisational recruitment and maintenance. As we shall see in Chapter 7, however, it might not be quite so functional for the achievement of movement goals.

Primary/secondary functions

While the strategy of the animal protection movement tends to focus on how best to influence decision-makers and the general public (see Chapters 7 and 8), there is a whole series of so-called 'secondary' functions performed by animal protection organisations. As Wyn Grant (1989: 9–11) points out, primary groups are those whose main purpose is to campaign for political change, whereas secondary groups are those who seek to provide a service to their members or to those on whose behalf a particular group is working. This provides a further classificatory refinement to add to the traditional sectional/ promotional distinction in that it allows for the fact that some promotional groups do, like sectional groups, have a service role, even though it is not aimed at those who are members.

   The extent to which animal protection groups offer a secondary service function varies. Those adopting a purely campaigning role are a relatively new phenomenon, deriving from the rise of mass-membership animal rights groups in recent years. Thus, groups such as Animal Aid have no 'hands on' role with animals. At the other end of the spectrum are those organisations which have little or no political role, such as the large number of independent animal sanctuaries which exist exclusively to help distressed animals, the nature reserves managed by the County Trusts for Nature Conservation overseen by the RSNC, the wildfowl refuges managed by the Wildfowl and Wetlands Trust and the voluntary work of those trained by the British Trust for Conservation Volunteers. Also in this category can be included the little-known activities of the numerous badger patrol groups who enforce the law by protecting badger setts.

Many primarily secondary groups will take on a political role intermittently when legislation particularly affecting them is in the offing or when government seeks advice on an animal-related matter. This applies to older organisations such as the Blue Cross, the People's Dispensary for Sick Animals (PDSA), the National Canine Defence League (NCDL) and Cats Protection, whose prime concern is to provide help to sick or injured animals. The PDSA alone provides over a million free treatments a year (*Guardian*, 12 October 2002). Finally, the International League for the Protection of Horses and the International Donkey Protection Trust conduct a more or less permanent campaigning presence but also spend a great deal of time directly caring for neglected equines.

Conflict has often revolved around the primary/secondary distinction whereby radicals within the animal protection movement have criticised the service focus of the older welfare groups. This conflict obviously relates particularly to the RSPCA (see below) but the LACS has also faced similar divisions. Under the chairmanship of Raymond Rowley who took over in the early 1960s, the LACS began to concentrate its efforts on the buying of land, often in strategic positions to disrupt hunts, which it turned into sanctuaries. As a result, it placed much less emphasis on trying to obstruct hunts in the field and in seeking legislative change to abolish hunting. By 1976, the LACS owned over 1,500 acres mainly on Exmoor. In the 1970s conflict (similar to that which was going on in the RSPCA) between the radicals, led by Richard Course, and the moderates, led by Rowley, came to a head. At a stormy AGM in 1977, Rowley (who had not helped his cause by being involved in Course's prosecution for receiving documents stolen from the British Field Sports Society) was removed from the chair to be replaced, at a recommended meeting later in the year, by the old animal welfare campaigner Lord Houghton. Houghton was acceptable to the majority because he emphasised the need for the LACS to seek the legislative abolition of hunting (Thomas, 1983: 89–91).

Despite intermittent disputes, the LACS now effectively balances its primary and secondary activities. It now owns about thirty separate sites covering over 2,000 acres in the West

Country, strategically placed to hinder deer hunting. As Thomas (1983: 99) points out, the sanctuary strategy has been a success at three levels. Not only does it directly prevent some animals from being killed by the hunt, but it can also lead to extensive publicity for the LACS's work whenever a hunt trespasses on its land, as well as providing a useful way of spending income from legacies. The RSPB has always successfully combined a political role with the owning and managing of nature reserves. It now has 170 reserves covering more than 280,000 acres (*Guardian*, 3 October 2001).

The RSPCA was created with the dual function of campaigning to change the law and public opinion as well as the secondary function of enforcing Martin's Act (Radford, 2001: 82–3). For much of its history, however, it has operated almost purely as a service organisation concerned, above all, with gratuitous cruelty or neglect towards animals kept as pets. Indeed, until the 1970s, any attempt within the RSPCA to seek legislative change (from the organisation of demonstrations even to corresponding quietly with ministers) was frowned upon. Only in recent years, primarily due to the influence of the radicals, has it begun to adopt an active political strategy as its founders intended (see below).

Although the campaigning side of the RSPCA's work has now expanded, it still performs a formidably effective service role, operating animal homes, hospitals and clinics in addition to assisting other independently run operations. The RSPCA is best known, of course, for its uniformed inspectorate and the enforcement of anti-cruelty laws. There are now ten regional headquarters manned until 10 p.m. every day from which 328 inspectors – responsible for investigating cruelty to animals, providing advice and information on their welfare and aiding those in distress generally – work (Radford, 2001: 375–81). The size of this operation is now under severe threat as a result of the RSPCA's declining income. A proposal to restructure the Society and make a considerable number of staff redundant was proposed and at the time of writing staff had voted to take limited industrial action (*Guardian*, 26 July, 5 September 2003).

Potential inspectors are trained rigorously by the RSPCA since a huge range of eventualities can be encountered. Thus, the seven month course includes not only classroom training and examinations in all aspects of animal welfare but also practical aspects such as mountain rescue, boat training, the use of firearms and hands-on experience of slaughterhouse methods. Finally, mention should be made of the Special Investigations and Operations Department founded in 1977. This 'undercover' arm of the inspectorate has proved particularly effective for monitoring the transportation of livestock abroad and, with the help of the police, raiding dog fights. Some spectacular successes have been achieved in the latter area, where intervention can be extremely dangerous, sometimes necessitating the presence of armed police (Beattie, 1990).

The radical criticism of the traditional animal welfare approach has a great deal of force. Not only does the service function absorb massive amounts of valuable funds that could be utilised for campaigning and influencing policy makers in a range of issue areas involving animals but, taking in and often killing abandoned animals (a practice which many in the movement abhor) is arguably dealing with the consequences of the problem rather than the problem itself, the resolution of which really lies in more stringent laws and a change in social attitudes. Indeed, by helping to disguise the problem, it may hinder a public policy solution which is part of the reasoning behind the NCDL's policy of refusing to kill healthy animals. Of course, the modern RSPCA recognises these problems. It has toyed with the idea of adopting the NCDL approach and its hard-hitting campaign for a dog registration scheme was an effective counter to the charge that the primary and secondary functions are mutually exclusive. In addition, can a movement which campaigns for animals really stand back and ignore their immediate needs in the interests of possible future gains? Finally, of course, few would dispute the valuable work done by the RSPCA inspectorate which not only acts as a deterrent against future cruelty (it is not the Society's fault that the penalties are often grossly inadequate) but also performs an essential educational role.

Animal protection groups undertake a variety of other functions which do not involve directly helping particular animals in need but which do constitute activities short of seeking political change. Compassion in World Farming (CIWF), for instance, set up a marketing company – the Athena Trust – which helps to finance its activities, the Humane Slaughter Association provides advice on slaughtering techniques and finances research into improvements and the Vegetarian Society has a research section which commissions academic studies to demonstrate the benefits of a vegetarian diet. Particularly important are those organisations who seek to promote alternatives to the use of animals in the laboratory. The Fund for the Replacement of Animals in Medical Experiments (FRAME) publishes a quarterly scientific journal *ATLA* which provides a forum for discussion on this issue and, together with the Dr Hadwen Trust for Humane Research (founded by BUAV) and the Lord Dowding Fund (founded by NAVS), finances research projects investigating alternatives.

Scope

There are a variety of dimensions relating to scope. The first is concerned with issue coverage. Here the most important distinction is between those groups – such as the RSPCA and Animal Aid – who are concerned with the whole range of issues affecting animals, and those that are concerned with a single issue or type of animal. Thus, for instance, CIWF in Britain and FARM in the United States are concerned with animal agriculture, NAVS and BUAV campaign against vivisection whilst the RSPB concern is equally self-evident. Some groups, such as the International League for the Protection of Horses, are more specific still and focus on a particular species.

Secondly, one can distinguish between groups on the basis of their geographical scope. Thus, whilst most groups focus on national issues, others have a wider remit. In the latter category, we can make a distinction between British-based groups who aim to protect animals in other countries by setting up sanctuaries and/or liaising with foreign groups, and genuinely international groups. Thus, in the former category are groups such as the International League for the Protection of Horses, the Greek Animal Welfare Fund (founded in 1959), the Society for the Protection of Animals in North Africa (founded in 1923) and, probably the best known, Brooke Hospital for Animals in Cairo (founded in 1932).

Genuinely international groups are of three main types. Firstly, there are those which exist in many countries but whose national organisations remain autonomous. The classic examples here are Greenpeace and FoE. Secondly, there are those groups which operate on an international basis and are open for individuals and national groups to join. Thus, the World Society for the Protection of Animals, based in London, has branches throughout the world with 400 societies in 66 countries affiliated to it. Similarly, both the International Council for Bird Preservation (founded in 1922) and the WWF are powerful groups in international conservation. Mention should be made here too of the International Fund for Animal Welfare (IFAW), founded by the Welshman Brian Davies in Canada in 1968. This is a unique group which has no formal structure, but simply maintains a list of supporters and activists in many countries. It is a dynamic 'commando-type' organisation which exists to move in on specific areas of animal protection as they arise, its most notable success being the campaign against the Canadian seal clubbing in the 1970s.

Finally, there are international groups which are totally or largely maintained by affiliated national organisations. Some, such as the International Vegetarian Union, exist merely to provide a means whereby animal campaigners in different countries can keep in touch through, for example, occasional conferences. Much more important are Eurogroup for Animal Welfare and the International Union for Conservation of Nature and Natural Resources (IUCN). Formed in 1980, Eurogroup for Animal Welfare exists purely to represent animal protection groups in the twenty-five member states in European Union institutions and also provides the secretariat for the Intergroup on Animal Welfare consisting of MEPs. Founded in 1948, IUCN (or the World Conservation Union) is only partly a non-governmental organisation in that membership is open to both national pressure groups and governments and their agencies. Sixty-four states, 111 government agencies and more than 400 pressure groups are affiliated members of it.

Animal rights/welfare

Of overwhelming importance in the classification of the animal protection movement is the distinction between animal welfare and animal rights. At a theoretical level, this distinction may not be strictly accurate because, of course, Singer (who, if anything, is quoted more often than Regan by the movement) is a radical but not an advocate of rights. Nevertheless, at a practical level, this philosophical nuance is largely lost and, as we saw, Singer is prepared to accept the rhetorical value of rights. Another problem is that some groups do not use these labels. It might, therefore, be more appropriate to use the terms radicals and conservatives instead, to avoid being accused of imposing a set of values for analytical convenience. Having said that, it is usually clear from a group's objectives where they stand. Put simply, if a group demands, as a short- or long-term objective, the complete abolition of animal use for science and/or food, they are opposed to the moral orthodoxy which justifies these activities. The essential point, then, is that the terms welfare and rights are indicative of the key division within the animal protection movement; between those who consider that animal interests should take a subordinate, albeit important, position and those who recognise a higher moral status for animals.

It should have become apparent by now that the revitalisation of the animal protection movement is inseparable from the radical character that this re-emergence has taken. The creation of radical and conservative wings has caused problems for the movement as internal divisions over objectives and strategies have, at times, seemed to take precedence over the acknowledged common enemy. Divisions in the animal protection movement, however, are not new. In the nineteenth century, for instance, Lewis Gompertz, who replaced Arthur Broome in 1828 to become the RSPCA's second secretary, eventually recognised the incompatibility between his uncompromising vegetarianism and anti-vivisectionist principles and the RSPCA's approach and left in 1832 to form the Animal's Friend Society (Turner, 1964: 142). Also worth mentioning is the Humanitarian League, founded by Henry Salt, one of the earliest advocates of animal rights as both a writer and an activist (Salt, 1980). The RSPCA's moderation, epitomised by its failure to oppose blood sports, was also the cause of the formation of the League for the Prohibition of Cruel Sports (later renamed the LACS) in 1924 by two disillusioned RSPCA members, Henry Amos and Ernest Bell (Ryder, 1989: 135).

The most serious splits occurred over the issue of animal experimentation. The RSPCA's failure to tackle vivisection head on led to the formation of the Victoria Street Society in 1875 (renamed NAVS in 1897) which (as did other groups such as the London AntiVivisection Society and the International Association for the Total Suppression of Vivisection) campaigned vigorously for the complete abolition of animal use in scientific research. The main force behind this was the leading Victorian animal activist Frances Power Cobbe who, as Richard French points out, 'became in the public mind the personification of anti-vivisection.' Cobbe left the RSPCA disillusioned at its moderate stance and in particular at its failure to lobby effectively for legislative restrictions (French, 1975: 62, 175). She was not, however, an animal rights advocate in the modern sense. In the first place, she, like many other opponents of vivisection, was not a vegetarian. In the second, she was not, in principle, an aboli-tionist but became one as a result of the recognition (due to the failure, in her eyes, of the 1876 Cruelty to Animals Act) that vivisection could not be effectively restricted (see Chapter 5) (French, 1975: 160–1). In the 1890s, a split developed within the anti-vivisection movement itself and Cobbe left to form the uncompromisingly abolitionist BUAV due to the NAVS's move, engineered by Stephen Coleridge, towards reformism (although this was a dispute over strategy as much as objectives) (Turner, 1964: 201–10).

What is clear though is that, nourished on a far more receptive social climate, the modern challenge to the dominant welfare ideology has been much more substantial. This can be seen, firstly, in the radicalism of many of the new societies. Groups such as Animal Aid in Britain and PETA, in both Britain and the United States, for instance, are uncompromising in their objective to see the end of all exploitative use of animals, whether by indi-viduals or institutions, and are not afraid of organising mass action to further this cause. Their moral case is clear. Thus, an Animal Aid policy document on vivisection in the 1990s stated that: 'Whatever the precise value of animal experiments are, and whatever alternatives may exist, the case against vivisection is first and foremost a moral one' and, lest one should be in any doubt about what this means, it goes on to say that: 'Discussion of alternative methods should not be allowed to imply that if there were no alternatives, vivisection is acceptable' (*Towards Animal Rights*, Animal Aid Report: 5).

Another distinguishing feature is the tendency for animal rights groups to recognise the parallels between different forms of animal exploitation. Their acceptance of animal rights, then, necessitates an attack on all fronts – vivisection, animal agriculture, zoos, the fur industry, blood sports – because they are all morally indefensible and to focus on one without the others seems to them inconsistent. As an indication of the wider concern precipitated by animal rights, the two Scottish anti-vivisection societies (namely the Scottish Anti-Vivisection Society and the Scottish Society for the Prevention of Vivisection) changed their names (to Animal Concern and Advocates for Animals respectively) to reflect their concern with other animal issues. Another symbol is that vegetarianism or even veganism is *de rigueur* for employment by the radical organisations even if a particular group is not directly concerned with farm animals. More to the point, those who work for the radical organisations are likely to be at least vegetarians anyway, since to be otherwise would compromise the moral principles on which their activities are based.

Even some of the single issue groups show some interest in other animal-related issues and are more likely now to be abolitionist. The LACS, for instance, are against all blood sports (with the exception of fishing upon which they have regularly refused to express an opinion). In addition, all of the British anti-vivisectionist societies (BUAV, NAVS, Animal Concern, and Uncaged), despite their historical differences, are now uncompromisingly abolitionists as are the bulk of the American anti-vivisectionist societies. Similarly, Advocates for Animals retains the ultimate goal of the abolition of vivisection even though it is prepared to countenance a reformist route as a tactic and, although CIWF concentrates on the worst excesses of factory farming rather than the promotion of vegetarianism, this is a tactic rather than an objective. The founders, Peter and Anna Roberts (who once ran a farm), are themselves vegetarians, as are the organisation's staff, and would like to see the end of the meat industry (see Chapter 7). The logic of animal rights, too, has led other groups, such as the ALF (in Britain and elsewhere) and the HSA, to adopt more direct methods. These will be explored in more detail in Chapter 8, but for now it should be noted that this kind of activity (whether it be breaking into laboratories or attacking the meat industry) would be unsustainable without the moral underpinnings of animal rights which many direct actionists believe (without necessarily having a sophisticated understanding of the theoretical debate) justify, and even necessitate, such activity.

Of course, a significant section of the animal protection movement still clings to the traditional welfare ideology. The RSPCA and the various American humane societies (some of which are exceedingly moderate) are the obvious examples. In addition, there is the Animal Welfare Institute based in Washington, DC. Founded in 1951, this organisation has a typical welfarist outlook – to 'reduce the sum total of pain and fear inflicted on animals', to promote the 'humane treatment of laboratory animals' and to 'reform the cruel treatment of food animals' (*Aims and Programs*, Animal Welfare Institute leaflet). Three other British organisations – FRAME, the Universities Federation for Animal Welfare (UFAW) and the Humane Slaughter Association – have the same outlook. FRAME was formed in 1969 to promote and finance research into alternatives to the use of animals in laboratories (a similar role is performed in the United States by the Medical Research Modernisation Committee). Its work is guided by the so-called 'three Rs' approach, derived from Russell and Burch (1959), which involves reducing the number of animals used, refining procedures so that animal suffering is minimised and replacing animals in the long term. For FRAME, though, animals should continue to be used until alternatives are found since the potential benefits to humans should not be put at risk. A similar approach is adopted by UFAW which historically has had 'an almost fanatical determination not to be fanatical' (Ryder, 189: 146). Thus, it aims to promote alternatives to animals but does 'not engage on either side in public controversies relating to the legitimacy of making scientific experiments of animals' (UFAW Report and Accounts 1989–90: 28). Similarly, UFAW's sister organisation, the Humane Slaughter Association, does not consider the moral debate about killing animals for food but focuses, as its name suggests, primarily on the promotion of humane ways of slaughtering animals.

The growth of the radical movement for animals in recent years has placed veterinary organisations in a difficult position. Because of the nature of their profession, they are obviously involved with animals in a variety of settings which animal rights

activists condemn. Inevitably, they have been criticised, sometimes from within the profession, for sacrificing their concern for
animals in return for retaining the business of clients involved in
animal use. Two of Britain's most senior veterinarians – a former
government assistant chief veterinary officer and a former president of the Royal College of Veterinary Surgeons – joined the call,
in the early 1990s, for the BVA to mount a much more radical
campaign particularly against some intensive farming practices
(*Guardian*, 8 January 1992).

In this climate, it is not surprising that veterinary groups have
sought to highlight their concern for animal welfare. Few are
radicals (although note an organisation in America called the
Association of Veterinarians for Animal Rights), but they are
becoming increasingly vocal in opposition to some modern practices involving animals. Thus, the BVA has become much more
interested in ethical issues in recent years, creating the Animal
Welfare Committee to formulate policy statements and the
Animal Welfare Trust which has raised money to fund a chair in
animal welfare at Cambridge, currently held by Donald Broom.
In the United States, similarly, Tufts University School of
Veterinary Medicine, in particular, has done much to publicise
animal welfare issues both within the profession and to a wider
audience.

Given the difference in outlook between the two wings of the
movement, it is hardly surprising that conflict has been endemic.
Quite often, it has not been the reformist – rather than funda-
mentalist – stance of animal welfare organisations that has been
most galling to animal rights activists but the failure of some
organisations to campaign at all, or much beyond a specific
concern for pets and strays. This is particularly the case with
some of the humane societies in the United States. A symbol of
their narrow focus is the apparently common tendency for
wealthy welfare groups to invest in the very companies that the
radicals attack. Thus, for instance, the ASPCA held shares in, and
the American Humane Association received financial donations
from, McDonalds, the very organisation which has almost demo-
niac status within the animal rights movement (*Animals' Agenda*,
November 1990: 4).

It should not be a surprise to learn that many of these welfare
groups reject totally the ideas of animal rights and regard the

radical wing of the movement with disdain. In a classic instance of this, the Presidents of the HSUS, ASPCA and the Massachusetts SPCA published a joint statement 'Resolution for the 1990s' in the *New York Times* in which animal rights activists were criticised. In an even more revealing incident, John Hoyt, President of the HSUS, wrote, a memo (which was later leaked) to the US Secretary of Agriculture, disassociating himself from a previous memo written by Alex Hershaft, the radical President of FARM. Hershaft, Hoyt wrote, 'in no way speaks for the US animal protection movement' which he described as the 'legitimate' part of the movement. Amy Freeman, one of his colleagues on the HSUS board, was even less reticent when she publicly declared that animal rights groups are a 'fanatical fringe' (*Animals' Agenda*, May 1991: 33).

The conflict between the opposing ideologies is at its most intense when it occurs within the same organisation. Animal rights activists have regularly attempted to convert the old welfare societies in both Britain and America, not surprisingly when once considers the wealth and influence at their disposal. The most perennial and fierce conflict, though, has occurred within the RSPCA and it is worth considering the nature of this conflict in some detail. As Harriet Ritvo (1987: 131–8) has convincingly shown, the foundations of the RSPCA's moderation lay in its Victorian roots where the rationale of its work against animal cruelty was, at least in part, a crusade against the perceived threat to social stability of working-class indiscipline and moral depravity. Bull baiting events, for instance, were opposed not just because they were cruel but because they encouraged both drunkenness and absenteeism amongst working-class factory workers. Thus, it is significant that the bulk of the prosecutions brought by the Society were against the lower classes – particularly drovers and butchers – whilst the cruelties to animals inflicted by the wealthy in the pursuit of 'sports' such as hunting and shooting were ignored. It was no coincidence that Richard Martin and Fowell Buxton, two key figures in the early days of the RSPCA, were themselves keen on field sports. The RSPCA, then, became very much part of the established order, enabling it to receive the approval mark of royalty and attract the support of wealthy patrons. These aristocratic connections were beneficial in the sense that they made the issue of animal protection fashionable, but the more reliant the RSPCA became on this patronage the more it was forced to turn a blind eye when it came to animal cruelties associated with the elite of Victorian society.

By the 1970s the rich and established RSPCA was the prime target for the new radicals aiming to transform its plodding respectability. As we have seen, challenges to the RSPCA had occurred before, but the modern version has been far more intense and has taken place within the organisation itself. Previously, disputes quickly led to either resignations or expulsions and the subsequent formation of new groups, not really challenging effectively the RSPCA's predominant position. This time, the attack came from both fronts and, as such, has had much more substantial consequences. It resulted in two decades of almost constant bickering with the Society's annual general meetings regularly degenerating into chaos. The general complaint of the radicals was the RSPCA's inactivity on most animal welfare issues, its genteel image as 'a rest home for old majors' and its concentration on cruelty to pet animals which had been acceptable to a majority of ordinary and Council members – the 'dog and cat brigade' as the radicals sarcastically called them (North, 1982).

The dispute, at least initially, crystallised around the issue of hunting. Throughout the 1960s, there had been attempts, particularly by the radical activist Vera Sheppard backed up by the well-known astronomer Patrick Moore, to carry anti-hunting resolutions but each time they were defeated. The RSPCA's refusal to take a stand against hunting was at least partly caused by its failure to exclude representatives of the hunting community from membership. Indeed, in the 1960s, senior members of the British Field Sports Society (such as the Duke of Beaufort and the Conservative MP Marcus Kimball) were actively involved in defending hunting within the RSPCA (Ryder, 1989: 189; Thomas, 1983: 70). This, of course, was regarded by the radicals as outrageous. They were, of course, right to claim that there was a concerted campaign by pro-hunting organisations to ensure that the RSPCA did not change its policy, but there was nothing clandestine about this campaign. Indeed, supporters of hunting thought that it was quite legitimate; the RSPCA had never previously interfered with their country pursuits and it had no business doing so now. For the radicals, of course, this was anathema and they sought to expel hunt supporters. Thus, in 1969 the AGM ended in uproar when a motion to this end was ruled out of order by John Hobhouse, the Chairman of the Council (*The Times*, 25 June 1971).

It was at this point that the Reform Group, made up of about twenty-five radicals, was formed to change the Society's direction. The primary means of doing this was to seek election to the ruling Council and in the 1972 elections the group succeeded in winning five of the eight contested seats on the Council of forty-six members. Buoyed by their success, Brian Seager, the Chairman of the Reform Group, hit at the heart of the RSPCA's respectability by demanding that an extraordinary general meeting be called to censure Princess Anne for fox hunting and to seek the resignation of the Queen and the Queen Mother as patrons unless they expressed regret at her hunting activities. The following day the RSPCA issued a statement supporting Princess Anne and disciplinary action was threatened against Seager. But, in a sense, the damage had been done. That august pillar of the Establishment, *The Times* (17 June 1972, 21 November 1972) was concerned enough to defend Royalty against what it saw as this form of unwarranted interference.

By this stage the divisions were so great that in 1974 an inquiry into the affairs of the Society was held under the direction of Charles Sparrow QC. Published in November 1974, the report confirmed the Reform Group's tactics and deplored their intolerance (*The Times*, 22–23 November 1972). The Reform Group, however, continued to make progress and in 1975, having achieved its aim of gaining a majority of sympathisers on the Council, disbanded. As Ryder (1989: 352), a central figure in the Reform Group and Chairman of the RSPCA in 1977, points out, the radicals were in a minority except for one brief period between June 1979 and June 1980. Nevertheless, with the support of other more moderate members of the Council who refused to side with the old guard, the radicals succeeded in changing the direction of the Society. The key change was that the Society began to formulate a written set of policies (which, incredibly, it had not done before) and decided to extend its campaigns to cover all the major areas of animal use, and not just strays. To meet the new requirements, specialist committees were set up to advise on policy and new departments created to initiate campaigns on the newly defined and expanded areas of concern (Ryder, 1989: 352, 192–4). These changes soon had an impact. In November 1975, the RSPCA officially criticised both Prince Charles and Princess Anne for fox hunting and in February 1976, despite opposition from the conservatives, the Society declared that its official policy now incorporated opposition to fox hunting and the shooting of birds for sport (*The Times*, 4 November 1975, 3 and 26 February 1976). A symbol of this shift occurred in 1977, when Ryder persuaded the Council to allow him to organise, with Andrew Linzey, a symposium on animal rights at Trinity College, Cambridge (proceedings of the conference were published as Paterson and Ryder, 1979).

Any thoughts of unity around a new more radical programme, however, were soon to be dispelled. The Council and the membership were still bitterly divided. This became painfully clear when the factions took sides over another issue in the late 1970s – this time over whether the RSPCA should be represented by its senior officials on the newly formed Farm Animal Welfare Council (see Chapter 4); unimportant in itself maybe, but another symbol of the wider divisions over policy and approach in the organisation. The bulk of the radicals opposed the move because the offer of representation was regarded as a sop to the animal welfare movement, unlikely to achieve any benefits for farm animals not least because it was dominated by representatives of those involved in the meat industry. The radicals won the day when the Council voted by eleven votes to ten against allowing representation. This decision provoked another round of bickering. Representatives of about 25 per cent of the membership adopted votes of no confidence in the Council and called for the expulsion of those Council members who voted for exclusion (*The Times*, 26 November 1979). At an acrimonious extraordinary general meeting the following February, 1,400 delegates (crowded into a hall meant for only 1,200) debated for five hours a resolution demanding the resignation of the eleven Council members. The radicals survived because the motion failed to receive the necessary 60 per cent support but the whole episode revealed the level of the support that the conservatives could still muster (Ryder, 1989: 202).

This support was confirmed later in 1980 when the moderates, under the leadership of Janet Fookes (the Conservative MP for

Plymouth Drake), regained control of the Council. But still the divisions persisted as old battles were re-fought. Thus, Richard Course was expelled from the Council in October 1981 for his outspoken attack on Princess Anne's hunting inclinations, which had apparently not dimmed, but was reinstated at the June 1982 AGM due to the influence of the radical delegates (Thomas, 1983: 79–80). Yet another major conflict occurred in the early 1980s when it became apparent that the RSPCA's finances were in dire straits. The radicals used this as an opportunity to attack conservative officials whom they accused of financial mismanagement. The Council initiated a report in 1981 but the conservatives were accused of trying to hide the results from its radical members. As a result of the findings, three senior officials including Julian Hopkins, the executive director, were dismissed (*The Times*, 28 June 1982). In the by now familiar exchange of gunfire, the Council then engineered the resignation of Richard Adams, the radical President of the Society, who, with Vice-Presidents Lord Houghton, Lady Dowding and Clive Hollands, left criticising the lack of democracy within the conservative camp and its unfriendliness 'towards the increasing number of younger members who demand more vigorous action against the growing commercial exploitation of animals' (*The Times*, 30 September 1982).

As the 1980s progressed, conflict within the RSPCA became less fierce and the media's attention was diverted to the more militant action of the ALF. As Ryder (1989: 206) explains, the radicals had all but disappeared from the Council but they had 'won the war of ideas' or at least partly so. The new challenge came from a younger, even more militant, group centring on the BUAV. Thus, Kim Stallwood and Angela Walder set up the RSPCA Action Group in 1985 which, following the pattern of the Reform Group in the 1970s, sought to promote a slate of candidates for the 1985 and 1986 elections. Despite attempts to determine the result by recruiting animal rights activists as RSPCA members, no Action Group candidates were elected. A new group with similar infiltrationist aims called Watchdog was set up in 1987 and five members of the group were expelled from the RSPCA in December 1988 (Henshaw, 1989; *The Times*, 1 December 1988).

As a conclusion to this section, it is clear that the RSPCA which emerged from these years of infighting was a very different organisation from the one that Ritvo described and the radicals in the 1970s sought to change. Not only does it campaign much more vigorously than it used to but it also now has a comprehensive programme of policies. On animal agriculture the Society is now opposed strongly to intensive systems, to the export of live food animals and to ritual slaughter. On experimentation, the moral validity of using animals if humans benefit substantially is recognised but it would like severe limits imposed. In addition, the Society is now opposed to animals in circuses, to the giving away of live animals as prizes, to any form of hunting with dogs and to shooting for sport. This is not quite the absolutist programme of a group such as Animal Aid, but it is much closer than it was.

The distance the RSPCA has travelled towards a strong animal protection agenda is illustrated by the fact that supporters of hunting are now very much on the outside of the organisation. The RSPCA's latest director-general, the former Liberal Democrat MP Jackie Ballard appointed in 2002, is a strong anti-hunt supporter. Moreover, the latest conflict within the RSPCA has concerned the, so far unsuccessful, attempt of the pro-hunting Countryside Animal Welfare Group, led by the former Olympic equestrian medallist Richard Meade (and closely linked with the Countryside Alliance), to infiltrate the Society. Having discovered the attempt at entryism the RSPCA won a high court judgment permitting the expulsion of, and denial of membership to, those who disagree with the organisation's anti-hunting policy (*Guardian*, 27 January 2001; 15 June 2001). Despite this, the problem was still apparent a year later when a number of pro-hunt supporters stood for election to the Society's ruling Council (*Guardian*, 26 May 2002).

One final point that should have become apparent about the conflicts within the animal protection movement is that the co-ordinating role of the animal rights challenge has been performed by a kind of animal rights elite who have been instrumental in both setting up new societies and attempting to radicalise the old ones. Alex Pacheco and Ingrid Newkirk have been the leading exporters of animal rights to more moderate groups in the United States. In Britain, Richard Ryder was not only involved in the attempt to radicalise the RSPCA but was also one of those who was involved in the revitalisation of the BUAV in the 1970s.

Ryder handed over the running of the BUAV to other radicals including Kim Stallwood who was co-founder of Co-ordinating Animal Welfare and, with Ryder, involved in the challenge to the RSPCA. To provide an international dimension to this circulation of elites, Stallwood emigrated to the United States where he became director of PETA, and subsequently editor of an animal rights magazine, *Animals' Agenda*. There are plenty of other examples too. Les Ward, the director of Advocates for Animals, has been on the LACS executive committee; both Richard Course and John Bryant were leading radicals in the RSPCA and the LACS, the latter still occupying a high-profile position; Peter Roberts founded CIWF and was also a member of the RSPCA Council in the late 1970s; Robin Webb was, until 1989, assistant director of Animal Aid, and was a Council member of the RSPCA until his role within the ALF became too obvious for the Society to overlook; and, finally, Jean Pink, who formed Animal Aid, was also President of the BUAV and one of the abolitionists who revived the organisation in the early 1980s.

New social movement?

One of the key reasons for the sustainability of the animal rights challenge has been the roots it has grown at the local level. Before the 1970s very few active local groups existed. Now, as we saw earlier, they flourish in all parts of the country. The vast majority of these local groups are the product of the emergence of radicalism since one of its major characteristics is the emphasis on grassroots campaigning. By contrast, animal welfare groups tend to be far more elitist and cautious, relying on expert opinions and preferring to leave campaigning to their own paid staff. A significant part in the development of local activism was played by Animal Aid whose initial campaigns in the 1970s were based entirely on their local groups. This set in train the widespread development of such groups which the older national societies, such as the NAVS and the BUAV, capitalised on. In America, similarly, the new radical groups have encouraged individual activists to participate in mass campaigns and civil disobedience. This was the fundamental characteristic of the Henry Spira-inspired campaigns which launched the modern animal rights movement in the United States (Singer, 1998). Likewise, Alex

Pacheco formed PETA in 1980 because of the need for a 'grass-roots group in the USA that could spur people to use their time and talents to help animals gain liberation' (Pacheco, 1985: 135).

An important characteristic of grassroots campaigning, as indi-cated above, is its very decentralised and unhierarchical nature. There are a number of recent examples in the animal protection field. One is the campaign against Shamrock, Britain's only primate importation and quarantine facility which, after a lengthy action by the Save the Shamrock Monkeys campaign, announced in 2000 that its primate facility would close. Another is the two-year campaign against Hillgrove Farm, a provider of laboratory cats, which culminated in its closure in 1998. In both cases, the campaigns were assisted by NAVS, among other national groups, but they were not run by any national organisation. Two equally relevant recent examples of British animal rights campaigns are those against live exports and the Huntingdon Life Sciences (HLS) company. In both cases, while the national groups have been involved, the initiative came from below.

The protests against live exports consisted, at their core, of people from the towns through which the animals were driven on the way to the port. Brightlingsea, in Essex, was typical. Here, Maria Wilby, a long-standing member of CIWF and daughter of its director Joyce D'Silva as well as being a local resident, founded Brightlingsea Against Live Exports (BALE) to which local people, many of whom had never protested about anything in their lives before, flocked. Local support for the live exports campaign was not evident everywhere, the local organiser in Dover, for instance, describing it as 'bitterly disappointing' (*Agscene*, 118, Summer 95: 6). In the case of HLS, allegations against the contract testing company (see Chapter 5) resulted in a campaign spearheaded by a group calling itself Stop Huntingdon Animal Cruelty (SHAC). Formed in November 1999 and now claiming 14,000 members, SHAC has mounted a campaign against HLS and anyone, such as financial institutions, who has anything to do with it. Some involved in the campaign have engaged in classic pressure group protest, aimed at publicising the issue. Others have stepped beyond this mark and have engaged in various forms of, legal and illegal, direct action (see Chapter 8).

Because of the characteristics noted above, the animal rights movement may be an example of a 'new social movement', distinguished from 'old' social movements by their decentralisation, disorganisation, rejection of the old political divisions based on capital and labour, and stress on wider cultural changes as opposed to merely seeking piecemeal legislative change (Bomberg, 1998: 22) This is a pretty accurate description of the animal rights movement, if not the animal protection movement in general. It should be noted though that some of the above characteristics imputed to new social movements are not particularly new – witness some of the animal protection campaigns in the nineteenth century, and there are some scholars, for example Jordan and Maloney (1997: 46–73) who doubt its explanatory utility.

Counter mobilisation

Perhaps the biggest tribute to the success of the animal protection movement in mobilising public support is the reaction of the movement's opponents. Content before to lobby government quietly, the organisations representing animal users have recognised the need to win over the hearts and minds of the voters. This has particularly been the case with animal experimentation. In the United States, the National Association for Biomedical Research was created in the mid-1980s and works particularly with the American Medical Association to counter the animal rights movement's public claims. A similar function is performed by the Research Defence Society (RDS) in Britain. Originally founded in 1908, the RDS was joined by the Animals in Medicines Research Information Centre set up by the pharmaceutical industry in the mid-1980s. Together with citizen groups such as Putting People First in the United States and Seriously Ill for Medical Research in Britain, these organisations have learnt from the animal rights movement and now use the same tactics – such as poster adverts, the use of snappy slogans, and more often than not images of vulnerable humans (usually children) who have benefited from animal research.

The most notable counter mobilisation in recent years has been the creation of the Countryside Alliance in the mid-1990s. The CA was formed from three groups, the British Field Sports Society (BFSS), the Countryside Movement, and the Countryside Business Group. The latter two were small, and the BFSS, which bequeathed its offices to the CA, essentially swallowed them up.

The clout of the CA has been revealed by a number of high profile marches in London, the one in 2002 attracting 400,000 people, and by its support for attempts to infiltrate the National Trust and the RSPCA (Younge, 2000).

Despite its claim to campaign on a range of countryside issues – the rural economy, transport, housing and so on – it is clear that the hunting issue predominates in the CA. As one former CA employee said: 'The idea was to wrap up hunting in the warm glow of the countryside and everyone will love it' (Younge, 2000). A leaked document revealed that in 2000, the CA allocated millions of pounds to the pro-hunting campaign and only about £250,000 on all the other issues in which they claimed an interest. In the run-up to the CA march in 2002, a coalition of high-profile countryside groups – including the Council for the Protection of Rural England – put out a statement criticising the predominance of hunting in the CA's campaign (*Observer*, 22 September 2002).

Explaining the rise of the animal protection movement

Why then has the animal protection movement prospered in recent years? Initially, of course, it should be asserted that pressure groups for animals have expanded, just as they have for other similar issues, because there is little opportunity within the party system in Britain for a concern for animals to be effectively expressed. There is, of course, the Green Party, which has embraced the concept of animal rights, but it remains a marginal party with little hope of electoral success. The role of political parties, though, does not explain why the concern for animals has been growing, only why it has taken the form it has.

One persuasive explanation for the increasing concern, which also helps to account for the character of the revival, is the postulate of the growth of a post-material political culture. This argument, as associated with Inglehart (1977), is that since 1945, as a result primarily of the welfare state and unprecedented economic growth, material needs have been largely taken care of. As a consequence, attention has been directed towards non-material quality of life issues, such as the state of the natural environment, and moral concerns.

Certainly, this approach would seem to have considerable

explanatory power as far as the animal protection movement is concerned. At a practical level, the more affluent society is, the more surplus income exists for membership subscriptions and donations to cause groups. At a more abstract level, concern for animals is a particularly appropriate cause for those who have turned their attention towards moral issues and for those who shun material values. A, slightly exaggerated, editorial in the *Independent* at the height of the live exports protest (21 January 1995) exclaimed, for instance, that it marked an end to the old politics of capital and labour, left and right. Instead:

> The new battle is over ethics and morality ... Great moral questions about the nature of man's relationship to the environment dwarf the old economic issues.

An acceptance of animal rights provides an opportunity to say no to the wearing of clothes, the use of cosmetics and the eating of exotic dishes if animals suffer as a consequence. And, of course, the sacrifice is even greater if one is not willing to let animals be used in experiments which may lead to profound human benefits, such as the cure for a currently fatal or debilitating disease.

That is not to say that the movement's ideals are necessarily anti-materialist or anti-science as is often claimed. Indeed, arguments for vegetarianism are rarely couched in the language of material sacrifice. Rather, a meat-free diet is usually extolled for its benefits to health and its variety and flavour. Similarly, as we shall see in Chapter 5, one of the principal claims of anti-vivisectionists is not just that animal experimentation is immoral, whatever the benefits to humans derived, but that medical science does not benefit from the use of animals and a reluctance to seek alternatives actually hinders advances. Even amongst those who do recognise that some benefit has, and may in the future, come from the use of animals, there is not a universal antipathy to progress, only to the belief that humans are justified in using animals to achieve it. Nevertheless, having said all this, it should be pointed out that the animal protection movement does provide an effective vehicle for those who do question the wisdom of the perpetual search for material and scientific advance.

The link between economic well-being and a concern for animals is further confirmed when one considers the historically uneven development of the animal protection movement. As we saw, the movement developed quite rapidly in the nineteenth century before stagnating somewhat in the inter-war years. The period of development coincided with a period of affluence and international security in mid-nineteenth-century Britain. Not surprisingly, the two world wars, separated by a period of severe economic depression, had the effect of turning people's attention towards human rather than animal suffering. Only in the past thirty years or so has the emphasis changed again, this time, perhaps, growing deeper roots that will not be completely unearthed in the event of future threats to economic and military security (Ryder, 1989: 152–4).

Inglehart associates the growth of post-material values with affluence. If he is right, one would expect to find that post-material values are likely to vary according to social class. He would appear to be right in the sense that empirical evidence of the social characteristics of animal protection activists shows a middle-class bias. However, the sector of the middle class most associated with animal rights, and environmentalism more generally, consists of those in the non-productive service sector – teachers, doctors and so on – who are not the most affluent parts of society (Greanville and Moss, 1985). It may be then that the explanatory variable is not, as Inglehart thought, affluence, but occupation. Cotgrove and Duff (1980) have made this suggestion, arguing that those employed in the non-productive service sector are more likely to have post-material values since they are more insulated from the market and likely to hold values – of caring and compassion – that reflect the nature of the work they do. Significantly, with the development of the welfare state and increased educational opportunities, this sector of the middle class has expanded dramatically since the Second World War.

Whatever the cause of the post-material culture, it should be noted that it is still largely rooted in an anthropocentric outlook. The dominant environmental issues are those which seek to improve the quality of *human* life, and this is often the case even when animals are involved. Wildlife conservation issues remain the most popular of all animal issues, primarily because there are various anthropocentric reasons for conserving wild animals (see Chapter 6). Similarly, the tone of the debate in the various agricultural disasters in recent years – most notably BSE and foot and mouth – has been almost exclusively in terms of the human problems encountered, despite the fact that the animal suffering central to them was largely caused by the practices of modern intensive agricultural practices (see Chapter 4). Not surprisingly, then, the radical movement on behalf of animals – which presages a fundamental shift in values and practices – has made relatively little headway. When the well-being of domestic animals is considered, the debate is conducted primarily in terms of welfare and not rights. Whilst humans are increasingly indicating their willingness to make sacrifices in order to reduce animal suffering, there is little evidence that they are prepared to recognise a moral status for them that would require more fundamental choices to be made.

We saw in the last chapter that there is now a body of academic literature seeking to extol the links between feminism and the protection of animals. The predominance of women within the animal protection movement suggests that it is worthwhile considering the explanatory validity of gender. Here, it might be argued that the culturally defined role of women, with its emphasis on nurturing and caring, and the greater consciousness women have of their political status, has led many to lend their weight to a cause with which they can identify. By contrast, compassion and even squeamishness 'does not conform with our macho culture's view of what is mature and manly' (Ryder, 1989: 321). It is surely no coincidence that many of the practices which the animal rights movement seeks to condemn, such as vivisection and hunting, are perceived to be male preserves since they promote culturally defined male values; the hard-headedness of the scientist, the virility of the hunter and the general indifference to pain.

It should be noted that both female and male values are independent of the actual validity of the various uses of animals so it is not the case that femininity here defined is equivalent to sentimentality, although one can agree with Marti Kheel (1990) that a 'unity of reason and emotion' is a crucial ingredient of an effective animal rights ethic. What can be claimed is that women are more likely to side with the moral claims being made for animals whether or not they are justified just as men are more likely to accept the use of animals for, for instance, food or science whether or not these practices are justified. The values associated with 'manliness' are dominant in Western society and to this extent the compassionate values crucial to animal protection remain subordinate. Nevertheless, the rise of the women's movement would appear to offer the potential for an effective challenge to macho values and one natural channel for this challenge is in the area of cruelty to animals.

The problem with the cultural, structural, and gender approaches to the rise of concern for animal well-being is that they provide no room for the independent explanatory validity of people's genuine concern for animals and what is done to them, as opposed to being by-products of affluence, occupation or gender. Surely of some importance, for instance, is the development of a radical philosophy for animals, explored in the previous chapter. This has given the movement academic respectability which has aided the recruitment of articulate people from academe and other professions. It has also provided the movement with a firm basis for action. There is a good deal of evidence that many activists are aware of the key writings, which is not surprising since the major theoretical exponents such as Regan, Singer and Linzey are also leading activists themselves and are therefore in an ideal position to influence others. Jean Pink – to mention just one piece of anecdotal evidence – is alleged to have founded Animal Aid after reading Singer's *Animal Liberation* and Henry Spira, a former leading American activist, enrolled on a course run by Singer at New York University after reading his first thoughts on animal liberation in the *New York Review of Books* (Hall, 1984: 212; Ryder, 1989: 300). Certainly, one only has to look at an edition of *Arkangel* – a journal published and largely written by members of the British ALF – to realise how far moral theory is utilised as a justification for action (now online at www.arkangelweb.org/).

Thus, just as Marxists have traditionally armed themselves with a copy of *Das Kapital*, animal rights activists have their Singer or Regan. The fact that most have probably not read the leading works and are not aware of the complex philosophising they contain is irrelevant. What is striking is the extent to which they are reducible to the level of slogans. The idea of animal rights is a useful asset to activists both in their search for an internal justification and also, in a more limited sense, in their quest to persuade others. Its moral absolutism may, as we shall see, be unprofitable in the decision-making arena and in the task of altering public opinion, but it is easy to see why it is attractive to activists and why it might appeal to youthful idealism. There is no need for complex and time-consuming analysis of the human use of animals. We are not entitled to exploit them even if there are human benefits to be gained. 'Meat is Murder.' That is all there is to it! This, coupled with the methods some are prepared to engage in to achieve their aims, has created a much harder image for the animal protection movement, a movement which, whilst still odd for many people, is not laughed at or ridiculed any more.

Of course, ideas by themselves do not have an impact without a receptive social climate. Many of the themes in the modern intellectual challenges to the moral orthodoxy owe a good deal to the ideas of Henry Salt writing 80 or so years ago, but his lone voice fell on deaf ears. Affluence and occupational structure may, of course, come into play at this point. One objective factor that has arguably made for a much more receptive climate is that far more now is known about the capabilities of animals. This has the effect of making the radical philosophical arguments more convincing. This greater knowledge goes beyond a simple recognition that animals can feel pain. The fact that they have been shown to have considerable cognitive ability makes it much harder to justify many of the practices which are described in this book. As Ryder (1989: 317) points out:

> It is possible to see the growth of animal liberation not so much in terms of increased overall compassion so much as an expansion of the family circle; the perception of other animals as our 'brothers and sisters', literally as our evolutionary kin to whom we feel 'kindness'.

The fact that the growing awareness of animal capabilities has coincided with the introduction and intensification of more severe ways of treating animals provides a juxtaposition of factors which, by itself, goes a long way towards explaining the increasing concern about animals.

Knowledge of animal capabilities, of course, leads to a greater recognition that animals are more like us than we had previously thought. The decline of theological separatism and the influence of Darwin's theory of evolution are crucial here (Rachels, 1990). More recently, greater knowledge of genetics has revealed how close human beings are to non-human primates. The staggering fact that the genetic differences between humans and chimpanzees are smaller than those between chimpanzees and gorillas, is a salutary lesson to those who continue to insist on a strict moral divide with all humans on the privileged side and all animals on the other.

That the public are now much more aware of both the capabilities of animals and what is actually done to them is primarily a product of the greater coverage of animal issues in the media, but this in itself is a product of the movement's efforts to get the issues on to the political agenda, to create a 'social problem' that needs rectifying (see Chapter 7). The press have found that the emotive nature of vivisection provides good copy and the development of television has greatly aided the cause of animal protection since it involves issues which can have a considerable visual impact. Just as coverage of the starving in Ethopia provoked a huge response in the West, the sight of animals in factory farms and laboratories would seem to offer similar prospects of public sympathy and revulsion.

The media tends still to focus on wild animals, and particularly endangered species, and the approach is often an uncritical, albeit educational, account of animal behaviour. There is reason to believe, however, that this is changing. The media's coverage of the Canadian baby seal clubbing in the 1970s (drawn to its attention by Brian Davies, the founder of IFAW) had a phenomenal impact resulting in huge public outrage and eventually the banning of seal products into America and the European Community. In recent years, too, more attention has been directed towards issues of animal protection on the farm and in the laboratory. For instance, as Porritt and Winner (1988: 52) point out, the broadcast (to over a million people) of the Animals Film (a harrowing account of the way animals are treated, narrated by Julie Christie) on British television marked 'an important moment in the growth of public awareness of animal exploitation'. This was followed by other television documentaries and the issues have even been aired in popular long-running drama serials such as Grange Hill (vivisection) and The Archers (organic farming and livestock transportation).

In this chapter, the modern animal protection movement has been introduced. It was noted that since the 1970s, there has been a greatly increased concern about the treatment of animals and part of this concern has manifested itself in the revitalisation of existing groups and the formation of many new ones, all of whom found a public which has become more attentive to the issues they raise. The radicalism of many of the new recruits, however, has produced a movement which has had its fair share of division and conflict. Disagreements about objectives are not fatal, given that all groups are heading in the same direction, albeit that some want to travel further down the road than others. Disagreements over strategy, however, would seem to be more damaging and we return to this in Chapters 7 and 8. Before that, in the next four chapters, the issues that most concern the animal protection movement are discussed in some detail.

3
Captives, companions and the law

The range of uses to which humans put animals is immense and the reasons given for these uses are equally varied. Of course, at least for the orthodox view, the extent to which these uses are valid largely depends upon an analysis of the level of suffering that animals endure as a result of them and the level of benefit that humans derive from them. As Chapters 4 and 5 (dealing with the use of animals for food and in the laboratory) will show, it has been widely argued that the sacrifice of animals is justified for the benefits produced for humans. Before assessing the validity of those claims, this chapter will be concerned with a very different category of activities involving animals: activities which would not, at first sight at least, involve the same serious consequences for animals but which at the same time would not appear to generate anything but superficial human benefits either. These are the keeping of pets, or companion animals, and the captivity of wild animals in zoos and circuses. Before we start, however, it is worthwhile, in the context of this and later chapters, considering the origins and scope of the general animal cruelty laws that exist in Britain and elsewhere.

The origins of animal welfare legislation

The least one can say about animal welfare legislation – and now it is a 'subject of well nigh infinite dimensions' (Cooper, 1987: 1) – is that it creates a much more favourable climate for animals. Before the nineteenth century, laws relating to animals did exist but their aim was exclusively to protect people from the damage

caused by animals owned by others or to protect animals as just
another piece of an individual's property. In Europe during the
Middle Ages, as a result of the widespread Christian belief that,
although they had no souls, animals could be possessed by evil
spirits, it was common for them to be put on trial and sometimes
even executed for 'crimes' supposedly committed whilst possessed
(Evans, 1987). At no time, however, were animals granted the
consideration that comes from recognition of moral standing.
Indeed, the welfare of animals was immaterial and any benefits
they gained were a by-product of laws regulating human activities
towards each other. Some modern legislation – many public
health measures, for instance – serves the same function of indirectly benefiting animals. Now, of course, it is also accepted that
animals need to be protected directly and particularly *against*
their owners.

Before legal protection, and in a social climate not conducive
to their welfare, animals, throughout the ages and in all parts of
the world, suffered abysmally at the hands of humans. Very
simply, virtually every atrocity imaginable was inflicted upon
them and much of this was not for food or scientific advance but
merely for human entertainment. The slaughter of millions of
animals in Roman amphitheatres is well known, but this represents the tip of a very large iceberg reaching down the centuries
(Turner, 1964: 18–22). Animals suffered, of course, from practices – such as being slaughtered for food and for the benefit of
scientific research – which we can recognise today (although even
here what we would regard as unbelievable cruelty took place).
What was completely different, though, was the scale and brutal-
ity of suffering inflicted merely for amusement. Thus, cock and
dog fighting and bear and bull baiting were, for instance, commonplace. Wagers on animals were often the impetus for such
activities. Indeed, there appeared to be nothing – from eating live
cats to biting the heads off birds – which individuals would not
do for a bet.

Gradually the climate began to change. By the eighteenth
century, greater benevolence towards animals was emerging,
particularly in the literary world, but the struggle for reform in
the 'real' world was long and often frustrating, albeit ultimately
fruitful (Ritvo, 1987: 39–42; Turner, 1964: 68–72, 77, 147).
Although some limited anti-cruelty measures can be found in

Ireland and America in the seventeenth century (Ryder, 1989: 53–4), the first sustained attempt to legislate for animal welfare occurred almost two centuries later in Britain. William Pulteney's bill to outlaw bull baiting was narrowly defeated in 1800, but after two other failures (in 1802 and 1809) some success was finally achieved with the passage through parliament of Richard Martin's bill in 1822. This made it an offence to wantonly and cruelly 'beat, abuse or ill-treat' a wide range of domesticated animals including horses and cattle.

Martin made several other unsuccessful attempts to prohibit other forms of cruelty, such as the baiting of animals not included within the 1822 statute, before losing his seat in 1826. His mantle in parliament was taken by Joseph Pease who secured the passage of a bill in 1835. Replacing Martin's act, it extended the number of animals to be protected against wanton cruelty and specifically prohibited cock fighting and the baiting of any animal. Together with legislation protecting certain wild birds, the prohibition of dog-drawn carts (1854) and the Cruelty to Animals Act 1876, which dealt specifically with vivisection (see Chapter 5), Pease's act marks the extent of the Victorian attempts to protect animals. Although limited, it was a great improvement on what had been allowed before and the scene was set for the twentieth-century expansion in animal welfare legislation.

The Protection of Animals Acts

The corner-stones of modern animal welfare legislation in Britain are the general laws relating to animal cruelty – the Protection of Animals Acts 1911–64. The key, most comprehensive, piece of animal welfare legislation in Britain remains the 1911 Protection of Animals Act which was a consolidating measure, replacing all of the general anti-cruelty legislation preceding it. Section 1 of this Act lays down the fundamental cruelty tenet. This has been interpreted to mean that to secure a cruelty conviction it is necessary to show that suffering (in the form of, for example, beating, kicking, torturing, terrifying or neglecting an animal) has taken place and that this suffering was both substantial and unnecessary (Cooper, 1987: 28). In addition to this general cruelty provision, the Act also lays down other more specific regulations. Confirming the 1835 statute, it rules out the fighting or baiting of any animal. Secondly, it prohibits transporting animals in a way which is likely to cause unnecessary suffering. Furthermore, it prohibits the deliberate poisoning of an animal without reasonable cause – a provision strengthened by the Animals (Cruel Poisons) Act 1962 and the Game Act 1970 under which certain poisons may not be used under any circumstances to kill animals, domesticated or wild. Finally, it prohibits operations performed on an animal without 'due care and humanity' – a provision which is strengthened by the Protection of Animals (Anaesthetics) Acts 1954 and 1964 which enforce the use of anaesthetics in cases where pain would otherwise occur. Exceptions to this are first aid in an emergency, experiments authorised under the 1986 Animals (Scientific Procedures) Act and the surgical castration of sheep under three months or of goats, bulls or pigs under two months (Todd, 1989: 21–4).

In the event of a conviction for cruelty, the Act, and subsequent legislation, gives the courts the power to impose a fine currently of up to £2,000 and/or imprisonment of up to six months, or both (Radford, 2001: 235). The 1911 Act also provides for the humane destruction of an animal if, in the courts' judgement, it would be cruel to keep it alive (or it is considered to be dangerous) in addition to the power to take an animal away from a person convicted of cruelty. Legislation in 1933 and 1954 introduced powers to disqualify a person convicted of cruelty from keeping animals. This was strengthened in 1988 to enable courts on a first, rather than a second, conviction to disqualify someone from keeping any kind of specified animal, an order which can be appealed against after twelve months of the ban has elapsed (Cooper, 1987: 29; Sweeney, 1990: 67).

One of the key difficulties with this legislation and, indeed, with the whole concept of animal welfare, is that it is based on the extremely ambiguous notion of 'unnecessary suffering'. As Radford (2001: 247) points out, it is how the courts interpret the notion that is the 'ultimate determinant of the degree of protection afforded by the law'. For some, legislation based on unnecessary suffering in reality provides little protection for animals, since human interests always trump those of animals (Francione, 1995). Conversely, Radford (2001: 258) suggests the flexibility of the concept of unnecessary suffering means it can be applied to many different situations, and gives the courts the opportunity to take into account ever-changing knowledge about animal suffering and changing public notions of what constitutes *necessary* suffering. It should also be noted here that, as we shall see in subsequent chapters, the unnecessary suffering model is not now the only, or even the main, model of animal welfare legislation, and the viability of animal welfare does not stand or fall with it. Indeed, the 1911 Act has in a sense fallen behind some other animal welfare regulations, particularly in relation to farm animals, since it only allows action to be taken once a case of cruelty has been discovered, rather than seeking to promote enforceable positive welfare standards to begin with (Radford, 2001: 400–1).

National and supra-national dimensions of animal welfare

Of course, it is inadequate to consider legislation affecting animals in the context of only one country. In the first place, legislation inevitably varies from country to country and, in federal systems, between different constituent units of the same state. The countries of northern Europe, for instance, have far stricter legislation than those in southern Europe where 'the concept of a moral concern or duty towards animals is much weaker, if not non-existent' (Jackson, 1989: 221). In the United States, most statutes relating to animal welfare derive from the fifty state legislatures since federal laws may only be formulated in the fields in which Congress has been given the authority by the US Constitution. New York was the first state to enact an anti-cruelty law (in 1828) followed in the next decade by Massachusetts, Connecticut and Wisconsin. By the end of the century, the vast majority of the other states had followed suit (Cooper, 1987: 169). Most federal law is concerned with conservation although the Animal Welfare Act 1966 (amended in 1970, 1976 and 1985) prohibits the use of animals in fights, regulates the inter-state transportation of animals and the supply and care of animals used in research. The 1958 Humane Slaughter Act regulates animals killed for food (Cooper, 1987: 170).

Since animals are an integral part of international commerce, there is an increasing need to standardise animal welfare legislation. It is extremely difficult to persuade the government of one nation to adopt stringent welfare measures if it is thereby put at

an economic disadvantage relative to other states with less stringent or non-existent welfare measures. Many of the attempts to
conserve species of animals are now undertaken at this supra-
national level (see Chapter 6) and on this and other issues
involving animal welfare, the World Trade Organisation (WTO),
and the European Union are increasingly significant institutions
(see Chapter 7).

Companion animals

The general framework of animal protection legislation dealt
with, we can now consider the specific areas indicated in the
introduction to this chapter. For most people, the only direct
contact with live animals is with pets or companion animals.
Domesticating animals and keeping them as pets is an age-old
practice although it was initially the preserve of the privileged
strata of society. Now, of course, it is such a common feature of
all cultures and all classes that it is largely taken for granted.
Within the EU alone, it has been estimated that, including fish,
there are about ninety million pets (over half of which are cats
and dogs) and that about half of all households contain at least
one pet. In America, there are over 400 million such animals. Pets
are now big business. The breeders and pet shops obviously reap
vast rewards but so also do the pet food industry, the veterinary
profession, the pharmaceutical companies and, particularly in
America, the various exotic animal services such as pet boutiques,
pet hotels (which provide luxury accommodation for pets whilst
their owners go on holiday) and pet cemeteries (Serpell, 1986:
11–12, 23–24).

The keeping of animals as pets *per se* would not seem to be a
problem from the perspective of the moral orthodoxy regarding
animals. Certainly, in the case of cats and dogs at least, well-
looked after animals (and these, from all the available evidence,
constitute the majority) seem to thrive. Some animals, of course,
make totally unsuitable pets. The trade in exotic wild birds, in
particular, causes great suffering and, given the limited benefits
that accrue to humans from keeping them, this suffering would
seem to be unacceptable. This trade, though, constitutes a small
proportion of the pet trade and there is an emerging consensus in
the West that it should be abolished (see Chapter 6). There is

certainly no division within the animal protection movement on this issue. More controversial is the keeping of caged birds in general. Whilst better protected in law than poultry (see Chapter 4), it is arguably the case that confining birds to cages, particularly when they are isolated from other members of their own species, causes suffering, although this is far from certain. The same kind of concern can also be expressed over smaller animals – rabbits, gerbils, mice – where they are kept in isolation in small cages.

On the other side of the cost–benefit analysis, in the past the ownership of pets was regarded as rather irrational, involving monetary cost, effort and time for no apparent benefit. It has been increasingly recognised, though, that the company of pets serves a very important function aiding the psychological and physical well-being of their owners. As Richard Girling (*Sunday Times Magazine*, 12 November 1989) points out: 'We feed emotionally on dog, cat or budgerigar, just as assuredly as we feed bodily on chicken, pig and bullock.'

It is widely accepted that the perpetrators of cruelty should be reprimanded and, as we saw above, legislation is in place to deal with offenders. As well as the Protection of Animals Act, there is a system of local authority licences for pet shops (Pet Animals Act 1951), dog breeders (Breeding of Dogs Act 1973), kennels and catteries (Animal Boarding Establishment Act 1963) and the ownership of wild animals classified as 'dangerous' (Dangerous Wild Animals Act 1976). Finally, three further pieces of general animal welfare legislation are worth mentioning. Firstly, the Protection of Animals Act 1934 banned bullfighting, and many aspects of rodeos, in Britain. Secondly, the Cinematographic Films (Animals) Act 1937 bans films, made in Britain or elsewhere, which involve the infliction of pain or terror upon an animal, and finally the Abandonment of Animals Act 1960 makes it an offence to abandon an animal in a situation which could cause it unnecessary suffering.

Despite this legislative framework, a number of problems with the sale and keeping of companion animals are apparent. In the first place, while pet shops are subject to a licensing system, the legislation is extremely permissive, providing no detailed guidelines for local authorities to base their licensing regime on. As Radford (2001: 315) remarks, since 'it is left to each individual authority to define the standards it considers to be appropriate', there may be 'considerable variation between different areas'. The variation in standards was confirmed by research commissioned by the Consumers Association which revealed that a quarter of pet shops keep animals in overcrowded and filthy conditions (*Guardian*, 5 December 2002). The indiscriminate breeding of dogs in so-called 'puppy farms' was also a source of much animal suffering, although the Labour Government elected in 1997 sought to deal with this problem by tightening up the conditions attached to a dog breeding establishment licence (Radford, 2001: 340).

Some pet owners also mistreat their animals, and cases of cruelty to domestic animals are still depressingly common. The RSPCA reports that it receives a telephone call reporting cruelty every 19 seconds. In 2000, the Society responded to 1.6m calls, and convictions for cruelty were 2,719 in 1999 and 2,473 the following year (*Guardian*, 28 June 2001). Equally worrying is the growing incidence of organised dog and cock fighting and badger baiting which, after a lull in the 1990s, was apparently on the increase again at the beginning of the twenty-first century (*Observer*, 29 April 2001, 16 June 2002). The cruelty figures cited above represent only the tip of an iceberg. They do not include, of course, those cases of cruelty not discovered (the owners of abandoned animals, for instance, are rarely traced). Furthermore, the RSPCA prefers, if at all possible, to issue cautions rather than immediately prosecute an offender. Cautions tend to be given in cases where an animal has been mistreated but its situation can be greatly improved by relatively simple measures. RSPCA inspectors will then make follow-up visits to ensure that these measures have been taken.

Cautioning offenders, as opposed to immediately seeking to prosecute them, is a product of the fact that more often than not, suffering is inflicted, not as a deliberate act, but due to a total ignorance of an animal's needs. In 1996, for instance, of the reported cases of cruelty to animals, no less than 1,650 were for neglect and only 28 for ill-treatment (*Guardian*, 24 April 1996). Locking dogs in cars on hot days for hours on end without the provision of food or water is a surprisingly regular occurrence, for instance, as is the chaining of dogs on the small balconies of high-rise flats. Yet, it is often not realised that this causes suffering. Finally, we ought to mention the suffering that is inflicted by the dog showing community – those, it might be added, who should know better. Amongst animals intended to be shown in competitions, surgical procedures such as tail docking and ear cropping are common and many breeds have congenital physical disorders caused by selective breeding (Serpell, 1986: 15). These are not covered by general anti-cruelty laws, although they may be included in the British government's proposed new Animal Welfare Bill, but there would seem to be a case for outlawing practices which cause suffering simply in order to fulfil artificial standards set by competitions.

The light penalties handed down by the courts for animal cruelty reflect the low priority given to animal protection. Only a tiny fraction of those convicted of cruelty, for instance, are given prison sentences: the figure was less than 2 per cent in 1990 (Sweeney, 1990: 69–73). Another problem, in addition, is the apprehending of offenders in the first place. Neither the RSPCA nor the police have the powers to search premises where they believe cruelty to animals is taking place. In addition, there is little chance of discovering the owners of abandoned pets, many of whom are simply thrown out of cars (even on motorways) or left on rubbish tips. It is not only animals who suffer from the callousness of those who discard their pets. Stray dogs are a major risk to the public through their contribution to car accidents (responsible for 54,000 a year in Britain), the injuries they cause through bites and scratches, the diseases that can spread through excrement and the damage dogs do to livestock.

To deal with this problem, the RSPCA have long campaigned, without success, for the introduction of a dog registration scheme. Up to 1988, owners of dogs had to license their animals but the licence fee (at 37$\frac{1}{2}$p) had remained the same since its introduction in 1878. As a result, the cost of collecting it eventually became more expensive than the revenue gained. A scheme to use microchip technology, it is argued, would enable the authorities to locate the owners of lost or abandoned animals and the fee would also make people think twice before buying a dog and would discourage multiple ownership which often leads to owners being unable to cope. One prosecution in 1990, for instance, involved the discovery by an RSPCA inspector of fifty-one starving dogs shut in one room in a South London house (RSPCA Annual Report 1990: 6).

The key point to note about the debate surrounding the dog registration scheme is that it is concerned with means and not ends. No one involved disputes that strays present a problem (although some may not appreciate its scale), but they disagree on the appropriate response. What *has* divided the animal protection movement in terms of ends is the issue of the destruction of healthy animals. Animal welfare organisations, and particularly the RSPCA, have, albeit reluctantly, continued with their destruction policy. The waste of animal life here is enormous as well as nothing less than disgraceful, both because of the scale of the problem and because of the pointlessness of it all. The RSPCA humanely destroyed a total of 71,596 animals in 1995 alone, and only about 25,000 were destroyed because they were too sick or injured to live (RSPCA Annual Report 1995: 11). In the United States the problem exists on a greater scale with a third of the dog population ending up in animal shelters and an estimated twenty million dogs and cats destroyed every year (Rollin, 1981: 158).

These animals are usually destroyed, not for science or because they provide food but because their owners too often treat them as throwaway objects to be discarded when they become inconvenient or cease to give pleasure. No doubt there are some genuine cases where, for instance, someone can no longer cope with looking after an animal, because of age and infirmity, but these cases are relatively rare. Rather, animals are taken to shelters by their owners for a whole range of trivial reasons – because they are moving house, going on vacation, the animal has become too big or even because it does not match the new decor.

According to the moral orthodoxy, humanely killing an animal is legitimate and the Protection of Animals Acts recognises this since it is not an offence to kill an animal provided it is killed without unnecessary suffering. There are two exceptions. Firstly, some endangered wild species are protected, but this is not primarily because they matter individually but because their death threatens the survival of the species (see Chapter 6). Secondly, it can be an offence for an animal to be killed without the permission of its owner but this, of course, is concerned with property rights rather than the welfare of animals. The long-term destruction policy of most animal welfare societies – the NCDL being the notable exception, in Britain, of an organisation which refuses to kill healthy animals – has, though, come under increasing challenge in recent years. In philosophical terms, the animal rights view, for reasons we have explored, regards this destruction as morally wrong (Rollin, 1981: 152). In practical terms, the 'new' morality has surfaced within the RSPCA where in the 1970s the Council agreed in principle to phase out the destruction of healthy animals (Hall, 1984: 171). This policy, however, has never been put into practice and the less controversial (although arguably even more morally dubious) practice of spaying and neutering all bitches and cats re-homed by the Society has been adopted. The RSPCA has, in recent years though, become much more vocal about a destruction policy it finds increasingly diffi-cult to justify. The registration scheme, if implemented, however, would have a negligible impact on the problem.

Captive wild animals

In terms of captive wild animals, we can make a distinction between zoos on the one hand – which usually claim to fulfil functions other than merely entertaining the public with displays of wild animals – and circuses and dolphinaria on the other which, although they have increasingly sought to justify their use of animals in other ways, remain primarily concerned with entertainment. Given that the moral orthodoxy demands that we balance the suffering of animals with the benefits that accrue to humans as a result, the predominance of the trivial benefit in the latter category would make the infliction of suffering morally illegitimate. The case of zoos, where it is claimed in particular that captive wild animals provide important conservation func-tions which will benefit wild animals in general, is more complex.

There is little doubt that many circus animals do suffer as a result of their captivity. There is evidence of deliberately inflicted cruelty particularly as a result of the training methods which often depend upon engendering fear in animals to make them perform (Johnson, 1990: 96–112). More important, though, is that even if circus employees did not inflict pain on their animals (and many no doubt do not) it is doubtful if circuses could ever provide a reasonable environment to prevent suffering. For obvious reasons, animals have to remain shackled or caged for most of the time between performances and are transported between venues in so-called 'beast wagons' which, by definition, have to be small and often basic (Johnson, 1990: 140–2). So even without considering the morally dubious nature of the 'tricks' that circus animals are expected to perform (the roller-skating elephant, for instance, or the ice-skating polar bear) the level of suffering inflicted on circus animals is high.

The law in Britain is remarkably lenient. Circuses and trainers have to be licensed by a local authority under the 1925 Performing Animals (Regulation) Act but this licence is given for life and, for the reason that circuses do not usually stay in the area where the licence is issued, there is little or no supervision (Johnson, 1990: 156). As a response to their inability to scrutinise effectively the circuses they have licensed, some local authorities have banned circuses from using land they own. At least some protection is afforded in Britain, which is more than can be said for the usual triumvirate of Spain, Portugal and Greece where no legislative regulations exist. In other countries though – such as Finland, Sweden and Norway – very strict regulations prohibiting circuses from using most species exist (Johnson, 1990: 318). Since circuses serve no significant human purpose, the moral orthodoxy demands that these strict regulations be enforced elsewhere. The moral orthodoxy does compel us to consider the livelihoods of circus employees, but it should be remembered that circuses can and do exist without using wild animals as part of the perform-ance. In addition, as William Johnson (1990: 318) has suggested, it is possible for governments to provide tax concessions and grants to enable circuses to develop non-animal shows and to retrain the animal handlers.

Similar arguments condemn the use of dolphins as a source of entertainment (Johnson, 1990: 165–313). Considerable stress is caused by the often brutal removal of the animals from the wild and their confinement, usually in small chlorine-filled pools, is surely unacceptable given that dolphins are intelligent creatures that thrive in complex social groups in the wild. There is substan-tial evidence that they do suffer in captivity. Many dolphins die young and few breed successfully. Abnormal behaviour, too, has been recorded. Tragic cases exist, for instance, of dolphins that die after continually ramming themselves into the side of their pool. Of all captive wild animals, the plight of the dolphin has caught the British public's imagination and dolphin displays have become a thing of the past, although they still exist elsewhere.

It is extremely difficult to assess the moral validity of modern zoos in general (from the perspective of the moral orthodoxy at least) because the conditions in which animals are kept vary to such a great extent, as do the non-entertainment functions performed by zoos. In addition, different species have very different needs (Jordan, 1987). Measuring the suffering inflicted on wild animals by captivity is a further problem. Clearly, suffering includes more than just physical pain and poor health, but because it may not be accompanied by visible signs it is often difficult to assess whether or not, or to what extent, an animal is suffering (this problem is examined in more detail in Chapter 4 in the context of farm animals). It is not enough to conclude that captive animals must be suffering simply on the grounds that they are unable to behave in ways that are natural to them. On the one hand, some captive animals are able to perform most of their natural behaviour and obviously the better the environment for them (in terms of space, contact with other members of their species and other stimuli) the more natural their behaviour will become. On the other hand, it is necessary to balance the restrictions which inevitably are placed upon captive wild animals with the security that captivity provides for them.

This is not to be complacent. Some zoos are extremely poor. In the early 1990s, for instance, only about one third of the 1,000 or so zoos in the European Union were reputable enough to be included within the International Zoo Yearbook. Some countries, such as Spain, Portugal, Italy and Greece, have no laws governing zoos. Britain has around 430 zoos, mostly privately owned, although some, such as Bristol and London, are run by charitable trusts and a handful are owned by local authorities. The Zoo Licensing Act 1981 sets minimum standards specified by the Secretary of State for the Department of the Environment, Food and Rural Affairs (DEFRA) and enforces these through a local authority licensing system and periodic six-yearly inspections (Radford, 2001: 305–6). As a result, a small number of zoos have been forced to close. In 1998 the Labour Government undertook a sweeping review of the legislation and announced the creation of a Zoos Forum, an independent body to advise on zoo-related matters, and a new set of standards requiring all zoos to provide for their animals a suitable environment allowing them to express, as far as possible, their normal behaviour (*Guardian*, 4 September 2002).

Critics have argued, however, that local authorities do not have the resources to carry out their obligations under the legislation and that they often face a conflict of interest because of the economic consequences to a particular area of closure (*Guardian*, 4 September 2002). Moreover, the standards enforced remain pretty minimal and, although the worst abuses are uncovered, still only barely touch upon the key issues of environmental enrichment and the purpose of zoos. On the other hand, the United States, in particular, has some very good zoos where large 'naturalistic' environments have been created. The evidence suggests that the public are increasingly turning their backs on the old-style urban zoos with limited space and unimaginative displays. Thus, the financial crises of many British zoos in recent years, including London, have raised fundamental questions about the purpose of such institutions and the way in which animals are kept.

That some animals obviously suffer in captivity can be seen by the exhibiting of abnormal stereotype (or repetitive) behaviour elicited by their captivity such as excessive grooming, inactivity, self-mutilation and rail sucking. For some, relatively minor adjustments to their environment can improve the situation (Dawkins, 1980: 36). For others, because of their size, the complexity of their social lives or their instinctive need to hunt over long distances, it is impossible to cater adequately for their needs. The classic example here is the polar bear (although other captive animals such as tigers and foxes also exhibit abnormal behaviour patterns) which in the wild will travel hundreds of miles in search of food. Reputable zoos now no longer entertain the idea of buying polar bears because they recognise that they are a species which cannot be kept in captivity. Similarly, it is being recognised increasingly that there can be severe welfare implications involved in keeping elephants in captivity. There are about 1,700 zoo elephants worldwide, 500 of whom are in Europe. A report by an Oxford zoologist found that Asian elephants can live up to 65 or longer in the wild, whereas the average life expectancy of these animals in European zoos is 15 (*Guardian*, 23 October 2002).

In Britain, zoos were created in the nineteenth century (the first

and most important in Regent's Park in the 1820s) as a symbol of
man's dominion over nature in general and the British dominion
over her empire in particular (Ritvo, 1987: 205–42). In recent
years, as the animal protection movement has begun to step up its
attack on the keeping of wild animals in captivity and as the
public's knowledge of wildlife has increased, defenders have
claimed a variety of roles for zoos. The four main benefits that
have been regularly cited are entertainment, education, research
and conservation. In so far as zoos exist purely for the amusement
of those who visit them – and this probably applies to the bulk of
them – their moral validity is extremely suspect. Only if they
provide exemplary environments for the animals, excluding those
species which cannot be kept in captivity without suffering, can
they be justified. Zoos also emphasise their educational value. In
so far as they do – and many zoos pay lip-service to providing an
educational content to their displays – it has to be asked whether
viewing animals in cages or in small compounds can really teach
anything of value – except perhaps that wild animals should not
be kept in this way. This is particularly the case now that excellent natural history films are able to show to a wide audience the
behaviour of exotic wild animals in their natural habitats.

Research involving captive animals is aimed towards arriving
at a greater understanding of the behaviour and anatomy of
animals which would otherwise be unavailable for study. This
research can be for its own sake or to improve the life of animals
in captivity or to benefit human health (Jamieson, 1985: 112–13).
The use of captive animals for research is again, though, limited
to very few zoos. In so far as it does take place, it is of limited
validity. Obviously, research to improve the quality of life for zoo
animals would not be necessary if the institutions did not exist. As
research tools to benefit humans, zoo animals are limited primarily because it is impossible (if they are to continue to be
displayed) to undertake invasive procedures. Simply observing
them is a poor substitute.

Finally, the strongest argument in favour of zoos concerns the
contribution they make towards conservation and the preservation of endangered species. Here, there have been some successes.
Without zoos, for instance, the Mongolian wild horse, the
European bison and the golden lion tamarin monkey would now
be extinct (Jamieson, 1985: 114). It should be noted, however,

that, by itself, the protection of a species against extinction is not an animal welfare issue (see Chapter 6 for a detailed examination of this point). Indeed, it may be preferable on animal welfare grounds to destroy humanely zoo animals which are suffering rather than keep them alive simply because they are members of an endangered species. Of course, it is often the case that the protection of endangered species serves various human interests which can then be measured for their importance accordingly.

Even as a conservation strategy, keeping animals in captivity really only scratches the surface of the problem. Thousands of species are endangered, not primarily because the animals themselves are killed directly but because their habitat is being destroyed. It is therefore unrealistic in most cases to hope that many species bred in zoos (and not all species, in any case, do breed successfully in captivity) can be released into the wild, simply because there is no longer a place for them. Finally, even if it is accepted that captive-breeding programmes are a useful conservation strategy, this need not be undertaken by zoos but by special centres which deal with one particular species and are not usually open to the public.

Companions, captives and animal rights

It is noticeable that the major philosophical advocates of animal rights have relatively little to say about the issues discussed in this chapter. Their focus on animal agriculture and laboratory animals is in part the result of the disproportionate numbers of animals utilised in these practices. It is also, arguably, because the conclusions from the application of animal rights philosophy to them are more clear-cut. Certainly, the deprivations involved in circuses and dolphinaria are equally illegitimate, but then even the moral orthodoxy demands the end of these practices. It is not so clear, however, that companion animals and zoos fall into the same category.

One well-known British animal rights activist – John Bryant – has come out very strongly against the idea that it is morally correct to keep animals as pets. 'I have not the slightest hesitation in saying,' he writes, 'that pet animals should be completely phased out of existence.' This is because, for Bryant, pets are 'slaves and prisoners' and the fact that they may be well-fed,

loved and not in pain is irrelevant just as it would be if we were
discussing human slaves (Bryant, 1990: 9–10). Although he does
not do so, he could apply the same analysis to captive wild
animals. Thus, however good the environment and however
absent are signs of suffering, zoos are wrong and always will be
wrong because the animals within them are, by definition,
captive.

   It is not clear to me, however, that these conclusions necessarily follow from the application of animal rights philosophy.
Prohibiting both practices only becomes morally required if one
adopts the view that the right to liberty should be granted to
animals on the grounds that it is a good in itself. As Rachels
(1990: 121–3) points out, however, it only makes sense to grant
rights in accordance with the harms that are likely to accrue if
those rights were to be infringed. Thus, it is not sensible to grant
to animals a right to vote or a right to worship since to deprive
them of this right is not to harm them. Similarly, we should only
grant to animals a right to liberty if to deprive them of it is to
harm their interests. In the same way, as Regan and others have
argued, taking a healthy animal's life is wrong because it harms
that animal's interest, as a subject-of-a-life, in continuing to live.
Taking the life of an animal racked with pain which is untreat-
able, short of rendering it permanently unconscious, is in a
different moral category (Regan describes it as preference respect-
ing euthanasia) since in this case it is in the interests of that
animal to be humanely destroyed because this is the only way we
can satisfy its preference to be rid of pain (Regan, 1984: 109–13).
Incidentally, the widespread practice of euthanasing animals
which are in pain and have little or no chance of recovery is
arguably the only instance where the law upholds the interests of
animals in a way which it does not for humans in the same
circumstances.

   In the case of zoos and pet keeping the extent to which captivity harms interests will surely be a matter of empirical
observation. Some animals, as we saw, do suffer from captivity by
an inability to perform their natural behaviour and it is likely that
for many of these – polar bears, for instance – no zoo could
provide an environment which did not harm their interests significantly. For other zoo animals, though, it is far from certain that
captivity does harm their interests to any great extent or that for

others, who at present are harmed, a more appropriate environment could not be created which would counter the harm objection. Similarly, we could apply the same kind of analysis to the keeping of companion animals. Thus, it is difficult to find an animal rights objection in the case of a dog which is well-fed, regularly exercised, and is never deprived (or deprived for long) of associating with animals of the same species. What interests, it should be asked, are being harmed in this case? The granting to animals of a right to liberty, therefore, will be a contingent matter since we cannot say a priori at what point for different species captivity does begin to harm their interests.

Bryant (1990: 16), and others, no doubt would reply to this by saying that the pet dog or cat is an aberration with all of the 'natural' dog or cat behaviour bred out of it for human convenience. But this argument suffers from all of the problems of a Rousseauesque notion of positive freedom – that the animals only think they are free whereas they will only truly be so if they recognise their real selves disguised by centuries of human trickery. As with zoos, of course, the liberty of some companion animals is deprived to such an extent that significant harms are inflicted and in these cases we can describe them as morally illegitimate. It is often difficult to say when this point has been reached, but that it is not reached in some cases is clear.

Another, and more valid, objection is that in order to maintain the pet population, other species have to be slaughtered to feed them. Strictly speaking, as *a consequence* of the existence of an artificially high level of companion animals, this objection has no bearing on the rights question as applied directly to companions but requires us to consider the extent to which killing animals for food is morally illegitimate. This very question is the subject of the next chapter.

The issues we have dealt with in this chapter are, for a number of reasons, less significant than those we turn to in the next three chapters. In the first place, infinitely more animals are involved in the production of meat and the practice of vivisection than in circuses, zoos and dolphin displays. Secondly, they have not produced the same kind of fundamental moral conflict. Even if we accept a fairly low moral status for animals, keeping suffering wild animals in captivity merely to amuse and entertain is illegitimate and growing numbers of people are recognising this.

Similarly, although there are many problems in the area of companion animals, these are widely recognised. Very few, even from an animal rights perspective, seek to prohibit the keeping of animals as pets and the disputes that have arisen centre on competing management strategies to ensure that unsuitable people are deterred from owning pets and that those who inflict suffering on domesticated animals are more effectively detected and punished. The destruction of healthy unwanted pets is clearly wrong if we accept that animals have a right to life, although not from the perspective of the moral orthodoxy. This potential conflict within the animal protection movement has been dissipated. This is partly because attention has tended to focus on the many more animals that are killed in slaughterhouses and laboratories and also because throughout the movement there is a growing feeling that it is a mistake, on practical grounds, for animal welfare societies to do society's dirty work since, by disguising the real scale of the problem, it hinders stronger collective measures being taken.

4

Animal agriculture

The rearing, transporting and slaughtering of animals for food is big business. In Britain alone it is estimated that about 450 million birds, four million cattle, eleven million sheep and fourteen million pigs are slaughtered annually, whilst world-wide it has been estimated that, excluding poultry, some 1,000 million animals are killed for food each year. In the United States, the meat industry is second only to the car industry as the biggest manufacturing and processing concern, with the cattle industry alone worth about $30 billion annually (Rifkin, 1992: 154).

This was not always the case. For much of its time on earth, the human species lived on a diet consisting of very little meat and it is only in this century that the consumption of animal flesh has taken on a pre-eminent position. After 1945, in partic-ular, consumption increased as incomes rose (Walker and Cannon, 1984: 69–71). To meet this rising demand, new, more efficient, intensive rearing methods were introduced. Much of the debate about farm animal welfare has centred on this new system of 'factory' farming, although the moral case for vege-tarianism predates these developments. This chapter considers these welfare problems. It seeks to describe the nature of modern intensive farming, assess the extent of suffering involved and asks, with the aid of the moral theories discussed in Chapter 1, whether animal agriculture ought to be reformed or even abolished.

Converting animals into food

Modern animal agriculture is dominated by intensive methods whereby larger numbers of livestock are kept together in a much reduced space. This has given rise to the term 'factory' farming since animal agriculture takes on many of the characteristics – rapid and efficient turnover, high-density stocking, high degree of mechanisation, little use of labour – associated with factory production. Animals are increasingly being kept confined indoors and treated more or less like machines. Such large animal 'factories' are now the norm although there are significant differences between countries. In America, for instance, the scale of factory farms, the concentration of ownership and the number of species that have been confined are much greater than in Britain. Nevertheless, the difference is one of degree rather than substance. In both countries, for instance, poultry is the most intensively farmed of all species. The poultry industry is vertically integrated, with the same companies owning the 'farms', the slaughterhouses, and the food processing plants. Poultry 'farms' are remarkably efficient machines for turning live animals into the cellophane wrapped chickens and turkeys found on the supermarket shelf.

It should not be thought that the treatment of farm animals was historically good. Indeed, like most other animals, they were subject to immense cruelty (Spencer, 1995: 214–15; Turner, 1964: 53–4). Since 1911, they have been 'protected' in Britain against the infliction of 'unnecessary suffering' initially under the Protection of Animals Act and more recently under legislation specifically designed for farm animals. Central here is the 1968 Agricultural (Miscellaneous Provisions) Act. This piece of legislation replicates the major provision of the 1911 Act by declaring it an offence for any person to cause unnecessary suffering to livestock and, in section two, enables the Agriculture Minister to make regulations for farm animal welfare.

It seems appropriate to start a brief examination of some common features of modern animal husbandry with poultry. Not only are the numbers of domestic fowls extraordinary (estimated at between nine and ten billion in the world) but they were the first animals to be subject to intensive farming methods. Not only that, they are also now the only species which is raised virtually exclusively in this manner. Of course, these intensive rearing methods include what has become the symbol of factory farming – the battery cage. Even though the first use of cages occurred in the United States as early as the 1930s, free-range management systems for laying hens were still common during the 1950s in most countries. Since then confinement has gradually come to dominate – firstly in indoor deep-litter systems and then, because of the ease with which units could be managed, increasingly in battery cages (Fraser and Broom, 1990: 370–1). 90 per cent of the 300 million egg-laying hens in the EU live in battery cages, whereas for Britain the figure is 71 per cent (*Guardian*, 26 June 2002), as compared to only 8 per cent in 1948.

Chicks destined for the cages are produced at hatcheries. Because broilers are a different strain of chicken from layers, all males hatched at a unit responsible for layers will be exterminated since they cannot lay eggs and are not efficient at putting on weight. In the United States, about 160 million chicks die this way every year. There is no legislation governing the methods of extermination. Most producers gas the superfluous day-old chicks in plastic bags but some simply allow the chicks to suffocate (Singer, 1990: 108). Clearly this is a practice which ought to be subject to legislation and inspection. Those chicks selected for laying are then sent to 'grow out' houses before, after about twenty weeks, they are ready to lay eggs.

It is easy to see why cages are preferred to free-range or even deep-litter systems by producers. Quite simply they are extremely cost-effective. Because such operations can be mechanically operated, labour costs are minimised. In addition, space is effectively utilised and disease and parasites are minimised particularly because the birds can be separated from their faeces. When birds do get sick they can be treated easily. Finally, egg collection rates are maximised because eggs are immediately removed through the front of the cages, which have sloping wire floors. Chickens can live for ten years or longer but battery hens last only about eighteen months, after which time their ability to produce eggs diminishes. They are then sent for slaughter and used to make soups and other processed foods. Some operators use a procedure known as 'force moulting' in order to shock previously spent birds into renewed egg productivity. This involves leaving the birds in the dark without food and water for several days.

Fortunately, this practice is now illegal in Britain and is not employed very often elsewhere because hens are cheap enough for a producer to simply replace a flock whose productivity has declined (Fraser and Broom, 1990: 372–3).

Battery systems are, of course, quite legal in most countries including Britain and the United States (although they have been illegal in Switzerland since 1991, Sweden since 1998 and Holland since 2000). At the European level, the focus has been on poultry welfare and in particular on battery hens. The European Community became a party to the Council of Europe Convention on the Protection of Farm Animals (1976) in 1978. Amongst the recommendations accepted by the Council of Ministers was a directive laying down minimum standards for hens kept in battery cages. Since then, regular debate within the EU has culminated in a decision taken in July 1999 to phase out 'barren' battery cages by 2012 (no new such battery cages have been permitted since 2003). However, at the EU level at least – if not in Britain – 'enriched' cages – larger and containing a nest box, perch and litter – will be allowed (*Guardian*, 25 June 2002).

The focus on battery systems disguises the fact that broiler chickens – those fattened for meat – are, if anything, treated less well than laying hens. As a result of vertical integration, the poultry industry, as eloquently described by Browne (2002), is a hugely efficient and mechanised system for 'growing', killing and processing chickens. Most broilers are kept in large deep-litter houses (commonly sheds with solid windowless walls), each usually containing between 10–20,000 birds, where they are fattened and sent for slaughter at about seven weeks. As many as 800 million broilers are produced each year in Britain alone (along with twenty-five million turkeys and nine million ducks) whilst the figure for the United States is three billion (Mason and Singer, 1990: 8). The welfare problems here can be acute. There may be as little space for the birds to move about as there is for battery hens, but in addition it is much more difficult, if not impossible, to locate and treat sick birds and, consequently, disease can spread. Birds in such close proximity are liable to engage in feather pecking, a practice which can cause serious injury or even death. In order to prevent this, both laying hens and broilers have traditionally been subject to beak trimming or debeaking, a controversial procedure first practised in the 1940s which involves the use of a heated blade to cut off about a third of a chick's bill. This practice will be prohibited within the EU from 2010.

It is rare for beef cattle to be confined indoors, particularly if, as the majority are in Britain, they are steers (castrated bulls) as opposed to bulls. In the United States, feedlots, or man-made concrete floored fenced areas with food troughs along one side, are now the norm, thus enabling the cattle to be fattened quickly on a diet of grain. Movement here is unrestricted but cattle have to endure a barren environment. In Britain, on the other hand, beef cattle are usually given considerably more freedom (Fraser and Broom, 1990: 355; Singer, 1990: 139–40).

In the United States there is a growing tendency to confine dairy cows in indoor stalls. In all countries, dairy cows are kept for as long as they are productive. This means a constant cycle of impregnation (usually by artificial insemination), birth and lactation. Cows spend eight months of each year pregnant, nine months being milked twice a day and six months both pregnant and lactating. This is achieved by removing the calf from the cow – usually after three days – and impregnating her again about six weeks later. This ensures a regular supply of milk for humans to consume. In fact, due to various factors including the growing use of hormones, cows produce almost twice as much milk as they did thirty years ago. As a consequence, cows now tend to wear out quicker than they used to, the average age before they are killed now being only five years (their natural lifespan being up to thirty years). As Webster (1994: 170) remarks 'to achieve the daily work rate of the dairy cow, a man would have to jog for six to eight hours per day, every day'.

The consequence of milk production, of course, is a supply of calves. Some calves are reared to join the dairy herds, others are raised for beef production and others are slaughtered immediately and the rennet removed from their stomachs used to harden cheese. By far the most controversial use of calves is to produce veal. Originally, the tender and pale veal meat came from calves slaughtered a few days after birth before they began to eat grass and their flesh darkened. The problem for the veal producers was that these very young calves were very small. In the 1950s veal producers in Holland hit upon the idea of keeping the calves alive longer without their flesh becoming any less pale or tender. During the 16 weeks of their lives, calves were fed a liquid diet which lacked the required amount of both roughage and iron and, because the animal could not be permitted to consume these elements naturally and develop muscles which reduce the tenderness of the meat, it was necessary for them to be removed quickly from their mothers and confined. The most notorious confinement was the so-called veal crate, a device which prevented the calf from turning round or grooming the whole of its body and which isolated the animal completely from external stimuli and even bedding which might be a source of iron.

Such has been the furore about these crates that they have been banned in Britain since 1990. Government regulations require that calves have enough room to turn around without difficulty and that they are fed adequate amounts of iron and fibre, although it should be noted that the law does not, as yet, outlaw single penning of calves. No such regulations exist in the United States, but an EU directive in 1994 stipulates that new and existing veal systems must allow enough space for calves to lie down, stand up and groom themselves. Moreover, they must be able to see other calves. Finally, in 1997, this directive was amended to prohibit, from 2006, calves being kept in individual crates after they reach eight weeks old (Wilkins, 1997: 17).

Pigs are reared in a variety of ways although there is a growing tendency in Britain towards free-range systems. Most controversy surrounds the way sows are treated. Like dairy cows, sows go through a continual round of giving birth to and feeding piglets and, soon after (whether they want to or not – hence the term 'rape rack'), impregnation again. As a result of a government regulation introduced in response to a Private Member's Bill sponsored by CIWF (see Chapter 7) the practice of confining sows in stalls tethered by metal chains has been phased out in Britain, and a similar measure will apply throughout the EU by 2005 (Wilkins, 1997: 21). Another controversial issue of pig husbandry is the so-called farrowing crate. This commonly used device is a self-enclosed area where sows are kept with their piglets. It does not allow the sow much freedom of movement but was designed with the welfare of piglets in mind since high mortality rates can occur through the sow lying on her young. By restricting movement and incorporating an area where the piglets can get away from their mother, the farrowing crate can alleviate this problem but at the cost of confining the sow.

Animals are transported to markets or slaughterhouses at home or abroad. In the latter case, the moving of very young calves from one European country (including Britain) to veal-rearing establishments in another part of the continent is common. Also prevalent is the shipment of live sheep, particularly to the Middle East and Asia from Australia, New Zealand and Ireland. In the early 1990s, about 300,000 calves and 500,000 sheep were exported from Britain each year, and there has been an EU directive on live animal exports since 1977 which was strengthened in 1981 to require a certificate from a veterinary surgeon showing that the directive has been properly observed (Humphreys, 1989: 96). In the United States, the transportation of animals by truck is still not regulated at the federal level despite the fact that 95 per cent of all farm livestock in the US is transported by road (Singer, 1990: 148).

The export of live animals from Britain has been one of the most controversial welfare issues in recent years. Animal welfare groups had long been concerned about the live export trade (see Stevenson, 1994) but major, and apparently spontaneous, protests against it in 1994 and 1995 catapulted it to centre stage in British politics for a while (see Chapters 2 and 7). The British government was urged to employ Article 36 of the Treaty of Rome which allows for exemptions from legislative harmonisation in certain circumstances, but, for whatever reason, ministers sought to gain more stringent regulations at the EU level instead. Groups such as the RSPCA and CIWF, recognising that an end to the trade was not an option, called for a blanket eight-hour limit to journeys. This was never going to be acceptable to many EU member states, however, and the 1995 directive mandated a 24-hour rest after an eight-hour journey, unless animals were being transported in 'special' vehicles which can carry food and bedding and have adequate ventilation (Wilkins, 1997: 4). For animals exported from Britain, the standards are more stringent with, for instance, any journey abroad over eight hours in duration requiring a route plan and itinerary to be approved by DEFRA (Radford, 2001: 320). As a final point here it was, ironically, not the protests that all but ended the live export trade from Britain, at least for a while, but first BSE and then foot-and-mouth which led to EU action to prohibit British exports (see below).

Most animals end their lives in the slaughterhouse, including dairy cows and laying hens which are slaughtered once they become insufficiently productive. Whatever the problems with modern slaughtering procedures, it is clear that they are a great improvement on the past. In Britain, it was not until Pease's Act of 1835 that a system of licensing for keepers of slaughterhouses together with a limited number of regulations was put in place. Slaughtering, though, remained primitive and cruel, being largely undertaken by small private enterprises subject to little or no supervision. Animals were typically herded into cellars, often after long journeys, and, since no effective stunning device was available, were butchered inhumanely. Sheep, for instance, were commonly knifed in the neck and sometimes skinned before death. Slaughtering on small farms was not much better as graphic accounts in novels by Thomas Hardy (particularly *Jude the Obscure)* and Flora Thompson demonstrate (Turner, 1964: 148, 220–2).

In the twentieth century, and particularly in the last thirty years, the way in which animals are slaughtered has been transformed. Gradually, local authorities built large public abattoirs (the first being set up in the nineteenth century) and more humane ways of killing – such as the stunning gun – were invented. Whereas animals were once hit over the head by a pole-axe (a sledgehammer) cattle are now stunned by a captive bolt pistol and pigs, sheep and calves usually by electric tongs. Similarly, poultry pass through electrical stunning baths before bleeding.

A considerable body of legislation now governs the procedures in slaughterhouses. The 1933 Slaughterhouse Act requires that animals be stunned so that they are unconscious before being bled. Central to the modern system is the 1958 Slaughter of Animals (Prevention of Cruelty) Regulations. This prohibits the slaughter of an animal in the sight of another awaiting slaughter. The requirement for lairaging, or waiting, areas, led to the end of the old 'booth' system whereby butchers could do their own slaughtering and the rebuilding of abattoirs to separate the waiting area from the stunning pen and the 'sticking' (or throat cutting) area (Davies, 1989: 66–7). As a result of the single market, slaughtering standards have been harmonised across Europe. In order to meet these, the British government announced a new set of regulations in 1990. The two crucial provisions were firstly that by 5 July 1992 the heads of cattle, sheep and pigs must be restrained before stunning and secondly the rule that animals should not see each other being stunned was abolished.

Controversially, the law in many countries, including Britain and America, allows Jewish and Muslim ritual slaughter even though it involves the cutting of an animal's throat with a sharp knife without pre-stunning. One ritual slaughter method is the rotary pen whereby animals are turned upside-down before their throats are cut. This method has been illegal throughout Europe from 1992.

In Britain, slaughterhouses, and those who do the slaughtering, have to be licensed annually by a local authority under the Slaughterhouse Act 1974 (poultry slaughterhouses only have to be licensed once, although the licence can be revoked, and poultry slaughtermen do not have to be licensed). Renewal of a licence depends upon the judgement of vets and environmental health officers. Most slaughterhouses in Britain did not comply with European regulations which require the antemortem (before slaughter) inspection of animals by a vet and, prior to the introduction of the Single European Act in 1992, meat from British abattoirs not complying with this regulation could not be exported. As a consequence of the Act, many British abattoirs not meeting European standards closed down. While more veterinary inspection of livestock can only be beneficial to their welfare, there is a downside in that fewer abattoirs has meant some animals have to travel much longer distances, creating additional welfare problems.

The suffering of farm animals

The vast majority of people, in the West at least, eat animals and therefore, in so far as they think about such things, are likely to accept, if they were asked, the validity of the moral orthodoxy – that animals are morally inferior to humans and, whilst taking account of their interests in not suffering, we are entitled to utilise them as a resource for food. As we have seen, the law adopts this position too, declaring it an offence to cause unnecessary suffering to livestock. According to this conventional morality, killing farm animals is not regarded as an issue, but the ways in which they are kept, transported and slaughtered are important areas of concern and legislative interference is justifiable.

The conventional morality, therefore, seeks to strike a balance between animal welfare and the benefits that accrue to humans. The problem is where to strike that balance. It would seem that the welfare side of the equation is relatively easy to assess given that it is an empirical question. Certainly, the development of animal welfare science in recent years has produced a far more rigorous analysis of farm animal suffering. It should be noted before this evidence is reviewed, however, that, because we are dealing with suffering which goes beyond the simple identification of physical pain, the evidence remains, in some part at least, contestable. A crucial initial point when reviewing the evidence on farm animal welfare is that suffering should not be seen as equivalent to pain. Even if animals are physically healthy they may still be suffering. In addition, an animal may be slaughtered before the signs of ill-health begin to show. This obviously applies, above all, to veal calves whose inadequate diet would eventually cause death (although it should also be noted that broiler chickens and pigs are slaughtered at an early age).

Physical pain, though, remains the starting-point for an analysis of suffering. In the first place, considerable pain occurs as a result of some behavioural abnormalities largely caused by confinement. These are described below. In addition, leg injuries are common in confined animals since their lack of exercise prevents leg muscles from developing to match their ever-increasing weight. This is particularly the case with broiler chickens who, in modern systems with little room to move, commonly multiply their body weight sixty times during their lifespan of six weeks (their natural lifespan is about seven years). As Colin Spencer (*Guardian*, 21 April 1992) pointed out:

> Imagine an eight pound new-born baby growing in seven weeks to the weight of thirty-four stone, and you will have a picture of this genetic and environmental monstrosity.

It is for these reasons that John Webster, Professor of Animal Husbandry at Bristol University, regards the treatment of broiler chickens and turkeys as 'the single, most severe, systematic example of man's inhumanity to another sentient animal' (Webster, 1994: 156). In battery hens, too, brittle bones are a common welfare problem. One study of about 3,000 birds found that, before slaughter, no less than 98 per cent had broken bones (on average six breaks each). This is not surprising given that, according to Webster again, the consistency of the bones of battery hens is akin to potato crisps (*Independent*, 29 December 1988).

Two legal practices which are known to cause physical pain are beak trimming and ritual slaughter. On a parallel is the tail docking of pigs, whereby the tails of young pigs are removed in order to prevent the common practice of tail biting (see below). There is little doubt that beak trimming is a painful operation even when done correctly, and its phasing out within the EU is welcome, particularly as there is evidence that economic pressures mean that often not enough care is taken and this can lead to additional injuries being inflicted (Fraser and Broom, 1990: 271). Ritual slaughter is also, the evidence suggests, a serious welfare problem. After the throat is cut, the animal remains conscious for anything up to three minutes 'during which the animal must be in great pain and distress' (Fraser and Broom, 1990: 286). Almost as important is the *way* in which animals are ritually slaughtered. Some animals in the United States, for instance, are shackled and hoisted – as stunned animals are – before having their throats cut whilst fully conscious. Finally, the pressure on dairy cows to produce more and more milk can lead to serious health problems, not least udder infections such as mastitis.

The transporting of animals, particularly across national boundaries, also gives rise to much concern. As one authority has pointed out: 'The welfare of animals is possibly more compromised by the requirement to move them from place to place than by any other human impact upon them'. The stress involved in transportation is a problem discussed below, but pain – caused by bruising, broken limbs and so-called 'shipping fever' – and even death are common features, particularly of international transportation. It is known, for instance, that the mortality rate of young calves transported over long distances can be as much as 25 per cent and that of adult cattle and sheep between 1.5 and 10 per cent (Humphreys, 1989: 85, 90, 96). Of course, the extent of this suffering will depend upon a number of variables including the distance travelled, the accommodation used, and the level of care provided by the operators. Often, it has to be said, standards are very poor. Within the EU, long journeys with the potential to cause animal suffering are still permitted, enforcement is lax and the regulations are regularly flouted in any case (Wilkins, 1997: 4). The trade between New Zealand and Australia to the Middle East is particularly problematic, with a proportion of animals always suffering and dying *en route*, with occasional huge losses of life reported, such as in September 2002 when 15,000 sheep perished on the three-week journey from Australia (*Guardian*, 4 September 2002).

The issue of slaughterhouses, in general, ought to be mentioned here too. In theory, given the regulations surrounding the slaughtering process, the suffering of farm animals in the last moments of their lives should be minimal, although there are some doubts about the effectiveness of electrical stunning equipment even if properly used (Singer, 1990: 152; Webster, 1994: 154–5). There have been many disturbing reports, however, that these regulations are regularly broken. As well as investigations by journalists, the British government's own advisory body on animal welfare – the Farm Animal Welfare Council – have published damning reports on the basis of extensive visits to slaughterhouses (FAWC, 1982; FAWC, 1984; see also *Guardian*, 8 March 1989, *Sunday Times*, 9 July 1989). In general, problems occur because animal welfare often takes second place to cost-cutting. Thus, the need to get animals through as quickly as possible results in inaccurate, or (in the case of electrical tongs) insufficiently lengthy, use of equipment and the failure to ensure that each animal is stunned in isolation from others. The pistol or electric tongs have to be in a precise position on the animal's head and it only takes a flick of the head at the last moment for an ineffective application to take place. The consequences of getting it wrong are considerable. Animals in agony may have to wait until the slaughterman reloads the pistol or animals may regain consciousness before, during or after having their throats cut. In addition, the equipment is not always properly maintained which is vital for its effective use. To cap all this, the slaughterhouse staff are often inexperienced and may care little for animal welfare. Not surprisingly, given the nature of the work and the poor pay, the turnover of staff is considerable.

Identifying suffering other than pain is not so easy. A common defence of factory farming is that the high productivity of the animals means they cannot be suffering. Marion Dawkins (1980: 27–32, 34) demonstrates, however, that this argument is seriously flawed. Productivity refers to the profit that can be made from animals and there is no doubt that the productivity of animal agriculture has increased dramatically. This is not, however, a necessary sign of a lack of suffering. The productivity of an individual animal may tell us very little about its welfare. For instance, the fact that an animal weighs more and is therefore worth more could come about as a result of lack of exercise due to severe confinement. Likewise, the egg laying of battery hens is not necessarily a sign of contentment. At the farm unit level, there is even less correlation between the welfare of animals and productivity. The profitability of intensive farm systems is dependent not just, or even mainly, upon the health and general welfare of the animals. It also has to include labour, heating and food wastage costs. In this context, intensive systems are more profitable even if some animals suffer as a consequence. Thus, for instance, a farmer may well opt to risk losing broilers since the death of a few birds will probably be cheaper than paying someone to inspect the birds for illness beforehand and paying for any subsequent treatment. This is not to say that the animals do suffer, but only that productivity is not the best means of deciding whether they do or not.

One alternative criterion of suffering is an animal's inability to perform the behaviour patterns normally associated with its particular species. Certainly, intensive rearing involves the unnatural confinement of animals with hens in cages, for instance, unable to stretch their wings, fly, roost, dust bathe, or build nests – behaviour which is common to the wild ancestors of the domestic fowl. As Dawkins (1980: 43) points out, however, to conclude from this that we should therefore not confine animals in this way assumes a number of things. In the first place, it is to assume that there are no significant genetic differences between the wild and domesticated species. Secondly, it is to assume that animals in the wild and in more 'natural' farming environments do not experience suffering. Yet clearly they do and this needs to be balanced against the suffering caused by the confinement of animals in intensive systems. Some of the problems, for instance, of returning to free-range chicken husbandry are that disease is more likely and less easily controlled, extreme weather conditions can cause serious problems and there is a higher degree of predation (Fraser and Broom, 1990: 371). Likewise, mountain sheep have to endure considerable suffering from being eaten alive by maggots in the summer to cold and hunger in the winter (Dawkins, 1980: 53). Although confined sows, in addition, do undoubtedly suffer both physically and mentally, it should also be recognised that group-housed sows tend to fight and injure each other, particularly when there is competition for food (Fraser and Broom, 1990: 363–4). These problems, it should be added, are not incapable of resolution, but they serve to illustrate that animal suffering is not exclusively the product of intensive farming. Finally, and crucially, the fact that animals are unable to perform behaviour natural to their species does not, by itself, demonstrate that the animals actually are suffering (Dawkins, 1980: 48–9). It simply begs the question of whether confining animals actually does cause suffering. To find the answer to this we have to look else-where.

A further indicator of suffering is physiological change which can be used to measure the level of stress animals are under. Such features as, for instance, higher ventilation rates, increased blood cortisol and noradrenaline levels, as well as an increased heart rate are signs that an animal is under stress, and such changes have been recorded in all stages of the birth to slaughter cycle (Fraser and Broom, 1990: 267–8). The transportation of animals to the slaughterhouse is particularly traumatic. Poultry are especially roughly treated, and are particularly disturbed by contact with humans. All animals intensively reared, though, are subject to stress because of the dramatic change of environment – from the stable, regulated world of the factory farm to the unregulated outside world with its unpredictability and extremes of heat and cold.

The problem here is that stress is not necessarily a sign of suffering. Indeed, stress is a natural reaction to an unfamiliar or threatening situation and stress symptoms are simply a way for the body to adapt to this environment, much like the boiler in a central heating system which switches itself on when the temperature falls below a certain level. An overheating boiler or one that does not work at all are more appropriate signs of a system not working effectively. The problem is it is difficult to define the point at which physiological changes amount to a breakdown in the animal's 'boiler' and therefore an indication of suffering. Certainly, stress-related deaths do occur amongst confined animals but this tells us little about those animals who do not succumb (Dawkins, 1980: 55–68).

Perhaps the most effective indicator of suffering is the observation of abnormal behaviour in confined animals. There is no question that this is a severe welfare problem and makes the case for the abolition of factory farming that much stronger. The abnormal behaviour of intensively farmed animals comes in a variety of forms. That which involves self-mutilation or the mutilation of other animals in the same species – including the licking and eating of an animal's own hair, wool or feathers, excessive drinking, feather pecking in battery hens which can result in cannibalism and tail biting in pigs – is a clear sign of severe suffering (Fraser and Broom, 1990: 318–28).

Abnormal behaviour occurs in other forms too. Examples of misdirected behaviour are homosexual acts amongst animals kept in single sex groups and teat seeking and sucking behaviour directed towards objects or other animals by young animals removed from their mothers at an early age. Here too, incidentally, we should mention the undoubted suffering caused to both mother and offspring which occurs as a result of very early weaning. Cows have been known to call for their calves for a considerable time and, in one celebrated incident, one actually succeeded in finding its calf after trekking seven miles through the night (Fraser and Broom, 1990: 328–31, 345–9). Apathy, too – particularly apparent in sows confined in tethers or stalls – is an indicator of poor welfare as is the hysteria that occurs amongst broilers and turkeys which can lead to the birds piling on top of each other and thereby causing deaths.

Perhaps the most well-documented form of abnormal behaviour is stereotypical behaviour, a phenomenon we encountered in the context of zoos (see Chapter 3). Many different types have been recorded (Fraser and Broom, 1990: 307–17). These include confined animals continually rocking backwards and forwards or from side to side, rubbing continually against an object, head shaking (occurring in caged birds), eye rolling (seen in veal calves), sham chewing for hours day after day (seen mainly in tethered sows), tongue rolling (seen most often in cows), licking or crib wetting and bar biting (again in sows). Clearly, this type of behaviour is a product of confinement. Whether it represents an attempt by animals to come to terms with their environment

or whether it is simply a sign that they are seriously disturbed is
not clear. Surely, though, we are entitled to describe it as suffering.

Improving the welfare of farm animals

In reality, despite the doubts expressed above, there is little question that intensive farming methods do cause suffering. Indeed,
this is recognised by contemporary legislation in Britain, the
United States and elsewhere since if ordinary members of the
public kept animals in the same way that many farmers do, they
would be liable to prosecution under general animal protection
laws. What becomes crucial, then, is the extent to which this
suffering is justified which, in terms of the conventional or orthodox morality, is to be judged in accordance with how significant
the human benefits produced by it are. If the human interests
served by animal agriculture are deemed to be significant, then we
are not entitled to protect animals to the extent that these significant human interests are undermined. Obviously, it is extremely
difficult to be precise here (which both demonstrates the inade-
quacy of the concept as a moral principle but also provides a
window of opportunity for reformers to justify change), but we
can, I think, assume that the abolition of animal agriculture
completely would affect human interests sufficiently severely for
it to be an illegitimate move as far as the orthodox morality goes.
In any case, killing animals is not a problem for the moral orthodoxy for reasons explored in Chapter 1 and, in theory at least, it
is possible to envisage a system of animal agriculture which
caused no welfare problems at all.

Of course, modern farming methods are employed, not
because those involved want to be cruel to animals, but because it
produces economic benefits to producers as well as consumers.
Thus, battery cage systems for hens produce cheaper eggs (it has
been estimated that eggs produced in low density free-range
systems are about 70 per cent more expensive than those
produced in battery systems meeting the minimum EU requirements) (Broom, 1989: 276). Likewise, economics are involved in
the transportation of live animals over large distances across
national boundaries, since live animals are worth more than
carcasses as they provide business for slaughterhouses and their

hides can be sold to leather manufacturers. Similarly, as we saw, a good deal of the mistreatment of animals in slaughterhouses occurs because of the economic imperatives involved in the throughput of livestock. If we then omit from consideration those practices which have an economic benefit for humans we are left with practices which cause suffering but which do not have an economic motive, such as ritual slaughter, as candidates for change. It has to be said that there really is no justification for this practice, and it has been banned in Switzerland since 1893, Norway since 1930 and Sweden since 1937 as well as in Ireland and most of the Austrian Lander.

This does not mean, however, that reforms to the present intensive system of animal agriculture are not justified, even though economic benefits may have to be sacrificed as a result. For the economic benefits produced by particular practices may not themselves (as opposed to animal agriculture in general) be significant enough to justify the suffering to animals that results. Most people, for instance, would not be harmed by the extra cost (or lower consumption) of animal products that resulted from less intensive forms of farming. Indeed, the search for economic benefit (for the producer and the consumer) has meant that the interests of farm animals are often given a low, if not nonexistent, priority. As Ruth Harrison (1964: 3) pointed out, 'cruelty is acknowledged only where profitability ceases'. Clearly, we are entitled to declare that this is unacceptable morally without departing from the orthodox position that human interests are of greater significance than those of animals. Thus, most of those philosophers who hold that meat eating is not morally prohibited accept that some of the modern intensive farming methods should be ended (see Frey, 1983: 207). In addition, Donald Broom, the Cambridge professor of animal welfare (not a radical by any means) can comment that:

> our current knowledge indicates that the welfare of very many animals on farms is so poor that there is a need for urgent action to change this situation. (Fraser and Broom, 1990: 279)

Certainly, therefore, one does not have to accept that animals have rights or interests which ought to be considered equally along with human interests in order to claim that modern animal agriculture has altered the balance between human and animal interests much too far in favour of the former, to the extent that relatively trivial human interests are being promoted ahead of vital animal interests. In addition, it has not gone unnoticed that the language used to describe intensive farming is reminiscent of the Cartesian theory that animals are little more than machines. Mason and Singer (1990: 1), for instance, in their critique of factory farming, illustrate the attitude of many in the meat industry by quoting disapprovingly a trade magazine which contained the following:

> Forget the pig is an animal. Treat him just like a machine in a factory. Schedule treatments like you would lubrication. Breeding season like the first step in an assembly line. And marketing like the delivery of finished goods.

It is significant in this context that painful procedures such as debeaking and tail docking are practised because the behaviour of animals is distorted by their confinement, a case of fitting the animal to the rigours of the husbandry system rather than the other way round.

In Britain, and some other European countries, as we have seen, gradual erosions of factory farming have taken place but the fundamentals remain despite much disquiet. It is in the United States, the birthplace of 'factory farming', that most remains to be done. No federal laws exist to regulate intensive farming and state anti-cruelty laws often exempt farm animals. It is clear, though, that there is much opposition to 'factory farming', or certain aspects of it, and this opposition is not restricted to radical animal rights activists. The public reaction to the detailed descriptions of modern animal agriculture contained in Ruth Harrison's *Animal Machines* led, in 1964, to the Labour Government setting up a committee, chaired by the noted zoologist Professor F. W. Brambell, 'to examine the conditions in which livestock are kept under systems of intensive husbandry and to advise whether standards ought to be set in the interests of their welfare, and if so what they should be' (HMSO, 1965).

The Brambell Report, published in 1965, was a damning indictment of factory farming. It called for new legislation to apply specifically to farm animals, thereby replacing the 1911 Act. Central to the critique was a recognition that animal suffering had to be more clearly defined in a way which included more than just physical pains. Given this wider definition, it proposed that the welfare of farm animals should be based upon what became known as the 'five freedoms' – freedom for an animal to turn around, groom itself, get up, lie down and stretch its limbs. Further, it recommended that the debeaking of poultry and tail docking of pigs be prohibited and that regular inspections of farms be made to enforce the law.

The 1968 legislation did take on board the idea of Codes of Practice, but these are not legally binding and tend to be disregarded by the courts. Brambell, in a letter to *The Times,* commented that the legislation was 'a compromise approximating to current practice; a compromise on a compromise for which no case otherwise than commercial expediency exists' (quoted in Sweeney, 1990: 36). However, it would be wrong to condemn the legislation out of hand. Crucially, it allowed for the introduction of regulations prohibiting certain practices, and it was under this legislation that veal crates and sow stalls and tethers were banned and under which battery cages will be phased out.

What the 1968 Act has not done is to create a set of minimum standards which farms would be expected to uphold. These standards could be easily upheld by inspection and would remove the need to prove the infliction of 'unnecessary' suffering in the courts which is time-consuming, expensive, often not successful and takes place *after* the cruelty has occurred. It could also involve a system of licensing which would control those who keep livestock necessitating, perhaps, the successful completion of a course of study (Radford, 2001: 262–6). Such proposals, of course, assume that some, or all, of the features of intensive farming would be prohibited.

BSE and all that

Most of the dominant issues in British agriculture over the past ten years or so have been concerned with animal husbandry. British agriculture has lurched from one crisis to another from the claim, in the late 1980s, that most British eggs were infected with salmonella to the BSE crisis in the 1990s and, more recently still, the foot-and-mouth outbreak in 2001. This litany of catastrophes for British animal agriculture has had many important consequences, but what can we say about them in terms of the welfare of animals?

At least three main themes can be explored. In the first place, it is significant that, whatever the implications of the issues cited above for animal welfare, they were usually couched in terms of their significance for humans, thereby reflecting the dominance of anthropocentrism. Concern in the salmonella outbreak was not primarily about the conditions in which battery hens were kept but about the effects on human health. Likewise, the media coverage of BSE really took off not because of the suffering of the animals infected with the disease but because of the discovery that there was a possible connection between BSE and CJD in humans. Similarly, the slaughter of millions of animals during the foot-and-mouth crisis was not for the benefit of animal welfare at all. Animals infected suffer only moderately and most make a complete recovery. Moreover, vaccination was an option. Rather, the mass slaughter was carried out because underweight animals would have been worth much less, and unless the disease was eradicated, which required slaughter rather than vaccination, the lucrative export trade would have been prohibited. There can be no better illustration of the arrogant anthropocentrism of human beings than the scenes of burning animal carcasses littering the British rural landscape at this time. Rarely has vegetarianism had a better recruiting ground.

The second theme concerns the generic cause of the outbreaks. For there is little doubt that all three cases were a product of agricultural intensification. It is somewhat ironic, then, that what was originally intended to produce human benefits, in terms of cheaper and more consistent food supplies, has ended up producing human costs. Salmonella, and other diseases, are so much more difficult to control in the cramped conditions of an intensive battery unit. BSE, likewise, was caused by the unnatural practice of feeding cattle with the brains and vertebrae of other animals. Finally, foot-and-mouth was caused by unscrupulous and reckless behaviour by one farmer, coupled with the centralisation of abattoir provision and the consequent need for animals to be transported greater distances, thereby making it more difficult to contain the outbreak (Fort, 2001).

Finally, it should be noted that the actual diseases themselves had a mixed impact on the welfare of animals. Salmonella is not a pleasant disease, but then the lives of battery cages are so short and impoverished that it barely registers as an additional welfare concern. Cattle with BSE, too, undoubtedly suffer, although it is difficult to estimate how much they were aware of their condition. In the case of foot-and-mouth, many millions of animals also lost their lives. Death, by itself, though is not a welfare issue. The animals were destined to die anyway of course, and being slaughtered on the farm was arguably preferable to the stresses involved in being transported, sometimes over long distances, to the abattoir. An added bonus to animals was the temporary bans on live exports and hunting during the crisis (*Guardian*, 28 February 2001). There were some disturbing reports of animals not being slaughtered correctly (see *Guardian*, 2 October 2002), or being left to suffer because of movement restrictions, but then, as we have seen, the transportation of animals often causes suffering and what happens to them in the slaughterhouse often leaves a lot to be desired.

Moral theory and vegetarianism

An obvious response to mark one's disapproval of some or all of the practices described above is vegetarianism (a meat-free diet) or even veganism (a diet free from any animal produce whatever). Indeed, those who challenge the moral orthodoxy – including both Singer's animal liberation and Regan's rights view – claim that vegetarianism is obligatory. We are, of course, primarily concerned here with vegetarianism as a moral response although there are a range of other reasons – from health to social status – for abstaining from eating meat. Indeed, much of the controversy over factory farming has focused on the public health aspects which are considerable but beyond the scope of this book (Frey, 1983: 6–16; Mason and Singer, 1990: 52–69).

A closer look at the philosophical challenges to the orthodoxy discussed above reveals that only those who hold the radical view that animals have a right to life can, without further investigation, say categorically that eating animals is, in almost all circumstances, wrong and therefore vegetarianism obligatory. To see that this is so we should examine this position followed by the alternatives.

Those, such as Regan, who hold that animals have a right to life can obviously establish that to kill an animal for food is violating that right and is therefore morally illegitimate. As we saw, Regan has been criticised for weakening his position by denying that humans and animals have equal amounts of inherent value so that in a hypothetical 'lifeboat' case, where either a human or an animal must be sacrificed, then it must be the animal. There is a great deal of difference, however, between such a hypothetical situation and the slaughtering of animals for food in modern societies since in the latter case it is not a question of life or death – a human life or an animal life. As is well documented, humans do not *need* to eat meat in order to survive and, indeed, can prosper on a meat-free diet.

Of course, the right to life is not absolute. There must be circumstances – your death, for instance, rather than someone else's – where it could be over-ridden. Meat eating does not for Regan (1984: 330–47), however, come into this category. Farmers and meat eaters, like everyone else as beings with inherent value, have the right to act so as to advance their own welfare. But this 'liberty' principle only applies in so far as those involved are treated with respect, and since animals are not treated with respect (and hence have rights which are violated) in the process of being reared and slaughtered for food, it is a practice which ought to be stopped – even though, as a consequence, those directly involved in the meat industry and those affected by its collapse are harmed.

Peter Singer claims equally strongly that his moral theory also obliges us to be vegetarians. The problem for Singer is that, as he is an act-utilitarian, we could consider animal interests as equal to human interests and still come to the conclusion that meat eating is justified. Indeed, theoretically, it would be possible to come to the conclusion that even the worst excesses of factory farming are justified. This is so because, as we saw, utilitarianism, as a consequentialist theory, requires us to measure our actions in terms of a cost–benefit analysis. It is far from clear that such an analysis would rule out meat eating.

What Singer omits to do, which is odd for a utilitarian, is not only to see if the benefits accruing to humans from factory farming outweigh the costs to humans and animals but also whether there are *any benefits at all*. Now one may dispute whether the costs of abandoning animal agriculture do outweigh the benefits. But it is simply not credible to say there are no costs. It is on this point that two leading figures (Frey and Regan) from opposite sides of the animal debate join forces against Singer, although, of course, they have very different motives for doing so. Frey (1983: 197–206), in particular, provides an impressive list of the consequences of an end to animal agriculture – from the direct loss of jobs in the farming and food industries to knock-on effects in education, publishing, advertising, the leather and wool industries and so on. In conclusion, Frey comments that these practical considerations 'cast serious doubt' upon Singer's utilitarian claim and for Singer not even to touch upon them gives his claim 'an air of fantasy, of make believe' (see also Regan, 1984: 221–2).

To be fair to Singer, Frey is equally guilty in that he implies that the only benefit from the abandonment of animal agriculture would be the elimination of farm animal suffering. This, of course, is a gross distortion. Indeed, Singer does provide an effective case against factory farming in particular. Firstly, there is the suffering inflicted on animals that we have already considered. But that is not all. We must also include the use of other resources by the meat industry such as water, heating and lighting (growing crops is much more energy efficient), its impact on the environment (particularly in terms of water pollution, deforestation and the destruction of wildlife habitats), and the human health problems associated in particular with the increasing use of drugs in the meat production process (Mason and Singer, 1990: 72–127; Singer, 1999: 166–9).

Perhaps most significantly, there is also the contribution that modern animal agriculture makes to the wastage of food resources with obvious implications for the impoverished in the developing world. Turning plant proteins into animal proteins is regarded as an extremely inefficient form of food production. Thus, it has been estimated that by taking into account the fertility, mortality and production costs of animal agriculture, beef animals, for instance, convert only 4 per cent of feed protein into animal protein (Mason and Singer, 1990: 74). If crops were grown purely for human consumption there would be far less waste, and extra food resources would be available at no extra cost. Not only does this waste occur in the developed world. Increasingly, developing countries too are growing crops to feed their own animals kept in intensive systems exported from the West. The meat produced is way beyond the price range of most local people and so a good deal of it is exported (Moore Lapper, 1971).

We might make two responses to this. One is that we would still need to weigh the economic costs to the developed world of ending animal agriculture with the benefits that might accrue to the developing world. In addition, famine is not a uni-causal phenomenon. More effective distribution of existing food resources or intensive birth control programmes, for instance, might be a more effective solution. In short, there is no guarantee that, even if more food was available, it would actually be utilised effectively to deal with the hunger problem.

These considerations, of course, go to the heart of the weakness of utilitarianism as an ethical theory. For even if we can come to a consensus about how to measure pleasures and pains and benefits and costs (which, of course, we cannot), there are so many imponderables to take into account that a conclusive guide to action is extremely difficult, if not impossible. Given the suffering inflicted on animals, the other costs of factory farming ignored by Frey, and the fact that it is possible to exaggerate the long-term economic damage caused by a switch to non-animal agriculture, I am inclined to think that utilitarianism does, on balance, justify an end to meat eating. But this is hardly a precise moral judgement. In particular, I simply do not know if or where there is a point at which meat eating becomes morally justified, only that, short of a clause declaring that it is wrong – *per se* – to take the life of an animal for food, utilitarianism does not rule out meat eating. Would, for instance, the removal of the worst excesses of factory farming do the trick and make it moral to eat meat or would more substantial changes be needed? And here, of course, is the problem with utilitarianism. It unrealistically depends not only upon being able to identify all the consequences – whether short or long term – of a particular action but also upon being able to quantify these costs and benefits in a meaningful sense. For our present purposes, like Regan (1984: 223), we must agree that:

> it is not *obviously* true that the aggregated consequences for everyone affected would be better, all considered, if intensive rearing methods were abandoned and we all (or most of us) became (all at once or gradually) vegetarians.

An alternative approach is to claim that rights can be justifiably applied to non-human animals but that this does not, for reasons explored in Chapter 1, include the right to life. One can then consider to what extent the right not to have suffering inflicted upon them rules out farming animals for food. Again, it is not clear that such a position does rule out meat eating *per se*. Certainly, under present conditions, the suffering inflicted on factory farms would be morally unacceptable but this does not rule out a system of animal agriculture which involved more humane practices. As Frey points out: 'The more animals that can be brought to lead pleasant lives, the more animals that escape the argument from pain and suffering ... may be eaten.' Of course, much depends upon how much suffering we are prepared to accept (and, indeed, what we regard as suffering) before calling a halt on the grounds that rights are infringed. Following Frey, it is possible to make a distinction here between a level of suffering which so affects 'an animal's quality of life as to make it miserable' and suffering which amounts to the infliction of occasional, short-lived and minor pain (1983: 176–9). If we adopt the former, then reforms to modern intensive farming methods would justify the continuance of meat eating. The latter, though, would seem to preclude any form of animal agriculture. For his part, Singer (1990: 160) thinks that viable commercial farming necessitates the imposition of considerable suffering and thus reform, rather than abolition, is not possible. This, of course, does not prevent reformers from seeking to minimise the suffering. They can be vegetarians as well.

From this analysis it has been shown that it is necessary to establish that animals have a right to life, which is not easy, for meat eating to be ruled out whatever the circumstances of its production. What should also have become apparent from this chapter is that even for those who do not accept this position there is much cause for concern. Considerable suffering takes place in animal agriculture and many aspects of intensive farming must be regarded as illegitimate on all but Cartesian grounds. Even exponents of the conventional moral position, whilst not prescribing meat eating as such, should question whether the significance to humans of many of the practices described are great enough to justify the level of animal suffering produced as a consequence.

5

Animals, medical science and consumer protection

For good reasons, the use of animals in the laboratory is the most emotive issue we will consider in this book. On the one hand, it provides some of the most severe examples of animal suffering (although it should be promptly added that the intensity varies enormously), whilst on the other it is claimed that the benefits to humans are so great as to make the infliction of this suffering justified. It should be said at the outset that this chapter is not an attempt to unravel the scientific complexities of the debate. Indeed, it is suggested that to a large extent the key to under-standing the polarised nature of this debate lies not in scientific evaluation in any case but in the ethical and political contexts in which scientists and anti-vivisectionists fight it out.

This is not simply to say that the participants bring with them differing perceptions of the moral status of animals. Certainly, like the other issues involving animals, there is a relatively straightforward, albeit contentious, ethical challenge to the moral orthodoxy which prohibits, in this case, animal experimentation *independently* of the human benefits that accrue from it. Unlike the other issues, however, the vivisection debate is conducted – for reasons that will become apparent – almost exclusively within the parameters of the moral orthodoxy itself. That is, the radicals have vigorously attacked the validity of the claim that animal experimentation produces human benefits whilst claiming to put to one side their ethical objection that, irrespective of such benefit, using animals in such a way is morally illegitimate. But, as this chapter will seek to show, the interpretation of the facts, by both sides, is so coloured by ethical judgements about the moral status of animals that there is little scope for a meeting of minds. Before these assertions are explored in greater depth the various ways in which animals are used in the laboratory setting and the extent of the legislative protection afforded to them will be considered.

The laboratory uses of animals

Animals are used for a bewildering variety of purposes in the laboratory. The terms 'procedure', 'experiment' and 'vivisection' have been used to describe these activities and it is important to distinguish between them. Only the first can really encompass all of what is done to animals. Not all procedures are experimental in nature. An experiment is one in which, by definition, the result is not known beforehand and could involve non-painful practices such as, for instance, determining what food an animal prefers (Dawkins, 1980: 4–5). Extracting products – such as antitoxins – from animals, the therapeutic value of which has already been determined, though, is not an experiment. The term vivisection refers specifically to cutting up a living body. Not surprisingly, the anti-vivisection movement prefers to use this term for all procedures because it obviously helps their cause to give the impression that the cutting and mutilation of live animals is the norm. Two points should be made about this. In the first place, most procedures involving animals do not, strictly speaking, involve vivisection. Secondly, it would be equally incorrect to equate vivisection with animal pain and suffering. Indeed, if anaesthetic is effectively applied and the animal is killed before being allowed to recover from a debilitating surgical procedure, then it is plausible to assume, all things being equal, that little pain and suffering is inflicted (although that, of course, does not make it right). On the other hand, other procedures in, say, toxicology testing or behavioural research, can and do involve the infliction of great suffering but do not, strictly speaking, involve vivisection. For ease of exposition, the terms we have discussed will be used interchangeably throughout this chapter.

Using animals in experimental contexts has a long history dating back to ancient Greece and Rome (Maehle and Trohler, 1987). It was only towards the end of the seventeenth century, however, that a large increase in the practice began to occur and the use of animals in scientific procedures, although often brutal, was, until our own century, conducted on a relatively small scale (Maehle and Trohler, 1987: 24–8; Ryder, 1989: 56–8). Since the 1930s, and the development of the petrochemical and pharmaceutical industries, the number of animals used has increased dramatically. In 1880, for instance, the Home Office licensed only 311 experiments whilst for much of the twentieth century there have been a million or more conducted annually in Britain. Robert Sharpe (1988: 16) has estimated that about 85 per cent of the animal experiments carried out over the past 100 years have been performed since 1950.

It is possible to classify animal experimentation in the modern era by identifying four dimensions; firstly the number of animals used, secondly the species used, thirdly the purpose of procedures and finally the procedures themselves. In Britain, the Home Office has, since 1876, collected and published, often incomplete, information on these dimensions. Such precise information is available in few other countries (the Netherlands and Switzerland being the exceptions) so we can only guess at the number of animals used world-wide. The United States Department of Agriculture does keep figures of animals used in research funded by the federal government and, in 1988, 1.6 million were recorded. However, this severely underestimates the actual numbers. It does not include rats, mice, birds, reptiles, frogs or domestic farm animals – since these are not protected by legislation (see below) – nor does it include animals used in secondary schools or those used by institutions not receiving federal funding. In total, a figure of twenty million annually would be a more accurate, although probably still conservative, estimate. World-wide, estimates vary from 50–150 million.

In Britain, animal procedures reached a highpoint in the 1970s when procedures using about five and a half million animals were conducted annually. Since then, there has been a downward trend so that by the start of the 1980s the figure had declined to about four and a half million and, as table 5.1 illustrates, around 3 million by the end of the 1980s, reaching a low point of 2.6 million in 1997. Since then the figures have remained relatively stable, with a slight rise to 2.7 million in 2002. The fact that the decline in the number of animals used began in the early 1980s suggests that the stricter legislation introduced in 1986 (on which see below) has had little impact on numbers. Perhaps more pertinent here is the recession, coupled with the cut-backs in public spending, diminishing research funds and the greater use of alternatives, which, it should be added, is encouraged by the legislation. Similarly, the slight increase in 2002 is caused entirely by the increase in genetically modified animals. At present, the Home Office includes in the statistics *all* genetically modified animals bred, and not just those used in scientific procedures. Not all genetically modified animals suffer and so, as the recent House of Lords select committee report on vivisection concluded, their blanket inclusion is not a particularly useful exercise (House of Lords, 2002: 42).

In terms of species, as table 5.2 reveals, rodents (and particularly mice) constitute the bulk of the laboratory animals used (84 per cent in 2002). Larger, and presumably more intelligent, animals are used more rarely although the use of any of them – and particularly non-human primates – raises acute ethical questions. In Britain, wild-caught primates and all of the great apes are no longer used in scientific procedures. All animals used for scientific procedures in Britain are purpose bred, but this is not the case in all countries. In the United States, laboratories are able to use animals provided by pounds. The use of unwanted animals, most of whom used to be companion animals, is problematic enough ethically, but added to this has been the existence of those prepared to steal companion animals for sale to laboratories. This appalling activity has caused such a public outcry that it was the subject of Congressional legislation (Garner, 1998: 208–9; Reitman, 1992).

Table 5.1 *Scientific procedures 1988–2002 (millions of procedures)*

1988	3.4	1996	2.7
1989	3.3	1997	2.6
1990	3.2	1998	2.6
1991	3.2	1999	2.6
1992	2.9	2000	2.7
1993	2.8	2001	2.6
1994	2.8	2002	2.7
1995	2.7		

Source: HMSO (2003) *Statistics of Scientific Procedures on Living Animals 2002*, Cmnd. 5886: 78.

Table 5.2 *Scientific procedures by species and primary purpose 2002*

Species	Purpose		
	Fundamental biological research	Applied studies human medicine	Protection of man, animals, or environment
Mouse	568,635	347,776	31,002
Rat	138,365	260,033	81,190
Cat	277	–	–
Dog	177	6,310	870
Pig	5,318	425	20
Primate	425	3,339	79
Total	864,277	669,946	185,626

Source: HMSO (2003) *Statistics of Scientific Procedures on Living Animals 2002*, Cmnd. 5886.

In terms of the purposes of scientific procedures, one can make an initial distinction between those that have direct therapeutic goals – in the sense that they are specifically aimed at under-standing and providing remedies for ill-health – and those that do not. Into the former category comes basic biomedical research, the more specific goal of developing substances for specific diseases and the use of animals for the extraction of therapeutic products (Rollin, 1981: 91). The fact that the figures reveal that most procedures are carried out by commercial concerns (as opposed to government laboratories or university departments) is not indicative of the predominance of non-therapeutic research since this also includes work done by, or on behalf of, drug companies. Indeed, the bulk of the recorded procedures are of a therapeutic nature.

Animals are used for a wide variety of non-therapeutic purposes, although, in some areas, a clear-cut distinction cannot be made. Firstly, there is basic biological research, 'the formula-tion and testing of hypotheses about fundamental theoretical questions' which do not have any direct practical application. Obviously, there is a considerable overlap between fundamental and applied research since the former can have profound implica-tions for human and animal health, but it is not conducted with just this intention (Paton, 1984: 24). Behavioural research on animals too can be both fundamental – in the sense of determining the meaning and likelihood of certain behavioural patterns – and therapeutic – in the sense that it seeks to explore the causes of certain mental states such as depression or neurosis. Finally, there is the use of animals in educational settings for demonstration, dissection and surgery practice. The training of surgeons is obviously therapeutic but the use of animals by undergraduate students in biology classes is not.

In the non-therapeutic category also comes the testing of non-medical products, weapons testing and space research. Although often unpleasant and controversial, these categories – including the safety testing of cosmetics, household products and food – have never constituted a particularly large proportion of the total procedures conducted. As table 5.2 illustrates, in 2002 less than 200,000 procedures out of 2.7 million were concerned with the 'protection of man, animals or environment'. Of these, only about 1,000 were for household products and 5,000 for food additives (HMSO, 2003: 57). In the 2002 statistics no procedures were carried out using tobacco, alcohol, or cosmetics, the latter following decisions in 1997 and a year later, with the consent of relevant companies, to end the testing of cosmetic ingredients and finished products (Radford, 2001: 301–2).

It is difficult to do justice to the variety of procedures adopted in the hope that the purposes identified above will be fulfilled. Many are unique to the particular purposes of the project. In this category is the use of animal tissues for the production of vaccines, physiological work involving actual vivisection and applied research involving, for instance, the implanting of tumours in order to test potential remedies. Particularly controversial is the research carried out by behavioural psychologists. This research can vary from painless procedures to the infliction of enormous suffering in, for instance, sleep and maternal deprivation work (on which see below), deliberately inflicted brain damage and electric shocks.

It is important to recognise, though, that similar procedures are used for different purposes. Thus, in particular, toxicology tests are conducted to test the safety of both non-medical and therapeutic products. Toxicology testing can itself take a number of forms. Historically, the two main – and most notorious – tests are the LD50 (introduced in the 1940s) and the Draize irritancy test (introduced in the 1920s). The classical version of the former simply represents the value of the lethal dose which is required to kill 50 per cent of a group of animals within fourteen days, arrived at usually by force-feeding several dose levels of a particular substance to different groups and calculating the result. This classical LD50 test is no longer licensed in the UK, if suitable alternatives exist (Radford, 2001: 302). The Draize test involves administering various substances, usually cosmetics, to the eyes or applying them to the skin of animals – usually rabbits – and examining the effects. Chronic toxicology tests – primarily for detecting the carcinogenic nature of substances – involve the long-term (up to two years) administration of small doses.

A key consideration of the procedures conducted is the pain and suffering inflicted. It is inadequate for this purpose to look at the number of procedures carried out without anaesthetic (about 60 per cent of the total in Britain) since many of these may have been harmless. The only guide available in Britain is the 'severity banding' introduced as a result of the 1986 Animals (Scientific Procedures) Act. Thus, in 1999, of the 3,481 project licences in force, 1,406 were graded as mild, 1,861 moderate, 66 substantial and 148 unclassified (Radford, 2001: 298). However, this Home Office information is difficult to interpret because it does not say how many animals were involved in each project or what procedures were involved (see below).

Genetically modified animals

Genetically modifying animals has begun, and will continue, to be a central issue in the animal experimentation debate. As we have seen, the slight increase in the number of procedures conducted in 2002 in Britain can be explained by the need to record the existence of genetically modified animals. This is obviously a hugely complex debate and we can do scant justice to the issue in this brief discussion (see Rollin, 1995).

A number of purposes are served by genetically modifying animals. Genetic modification can be used in agriculture to generate animals that will produce more meat, wool, eggs and milk. It could even be used to create distinctive pets – the translucent fish is one example that actually exists. More significantly, though, it can be used in a variety of ways as a means of improving human health. The principal use of GM animals is in basic scientific research, typically to understand more about the functioning of human genes, particularly in cancer research. It is argued that GM animals are a better model for human diseases because of the inclusion of human genes. Added to this is the possibility of redesigning animals to secrete useful drugs in their blood, milk or eggs. More recently, scientists have explored xenotransplantation, the transplantation of cells, tissues and organs from one species to another. Because of the perceived ethical problems over using non-human primates, the preferred animal is the pig. The biggest scientific problem here is organ rejection, which necessitates the genetic alteration of animals to be used for transplantation.

From an animal rights perspective, the genetic alteration of animals is unacceptable because it infringes their fundamental rights. From a welfare perspective, the issues are more complex. It need not necessarily be the case that genetically modified animals suffer, although it is clearly the case that many do, either because it is inherent to the project or where the process has gone badly wrong, as in the infamous experiments in the United States to create more productive pigs which resulted in animals with crippling arthritis, deformed skulls and poor vision (*Guardian*, 5 March 1997). To the extent that they do suffer, this suffering has to be balanced against the benefits to humans. These could be considerable, as in the creation of animal models of various human diseases. In addition, the desperate shortage of human organs available for transplants means that the existence of a ready supply of animal alternatives could result in the lengthening of many human lives. A common argument is that keeping animals for their organs is little different from keeping them for food, but of course it might be very different, not least because of the need in the former case to keep the animals in a sterile, and barren, environment before hand. Attempts at xenotransplantation have so far been unsuccessful, and as we will see below have been the cause of much severe animal suffering already. Moreover, added to the potential costs should be the potential for the transfer of viruses from animals to humans which could have a devastating effect on the human population.

Animals, laboratories and the state

Legislation regulating the use of animals in the laboratory varies widely throughout the world (Orlans, 1993: 131–47). Some countries, such as Spain and Portugal, have initiated little or no legislation of their own. In France, very little detail is required for the award of licenses and inspection is patchy, and in Japan there is no formal inspection of animal labs and no reporting requirements for the number of animals used (House of Lords, 2002: 12–15). Other countries, such as Britain, the Netherlands, Denmark and Germany, have detailed statutes. A European Union directive adopted in 1986 at least provides minimum standards with which all member states must comply but inevitably reaches for the lowest common denominator. It should go without saying that no country has completely prohibited the use of animals for scientific purposes, although Switzerland came the closest when a referendum on the issue in December 1985 produced a 70 per cent–30 per cent vote against abolition.

Whatever the faults of the British legislation, and, as we shall see, there are many, it does provide much greater protection for laboratory animals than that of most other countries. This includes the United States where the only existing legislation is the Animal Welfare Act 1966, amended in 1970, 1976 and 1985, although grant-awarding bodies such as the National Institutes of Health also regulate research on animals through their own administrative procedures which have been tightened up in recent years (Garner, 1998: 202–28). The Animal Welfare Act has a number of serious weaknesses from an animal welfare point of view. In the first place, its aim is not primarily to regulate the kind of procedures adopted, but only the supply and care of animals destined for research institutions (purchase, transportation, housing and handling). Secondly, a whole range of animals is completely excluded from protection, including, most importantly (since they constitute around 80 per cent of the animals used in the laboratory), rats and mice. Thirdly, the legislation covers only those institutions who receive federal government funding.

Most importantly, it has been widely recognised that the Act is not effectively enforced (Garner, 1998: 223–7). All research institutions funded by the federal government have to be registered with the Department of Agriculture and theoretically are subject to periodic inspection, but the USDA does not have the time or the expertise to fulfil this task effectively. Stung in the 1980s by revelations (usually provided by the animal protection movement) of extreme cruelty to animals by some researchers (see below), Congress carried the 1985 (Improved Standards for Laboratory Animals Act) amendment which sought to tighten up the regulations. In particular, it provides for the first time a requirement that animal pain and distress should be minimised in experimental procedures including, if possible, the use of alternatives and the creation of so-called 'institutional animal care committees' within each establishment using animals for scientific purposes. These committees must contain at least one lay person and are required to review experiments being carried out and conduct regular inspections of research facilities and report any violations of the regulations to the federal authorities.

Given the weak national protection, the prosecution of scientists is dependent upon state anti-cruelty laws but even if evidence of animal abuse is discovered (and this is difficult enough) it is not clear whether it applies to laboratory animals. In 1982, for instance, Edward Taub's conviction for animal cruelty under Maryland state law (see below) was quashed on appeal when the court ruled that it did not apply to those scientists whose work was funded by federal bodies (Finsen and Finsen, 1994: 62–7). Given these problems, it is interesting to note that some states have considered introducing legislation specifically concerned with vivisection, usually involving particular procedures such as the Draize eye irritancy test.

In Britain, there have been two pieces of legislation regulating scientific procedures on animals; the 1876 Cruelty to Animals Act and the 1986 Animals (Scientific Procedures) Act which replaced it. Remarkably, no amendments were ever made to the former before it was repealed. The Cruelty to Animals Act came about as a consequence of a complex set of factors, most important being the public disquiet at the techniques and attitudes of continental vivisectors – particularly the Frenchman Claude Bernard – and their growing influence in Britain (French, 1975; Ryder, 1989: 169–90). Under the Act, anyone who wished to undertake experiments upon living vertebrate animals had to be licensed by the Home Secretary and had to perform the experiment at premises registered with the Home Office. The main body of the legislation placed severe restrictions on experimentation but these were all but removed by a system of certificates granting exemptions from most of the restrictions. The main provision not subject to exemption was the purpose of an experiment which was to be useful, in terms of the development of physiological knowledge or for knowledge which would save or prolong human life (French, 1975: 179–215). Whatever the details of the legislation, it quickly became apparent that Home Secretaries would rely on the advice of the scientific community when considering applications and so, in effect (despite the creation of the more formal Advisory Committee on Animal Welfare in 1912), scientists still regulated their own activities.

The process of reforming the nineteenth-century legislation extended over a long period of time. The departmental committee set up in 1963 by the Home Secretary under the chairmanship of Sir Sidney Littlewood was the starting-point. The Littlewood Report (HMSO 1965a) made eighty-three recommendations including the prohibition of severe and enduring pain, a recognition that animal suffering includes more than mere physical pain and that the advisory committee should contain lay members. No fundamental changes were envisaged, however, until a commitment to repeal the 1876 Act appeared in the Conservative manifesto at the 1979 general election. A bill finally appeared towards the end of Margaret Thatcher's second term and the new legislation entered the statute book on 20 May 1986.

The 1986 Act is much stricter than its predecessor (Morton, 1989). It includes all vertebrates (except humans), but also, for the first time, the foetuses of mammals, and birds and reptiles more than 50 per cent of the way through gestation. A number of previously unregulated scientific procedures – such as the production of sera and vaccines – are brought under legislative control, breeding and supply establishments are subject to its provisions and, following on from the Littlewood Report, the cost to animals is not to be measured only in pain but also in terms of distress, suffering and lasting harm. Furthermore, the way in which animals are killed in the laboratory is now regulated. The centrepiece of the Act is a three-fold licensing system whereby research, breeding and supplying establishments are licensed if they meet the requirements of the Act (in terms of adequate housing);

individuals are licensed if they are assessed as competent to perform particular procedures; and projects are licensed (for a five-year period) if they meet the criteria laid down.

Each project is assessed by Home Office inspectors in accordance with a utilitarian cost–benefit analysis with the level of suffering inflicted – categorised in the legislation as mild, moderate and substantial – related to the aims and objectives of the procedure. Thus, each licence granted has a 'severity banding' assigned to it which is assessed against the benefits envisaged. Even if there *is* a benefit to be had, the use of animals must only be sanctioned if it is not possible to carry out the work some other way. Again, unlike the Cruelty to Animals Act, there is an upper limit or 'termination condition' whereby if the suffering becomes severe the procedure must be stopped – irrespective of whether or not it has been completed – and the animals humanely destroyed or the suffering alleviated. The legislation, then, gives the Home Secretary a statutory right to reject or alter applications, a power he technically did not have before.

Project applications are scrutinised by Home Office inspectors, now with statutory powers and responsibilities, who are assisted by a panel of independent expert assessors and, although the Act does not specifically prohibit any procedure, the Home Secretary can refuse to license particular projects without recourse to further legislation or even regulation. To aid enforcement of the Act's provisions, each designated establishment, in addition to the certificate holder, has to nominate two named persons – a veterinary surgeon and someone with day-to-day responsibility for the welfare of the animals. The certificate holder, or, if not available, either of the named persons, has a statutory responsibility to stop a procedure at any time if he feels that the suffering inflicted is severe or is otherwise not warranted under the terms of the project licence. In order to prevent 'malicious' prosecutions, the consent of the Director of Public Prosecutions has to be given before court action is taken under the Act. The maximum penalties on conviction are an unlimited fine and/or two years in prison. Section 24 of the Act is a catch-all confidentiality clause which prohibits the public communication of any information under the jurisdiction of the Act unless it is officially sanctioned.

A further innovation is the creation of the Animal Procedures Committee (which replaced the Advisory Committee on Animal

Welfare). This is a statutory body independent from the Home
Office, unlike its predecessor, and has the power to act on its own
initiative, publishing an annual report which is laid before parliament. Its role has been further enhanced as a result of the decision
of successive governments to refer to it applications seeking to
undertake particular procedures, such as tobacco research and
those involving the use of non-human primates. Appointed by the
Home Secretary, the committee now consists of a chairman,
currently Professor Michael Bannister, and eighteen members,
two-thirds of whom must be doctors, veterinarians or biological
scientists. Not more than half can hold licences under the legislation, and it has become the norm to invite members of animal
welfare groups to serve on the committee. These have included, in
recent years, Mike Baker, at one time chief executive of the
BUAV, Les Ward, from Advocates for Animals and Maggie
Jennings from the RSPCA.

One final part of the administrative machinery surrounding
animal experimentation in Britain is the ethical review process
which all licensed research institutions have, since 1999, been
required to set up. Suggested by the Boyd Group of individuals on
both sides of the animal research debate (see Chapter 7), the
process involves a committee of employees from the designated
establishment who scrutinise and advise on research proposals
before they are submitted for approval to the Home Office inspectorate. Critics argue that these committees have little power, and
there is no requirement to have lay members appointed from
outside the institutions concerned, let alone those with an interest
in animal welfare or even animal rights (House of Lords, 2002:
34–6).

Assessing the 1986 Act

Before discussing the rights and wrongs of animal experimentation in general, it is worthwhile assessing the British legislative
regime in particular. The opening gambit here is a House of Lords
Select Committee investigation on animal experimentation in
2002 which reported that 'virtually all witnesses agreed that the
UK has the tightest system of regulation in the world'(House of
Lords, 2002: 12), somewhat of an exaggeration given the stringent statutes existing in Germany and the Netherlands (Orlans,

2002). We saw above that the legislation on animal experimentation in many developed countries with large pharmaceutical companies, including the United States, leaves a great deal to be desired. By contrast, not only does the UK system have detailed reporting requirements for the number of animals used, meticulously documented in the annual statistics, but it is also the only national system 'to require an explicit cost/benefit assessment of every application to conduct animal research' (House of Lords, 2002: 12). Moreover, although parts of the animal protection movement were very critical of the legislation at the time of its passage through parliament for its failure to ban any particular procedure, such as the use of animals for cosmetics testing, its flexibility allows for significant strengthening without any further legislation. This has what has happened, as we saw, over the testing of cosmetics, alcohol and tobacco; the use of great apes and wild-caught primates; and the creation of the ethical review process, all achieved without additional legislation.

However, the legislative regime does have some significant weaknesses. Firstly, there is a great suspicion that lip-service is paid to the search for alternatives to the use of animals in scientific experimentation. This is partly a product of the wider scientific community, where work on alternatives does not appear to have a particularly high status, but it is also the case that insufficient attention to the issue is paid by the Home Office which does little to promote alternatives. Secondly, despite being the centrepiece of the legislation, the cost–benefit clause remains insufficiently developed so that it remains unclear what exactly it is that the Home Office Inspectorate base their licensing decisions on.

This lack of clarity is linked to another criticism: that what is done under the authority of the Act is shrouded in a great deal of secrecy, because of the all-pervasive use of Section 24. Currently, no information is provided on individual project licence applications, so that we have no official knowledge of what inspectors regard as acceptable levels of suffering for the achievement of particular objectives. All that is provided is the number of procedures (not number of animals) calculated to be in moderate, severe, and substantial categories. This excessive secrecy has been a major target of anti-vivisection organisations (particularly NAVS) over the past decade. Partly, at least, as a result of this, the House of Lords select committee (2002: 6, 45–7), and the Animal

Procedures Committee (APC), recommended greater openness, which necessitates a repeal of Section 24 of the 1986 Act. The government subsequently conceded some ground here and announced that summaries of successful applications for project licences will be made public in future (*Guardian*, 21 June 2003). However, this still falls short of what the anti-vivisection community want, which is an opportunity to comment on applications *before* they are approved.

Perhaps the major criticism of the legislative regime concerns issues of enforcement. Doubts about the enforcement regime occur largely as a result of the publicity given to cases of suffering being inflicted on animals which was not authorised by the project licence, and which was not discovered by the inspectorate but by whistleblowers or animal activists working undercover. Three major cases are usually cited. Firstly, the case, in the early 1990s, of Wilhelm Feldberg, an ageing researcher at the Medical Research Council's Institute for Medical Research who was found to have vivisected live rabbits without applying anaesthetic effectively (MacDonald, 1994). Even worse was the undercover discovery, in 1997, of instances of cruelty to animals at the Huntingdon Life Sciences (HLS) laboratory in the East of England, broadcast on a Channel 4 television programme 'It's a Dog's Life'. The subsequent Home Office investigation resulted in prosecutions of two technicians, and the start of almost ten years of ferocious campaigning by the animal rights movement almost bringing HLS, Europe's biggest contract researcher, to its knees. Finally, leaked documents about alleged abuses of animals during xenotranslantation experiments conducted on pigs, macaque monkeys and baboons by Huntingdon Life Sciences for the company Imutran between 1994 and 2000 were widely publicised by the media and the Uncaged Campaigns organisation in 2000, and resulted in a Home Office investigation, which all but exonerated the company, but has not stopped the call for an independent public enquiry (see below).

As we shall see below, the anti-vivisection campaign has, deliberately or not, often failed to distinguish the often grim, but quite legal nevertheless, reality of animal experimentation, and behaviour which contravenes the licences granted. The cases described above, however, do provide evidence of the latter, and were a severe embarrassment to the Home Office Inspectorate, and all of those who have defended the legislative regime. Critics have focused on the limited number of inspectors employed. In 2002, for instance, only twenty-five inspectors existed to monitor 3,180 project licences in 240 designated establishments (HMSO, 2003: 84–5). Although the government has indicated this will increase to thirty-three over a three-year period (*Times Higher*, 30 March 2001), it is doubtful if there could ever be enough inspectors to police the system as anti-vivisectionists want them to. A great deal of reliance is placed upon the ability of the research community to regulate itself, to have due regard for the welfare of the animals they are using. This is coupled with the possibility of being found out. The loss of livelihood that may result from the removal of an individual's licence, added to the stigma (and vilification) that would be attached to anyone caught breaking the rules, particularly in a way which substantially increased animal suffering, provides a strong incentive to comply. Many anti-vivisectionists, of course, do not, to say the least, have a very high opinion of researchers and do not trust them to regulate themselves.

Having said that, inspectors *have* acted against researchers found to be infringing the Act. The penalties, however, have appeared to be lenient, although very limited information is made available (see APC, 2002: 6). Animal protection groups have a suspicion that inspectors are too close to researchers in the sense that they are largely drawn from the research community itself. Whether or not this is the case the Home Office does not do itself any favours by its continual reliance on the inspectorate to investigate cases of cruelty drawn to its attention by animal rights groups, even when the cases involve criticisms of the inspectors themselves. This was particularly evident with the Imutran case where, despite calls for a public inquiry and the willingness of the APC to be involved, and despite a previous suggestion by the Home Office minister responsible for animal experimentation that the APC act as a quality assurance check on inspectors' reports, the Home Secretary not only refused to comply but insisted that the Chief Inspector look into the case in the course of his routine review of procedures undertaken. As a result of this, the House of Lords Select Committee on animal experimentation recommended (2002: 6, 29) that the inspectorate should be subject to periodic review by another body. The government has so far failed to act on this.

Vivisection and ill-gotten gains

One form of the modern challenge to vivisection does not depend upon the benefits that allegedly accrue to humans as a result, and would therefore regard the regulation of it as anathema. A major exponent of this *ethical antivivisection* is Tom Regan (1984). Since at least some animals are subjects-of-a-life, for reasons that we explored in an earlier chapter, all laboratory uses of animals for Regan should be prohibited since they violate rights. Importantly, this also includes experiments which cause an animal no pain either because anaesthetic is used or because the procedure, by design or circumstances, is harmless. To take the life of animals is to deprive them of the 'opportunities for obtaining the satisfactions their capacities make available to them', something 'no amount of anaesthetic will numb' (Regan, 1984: 370). To use them at all (except perhaps in the most benign ways) is to treat them 'as if their value was reducible to their possible utility relative to our interests' and since animals 'have a value of their own, logically independently of their utility for others, it is morally wrong to do so' (Regan, 1984: 384–5). This, of course, applies equally to cases where benefits do result and to those where they do not. As Regan (1984: 393) states:

> the harm done to animals in pursuit of scientific purposes is wrong. The benefits derived are real enough; but some gains are ill-gotten, and all gains are ill-gotten when secured unjustly.

We examined Regan's general claims in Chapter 1. Here, it is worthwhile dwelling upon a particular part of his theory which focuses on the internal logic. It will be remembered that Regan seems to weaken the claim he makes for animals by suggesting in a hypothetical lifeboat example that we should dispense with an animal, if by so doing a number of humans survive, because the animal has *less* inherent value than each individual human. A number of commentators, including Singer, have stressed, rightly it seems to me, that this would justify using animals in medical experiments if human lives could be saved as a result. H. J. McCloskey (1987: 80) wants to go further than this. If, he argues, the rights of mammals are less stringent than those of humans, then 'the floodgates are opened to justify animal experimentation' since it is not just the right to life that is more stringent but also the 'rights to health, to bodily integrity, to self-development of persons'. For the record, when discussing animal experimentation specifically, Regan (1984: 385–8) uses a similar lifeboat scenario but this time claims that the animal should not be sacrificed because to do so would not be consistent with the 'recognition of the equal inherent value of all those who have inherent value'.

It would be pernickety to concentrate unduly on this apparent inconsistency in Regan's impressive tract. More to the point is the more substantive moral claim that we can *never* use animals (or humans) in medical research in order to benefit animals (or humans) since to do so is to violate their rights. Now, as Regan obviously recognises, utilitarians would clearly disagree here and, although one can see the important protection to the individual the rights view affords, we can agree with utilitarianism in as far as it is surely possible to conceive of cases where our moral intuition would be reluctantly willing to accept the sacrifice of individuals if the aggregate benefit was sufficiently large. The problem is, of course, that utilitarianism is not so selective and would sanction such sacrifices even if the benefits were only marginally greater than the costs – to the victims and other interested parties.

One of Regan's targets in his criticism of the application of utilitarianism to vivisection – although he does not mention him by name – is clearly Peter Singer. Although Singer's utilitarianism would sanction experiments on sentient beings, it does provide an equally powerful critique of the present use of animals in the laboratory and in this sense serves as an alternative version of the ethical antivivisection position. At first glance, utilitarianism would seem morally to sanction the use of animals if the result is that the pleasure or happiness thereby produced through, say, the development of an effective remedy for a human and/or animal disease, outweighs the pain inflicted upon the experimental subjects. Indeed, as we saw, the British legislation regulating vivisection adopts precisely this kind of cost–benefit analysis.

There is a significant difference, however, between this version of utilitarianism and the form adopted by Singer. The key phrase here is 'experimental subject'. For Singer, given that the capacity to suffer is the only valid moral criterion, there is no reason to exclude the interests of animals from being considered along with human interests and if we do that there are no valid grounds for *always* sacrificing animals for the benefit of humans and *never* sacrificing humans for the benefit of animals and other humans. To do this is to grant humans a higher moral status and since this is based on nothing more than an irrational and prejudiced claim for preference to be given to our own kind it is speciesist (Singer, 1990: 78). It is for this reason that the debate about the benefits of vivisection is illegitimate unless we also consider using humans in such tests.

Of course, whether one accepts Singer's claim depends upon an assessment of his underlying moral theory which itself depends, to a large extent, on being unable to find a human characteristic which enables us to claim that our own species is morally superior. As we saw in Chapter 1, many philosophers claim that it is the quality and richness of human life that distinguishes us from non-human animals and because of that it is always wrong to use humans in experiments when animals are available. As we also saw, however, this approach has problems in dealing with marginal humans, whose richness and quality of life is severely diminished. Are we still to treat those humans as though they were morally superior to animals?

With this in mind, it is interesting to note that the philosopher R. G. Frey (who is generally critical of Singer on precisely the lines indicated above) is forced to accept that the answer to the question posed is no. Frey, as a utilitarian, recognises the logic of the benefits argument of experimentation on live subjects. But if we are to use animals and not concede the anti-vivisectionist case, he argues, there is no justification for not also using those marginal humans who have no greater quality of life (and some no doubt less) than many species of animals used now (Frey, 1983: 111–15).[1]

A further point should be added here. This concerns the consequence of accepting Singer and Frey's position. Most would agree that the best way of maximising the benefit to humans from experimentation is to use humans since the difficulties of extrapolating results from one species to another are acute. This being so, we should be obliged (if Singer and Frey's position holds) to use humans in preference to animals *whenever we get the chance*. Of course, the effect of this argument is to make the granting of inviolable rights more attractive, but then, if they are granted to humans, why not to animals? This is perhaps Singer's real intention since the end result is much the same. His fundamental aim is to deny that humans and animals should be treated in a morally different way. Thus, either we experiment on both or we experiment on neither and Singer does not seem too concerned if we adopt the latter approach. Frey, in what on the face of it is an odd position for someone seeking to defend widespread and socially accepted practices regarding animals (if not humans!), is put on the defensive since our moral intuition, for what it is worth, suggests (and public opinion would surely comply) that we should not use marginal humans in such a way. Yet Frey thinks that the use of marginal humans is a price worth paying for continuing to benefit from experimentation (Frey, 1983: 115).

Unnecessary suffering and animal experimentation

Of course, public debate about animal experimentation is conducted largely at what for Singer and others is the speciesist level. That is, the use of animals should be judged according to a cost–benefit analysis with the cost referring exclusively to the animals and the benefits referring to humans (and, to a lesser extent, animals). It is fairly easy to define theoretically what would count here as unnecessary suffering. Ruled out are procedures using animals where alternative methods are available and able to produce comparable results; procedures which are unduly repetitive, where, that is, the results are already available even if the researcher is not aware that they are; procedures which do not serve the purpose for which they were designed – where, that is, they are not applicable to humans through species differences or so badly designed that no meaningful conclusions can be reached; and procedures where the benefit for humans is not important enough to justify the suffering inflicted on the animals in terms of individual levels of suffering and the number of animals used.

It should be noted here, too, that, according to this view, the death of an animal, as long as it is killed humanely, is not by itself a matter for moral concern. Similarly, there is no welfare problem if an animal is effectively anaesthetised before a procedure and killed without regaining consciousness. For the moral orthodoxy (and indeed, it appears, for Singer's version of utilitarianism) the suffering inflicted on a sentient being measured against the benefits accruing is the key moral criterion. For Regan, of course, the very use of a bearer of rights as a means to a human end is itself objectionable irrespective of what the content of the procedure is.

It would seem from this that the existing legislative regime in Britain, at least in principle and ignoring for a moment the problems identified above, complies well with the terms of this moral orthodoxy. As we saw, its central mechanism is the provision of a utilitarian calculation – involving the factors described above – which is to be used to determine the validity of a particular project. Indeed, by also providing a 'termination clause' (whereby a procedure must be stopped if the suffering inflicted is severe whether or not human benefits, and presumably even substantial benefits, would accrue from continuing) the legislation goes beyond the requirements of the moral orthodoxy which would allow even severe suffering if the benefits were substantial enough.

In the context of a discussion of the moral orthodoxy it is important to note that, in addition to ethical theories, referred to above, which challenge the moral legitimacy of animal experimentation, there are those who want to challenge the whole validity of animal experimentation from within the moral orthodoxy itself. That is, a fundamental feature of the modern debate about the use of animals in laboratories is that it is not ostensibly about ethics at all but about empirical claims as to its utility for humans. To understand more clearly what is being claimed here we need to consider what might be called the *practical anti-vivisection* case (in order to distinguish it from the ethical anti-vivisection we identified earlier). According to the definition being adopted here, practical anti-vivisection refers to those who hold that, morally speaking, animal experimentation is illegitimate but who also seek to show that in any case it produces (or has produced) few, if any, benefits for humans. The level of benefit each author is prepared to admit varies. Both Richard Ryder and Peter Singer are prepared to accept that humans have benefited from animal experimentation whereas the 'purest' practical anti-vivisectionism is provided by Robert Sharpe (1988) who is not prepared, it seems, to give any ground to the research community (see also Francione, 2000: 31–49). For these practical anti-vivisectionists, then, the British legislation regulating animal experimentation would be working effectively only if, as a result of the cost–benefit analysis, *no* scientific procedure using animals were ever allowed.

It is important to distinguish this practical anti-vivisection, which has also been adopted by most anti-vivisection groups, from another approach prevalent in the animal protection movement. This is provided by those who accept the moral orthodoxy (that if animal experimentation produces human benefit then it ought to continue) and accept that a good deal of experimentation is beneficial. Thus, the main aim, apart from prohibiting that research at the periphery which is of dubious utility, is to find replacements for animals in the laboratory. But until that can be done, the use of animals must continue. This is the approach most notably adopted by the British group FRAME who take their stance, in particular, from the 'three Rs' suggested by Russell and Burch (1959).

Ethics masquerading as fact

Superficially, it may seem that an assessment of the practical anti-vivisection position is dependent upon an empirical analysis of the value and necessity of vivisection. Things are not as simple as this, however, as the protagonists bring with them a great deal of ethical baggage and the debate is polarised, and ultimately irresolvable in a number of areas (without a consensus emerging on the moral status of animals), precisely because ethical perceptions intrude into the interpretation of the facts.

The first obvious point about practical anti-vivisection is that it has an underlying moral objection which is not alterable by empirical arguments dealing with the utility of scientific procedures using animals. The case of an exponent, therefore, is not diminished if his empirical analysis is exaggerated or just plain inaccurate (a common complaint from scientists is that the anti-vivisectionists regularly quote out of context from the published work of animal researchers) (Bateson, 1986). That is not to say that such exponents deliberately lie about the value of vivisection, although some claim that they do (Gray, 1987: 222). At the very least, though, it should be remembered that anti-vivisectionists are engaged in a political campaign and a moral crusade against animal experimentation and since it is their moral objection which is fundamental they are arguably justified (and, more to the point, feel themselves justified) in furthering the goal by such tactics.

It is important, of course, to distinguish between what is and is not done in animal experimentation. Because procedures do involve cutting (that is, vivisection proper), it is easy for the anti-vivisectionist to trade upon the public distaste for mutilation whilst neglecting to say that a particular procedure was conducted painlessly under full anaesthetic. There is no doubt that this neglect does take place although not necessarily intentionally since the practical anti-vivisectionist regards this kind of procedure as just as illegitimate as any other. The point is not that anti-vivisectionists deliberately mislead by claiming that a particular 'invasive' procedure was conducted without applying anaesthetic or analgesics (pain killers) when it was (at least I have not come across any examples), but that much of the literature fails to say whether they were applied or not. A similar approach is adopted in anti-vivisection literature when discussing the Home Office figures which reveal that the majority of procedures are conducted without anaesthetics (see Ryder, 1975: 29). Simply stated, it is true but, without the rider that many (although by no means all) of these procedures are relatively harmless and do not require anaesthetic, it is misleading.

More often than not, though, anti-vivisectionist literature does deal with 'real' evidence and anti-vivisectionists can hardly be blamed for highlighting the worst aspects of a practice they seek to condemn. A common theme, though, is the failure of anti-vivisectionists to distinguish between the suffering which is an integral part of a particular procedure (however valid it might be) and obvious cases of cruelty beyond the procedure itself. The latter, it might be suggested, are much rarer than the former, but where evidence of the latter is found, it is more often than not conflated with the former. Take the case, for example, of Edward Taub who has gained notoriety as a result of the activities for which he was prosecuted under Maryland State anti-cruelty laws (see above). His research was aimed at finding a means for stroke victims to rehabilitate themselves and his experiments involved crippling monkeys in order to see if they could be taught to reuse their impaired limbs. These experiments, of course, are distressing and likely, by many, to be criticised, but he was not prosecuted for these procedures, however, but for his general treatment of the monkeys. They were kept in filthy conditions, not fed for days on end and denied veterinary treatment.

Another example is the Imutran case mentioned above. The Uncaged Campaigns report on the procedures ('Diaries of Despair') made great play of their gruesome nature and the fact that they were not particularly successful (*Observer*, 20 April 2003). However, these experiments (unpleasant though they undoubtedly were) were not illegal – they were documented in the project licence – and experiments are precisely that: they do not always work. There were some serious misdemeanours but, as the Chief Inspector's report pointed out, these were relatively minor compared to the inherent suffering involved in the procedures themselves. An *Observer* report described how 'monkeys and baboons died in fits of vomiting and diarrhoea. Symptoms included violent spasms, bloody discharges, grinding teeth and uncontrollable, manic eye movements. Other animals retreated within themselves, lying still in their cages until put out of their misery'. The fact that these experiments were classified by the Home Office as causing moderate suffering would seem to be, at the very least, a mistake, although this was the judgement before they took place. By itself, however, this does not mean they are morally illegitimate.

It is quite understandable why Imutran tried to prevent Uncaged Campaigns publicising such appalling suffering, and there was much more than space permits here. But this is the grim reality of animal experimentation, and anti-vivisectionists do their cause a disservice by implying that the Imutran case was somehow an aberration from what animal experimentation is usually like when it causes substantial suffering. It might, and probably should, strengthen the case for animal rights, at least to be applied to non-human primates. From an animal welfare perspective, though, this suffering has to be balanced against the enormous financial and medical benefits that would result from the successful development of animal to human transplants. The Home Office inspectors, at least, thought the benefits outweighed the costs in this case, although others, of course, disagree.

These particular cases do not demonstrate that the experiments themselves had no value. They may not have, but that is an entirely different question. What we can say is that the regulatory mechanism is failing to root out the extreme examples of cruelty, defined here as the infliction of suffering on animals not as part of the procedures licensed for. It is difficult to say how common this abuse of animals is. In Britain it is probably rare. In America, there is perhaps more cause for concern. A report published by an animal welfare group in the 1980s, for instance, contained veterinary reports compiled by the Department of Agriculture from inspections of 214 research facilities visited during a four-year period. They make grim reading, particularly as these facilities, unlike others, are meant to be regulated! Abuse or neglect of animals – including inadequate caging and veterinary care – was reported in no less than 80 per cent of the places visited (Animal Welfare Institute, 1985).

The practical anti-vivisection case

The practical anti-vivisection case stands or falls on the claim that animal experimentation is invalid because it either does not work or it is for trivial, or unnecessary, purposes. We should note firstly that it is clearly the case that there have been some procedures which are extremely dubious in terms of both their apparently trivial nature and the extent of suffering inflicted. The litany of cases is well documented in the anti-vivisection literature. Both Sharpe and especially Singer start their expositions by documenting, often without comment, particularly horrendous experiments. The first three pages of the latter's chapter on animal experimentation, for instance, describe in detail the irradiation of monkeys at a US air force base, followed by another four pages on other military experiments and a further five on psychological research (Singer, 1990: 25–36).

Particularly targeted are the behavioural experiments designed to study maternal and sleep deprivation. The aim of the former is to discover the long-term effects of child neglect. This is a worthwhile object in itself but, with all due respect to Professor Paton's point (1984: 129) that what may seem trivial to the layman may be important to scientists working in a particular specialist field, it is extremely debatable whether the severe suffering inflicted, in these cases at least, is really warranted, particularly as there are, unfortunately, plenty of humans around who have been subject to childhood neglect.

The experiments of the late Harry Harlow, professor of psychology at Wisconsin University in the 1960s, are the most infamous. Harlow pioneered the use of cloth surrogate mothers which turned into 'monsters'. Thus, infant monkeys would be encouraged to cling to the machine which would then be made to rock violently or eject compressed air or sharp spikes in order to measure the animals' reactions. It is hard to avoid Sharpe's (1988: 214) conclusion that these were 'some of the most sickening experiments ever recorded'. Not far behind are the sleep deprivation experiments of John Oren, professor of physiology at Texas Tech University, which have been criticised by other scientists. To create sleep-deprived cats, he has adopted methods such as forcing them to run on a treadmill for up to sixteen hours and placing them on a narrow plank inside a tank of water so that they are unable to lie down to sleep for fear of overbalancing and drowning (Orlans, 1993: 188).

Whilst such dubious procedures (and there are many others) do raise genuine concern about the largely unregulated system in the United States – and without the efforts of the animal rights movement they might never have come to light – they do not demonstrate that all animal experimentation is worthless. Indeed, Singer (1990: 91) himself admits as much when, right at the end of his chapter on the subject, he comments that: 'No doubt there have been some advances in knowledge which would not have been attained as easily without using animals.' What, one wonders, would have been the impression had this been included at the beginning instead? Singer's tactics are really given away by his final thought (on animal experimentation) that the 'ethical question of the justifiability of animal experimentation cannot be settled by pointing to its benefits for us' (Singer, 1990: 92). If that is the case, why bother to document how much animal experimentation *is not* beneficial to us, unless it is a tactic, part of the political campaign?

All this is perhaps a little disingenuous to anti-vivisectionists. Their fundamental aim is not to manipulate information in the interests of an ethical theory. They genuinely believe that the benefit to humans from work on animals is seriously exaggerated, if not non-existent. This anti-vivisectionist case is built on a number of assertions. Firstly, that the infectious diseases of the nineteenth century were wiped out, thus producing greatly increased life expectancy, not because of the development of effective treatments, but because of improved environmental health; that no effective medical remedies have been developed for the modern killer diseases which are in any case to a large extent preventable; that many millions of animals die in tests on unnecessary products; that research on animals was not fundamental for many of the key medical breakthroughs in the past which were the product of a combination of clinical observation and pure chance; that there are major flaws in animal experimentation particularly because of species differences which not only makes many results obtained worthless (because it is impossible to extrapolate them to humans) but also can have disastrous consequences in addition to hindering the development of effective treatments.

The claims made by advocates of the practical anti-vivisection approach have produced a backlash from the animal research community. Their response is often to make equally exaggerated claims such as that medical research would completely collapse without the use of animals. The reaction of the research community in the United States to the Taub affair was, at best, insensitive and, at worst, disgraceful. Particularly remarkable was the concerted legal battle for custody of the so-called 'Silver Springs monkeys' with the National Institutes of Health unwilling to hand them over to the animal protection movement, despite the fact that good homes for them had been found, apparently for fear that they would be seen to have given ground to their opponents. Incredibly, some of these monkeys were used for further experiments before being killed (see Blum, 1994).

Even in Britain, the relentless anti-vivisection campaign has led to a fierce response. Sir John Vane, a Nobel prizewinner for his work on heart disease and strokes, for instance, was reported as saying that 'there is no modern medicine or vaccine that would be on the market without the use of animals for experiments' (*Sunday Times*, 10 November 1991). This is surely correct only in the simplistic sense that the regulations require animal testing for therapeutic products. Understood in the sense in which it was almost certainly meant (that all modern medicine could not have been discovered without the use of animals) it is surely not true.

In the ways illustrated, then, the debate has become polarised, with neither side willing to give an inch and little constructive debate taking place. For the anti-vivisectionists, of course, this is not seen as a problem. Indeed, it is, at least for those who want massive reductions or even the complete abolition of animal experimentation, good politics. By challenging the validity of the scientific claims head on, it is more difficult for them to be labelled as 'anti-science' and to be accused of putting animals before humans, tactics regularly used by their opponents. In addition, since only complete abolition is sufficient, a constructive debate is pointless anyway. Indeed, their best chance of success lies in discrediting the work of animal researchers in the eyes of the public, an aim which is hardly likely to further a spirit of compromise.

What should we make of the claims made by exponents of practical anti-vivisection? To a certain extent, of course, they are based on empirical facts which can be praised or criticised for their accuracy. In this sense, there is little doubt (if the notion of benefit is to have any meaning) that the assertions underestimate the benefits that have accrued to humans from medical advance in general and animal research in particular. In another sense, though, that is not the biggest difficulty in assessing them. Many scientists and others involved in research with animals would probably agree with a surprisingly high proportion of Sharpe's factual analysis. They would not agree, though, with many of his conclusions because they approach the arguments with very different assumptions about the moral status of humans and animals. What we will try to show here is the way in which this occurs.

Most informed people would not deny the truth of the first two assertions which are challenges not to the utility of animal research as such but to the necessity of medical treatments. Improved diet, living and working conditions, and sanitation surely played a key role in reducing the impact of the major infectious diseases of the nineteenth century – bronchitis, pneumonia, influenza, cholera, typhoid and so on. It is probably also the case that the death rate from many of these diseases had fallen rapidly before the arrival of effective medical treatments (McKeown, 1979; Sharpe, 1988: 21–40). Nevertheless, it still remains the case that the development of medical treatments – of antitoxins and immunisation – through the use of animals, played a part and that many people benefited from their availability (as they still do in some cases). The fact that they only played a part would be sufficient justification for someone who regarded humans as being infinitely more important than animals. For the practical anti-vivisectionist, however, animals should have been used only if absolutely necessary and since, in this case, alternative means of eradicating many of these diseases existed, and there have been doubts about the effectiveness and safety of some vaccines, the necessity was not great enough.[2]

The second assertion too, that the modern 'diseases of affluence' – primarily cancer and heart disease – have been shown, largely by epidemiological studies, to be largely preventable is also true and recognised by proponents of animal experimentation (see Paton, 1984: 139–40). Smoking alone accounts for 40 per cent of British cancer deaths, and there are significant correlations between poor diet, alcohol abuse, poverty and the incidence of these diseases (Sharpe, 1988: 45–55). Given this, there is a good case for saying that more money (from government and medical charities) should be diverted from animal research aiming to find effective treatments for such diseases, to public health campaigns to persuade people to change their diet and give up smoking.

But then are we to give up on those who have these diseases whether or not it is their fault? Even if lifestyles were changed considerably, cancer and heart disease would still exist (in addition to other crippling diseases such as muscular dystrophy and multiple sclerosis), and the number of people suffering would not, in theory at least, affect the number of animals used in experiments if the same number of diseases existed. There is an element, intended or otherwise, of puritanism here amongst anti-vivisectionists in that the impression is given that animals should not suffer for humans who wreck their own healths through drinking, smoking and eating to excess. Some anti-vivisectionist literature actually makes this point explicitly. Thus, a BUAV slogan reads:

> Animals don't smoke. Animals don't drink. Animals don't wear make up. Animals don't use paint. Animals don't drink alcohol. Animals don't drop bombs. Because we do, why should they suffer?

They might, of course, be right. Should animals continue suffering, for instance, just so that we can reduce the risk of disease from a (smoking) habit that is far from necessary? This, though, is a matter of ethics and not fact. The facts are that people do get cancer and heart disease (many through no fault of their own) and, more or less, effective treatments (bypass surgery, cardiac pacemakers, transplants and so on) have been developed and research on animals has, at the very least, contributed to these developments.

It has long been the claim of anti-vivisectionists that many experiments have been conducted to assess the safety of products which do not strictly need to be developed because they are trivial or already available. Although the numbers of animals used now are relatively small, it is true that many products – from household detergents to cosmetics – are tested on animals for their toxicity. Do we really need, it is argued, another new eye shadow or washing powder when suffering is inflicted on animals as a result? In recent years, at least partly due to the pressure from the animal protection movement, many manufacturers of cosmetics and toiletries have stopped animal testing, and in Britain there is a consensus that cosmetic products and their ingredients will no longer be tested on animals, although they continue to be so tested elsewhere. In 2002, the Council of Ministers agreed to ban the sale of animal-tested cosmetics after 2009, although some testing may still be allowed where no alternatives exist, at least for a while. More controversially still, there is a plan to introduce an EU-wide ban on imports of animal-tested cosmetics from non-EU countries, although such a move may still fall foul of the WTO (see Chapter 7) (*Guardian*, 8 November 2002).

But even with cosmetics and household products, there is a difference of emphasis which reflects different ethical perceptions. In the first place, there are those who would defend the value of cosmetics as 'semi-medicinal' – in the case, say, of salve to relieve chapped lips – or as important aids towards 'social and sexual communication' (Paton, 1984: 139–40). Those who regard animals as having a very low moral status will always put public safety above animal welfare, providing, of course, that animal testing does protect the public (a matter which is discussed below). If new products, containing new ingredients or new combinations of ingredients, are to be marketed they must be tested in order to prevent human suffering. Animal advocates might respond to this by saying that fewer new products should be produced, but their adversaries are likely to retort that these new products can be justified by reference to the economic benefits accruing from them. Clearly, then, within what we have called the moral orthodoxy, there is a great deal of scope for debate centring only partly on a purely empirical analysis.

The issue of drugs is more controversial. As the battle over non-therapeutic products has declined, anti-vivisectionists have increasingly turned their attention to the medical benefits of animal experimentation. Here, it is the number of new, so-called 'me-too' drugs that has been the main cause for concern (Sharpe, 1988: 129–30). It is true that very few drugs are essential and that a great deal of animal suffering could be eliminated if new medical products were restricted to areas of real need where similar formulations were not already available. There is a great deal to be said for this and some scientists who otherwise defend animal experimentation in general concur (Shuster, 1978: 81–2). But there is still a problem. Who is to say what a 'real need' is? For the anti-vivisectionist, of course, the line would be drawn very high up the list, with products which have life-saving potential the only ones guaranteed a pardon. Others, though, would be prepared to allow many other drugs which, although not strictly speaking essential, do have important medicinal properties. The answer of course will depend upon a prior assessment of the moral status of animals since the higher we regard animals, the higher must be the human need before we are prepared to sanction causing them to suffer. Of course, it is not so much the kind of drugs available as their duplication which is the problem. Here, there would seem to be a good case for reform, although one should not neglect the economic benefits that accrue from the activity of pharmaceutical companies. For the anti-vivisectionist, such a consideration is anathema but for others, with a lower opinion of the moral status of animals, the wealth created may be the deciding factor.

The first three assertions relate to the necessity of using animals in the laboratory rather than the effectiveness of doing so. Anti-vivisectionists also deny that even when medical science does have a role to play in public health – such as finding an effective treatment for those who have developed cancer – animal research has had, or does have, much to offer. Determining the role of animal research in key medical discoveries in the past is difficult. For one thing, the exact point at which a particular breakthrough was made is disputed. Sharpe refers throughout, for example, to the 'crucial' or 'most important' breakthroughs which did not involve animals. Much dispute has occurred, for instance, over the discovery of the treatment for diabetes. Sharpe (1988: 173–4) claims that the 'really important discoveries came through clinical investigation and chemical purification' whilst others point to the experiments on dogs undertaken by Banting and Best in the 1920s as the fundamental work.

What is indisputable is that animal research has made *a contribution* to the development of medicine and for the pro-vivisectionist, armed with his ethic that humans are superior to animals, this is enough to justify their use. The very nature of science is that a variety of work, including the use of animals, contributes to a particular discovery providing, brick by brick, a more complete structure of knowledge. In addition, only occasionally may an experiment with animals bear fruit, but this will often be the consequence of other unsuccessful experiments. As Paton (1984a: 93) states, this is the 'great objection to any legal provision which requires the beneficial outcome of an experiment to be precisely specified; it would not be an experiment if that were possible'.

The problem is that, for the anti-vivisectionists, this is not a clear enough justification for using animals. If there is any chance that discoveries could have been made in other ways, then animals should not have been used. But this is to misunderstand the nature of scientific progress where all available methods often have been tried. This is not to claim that by prohibiting the use of animals medical science will grind to a halt, only that if they are to be used it is difficult to say, even after a particular experiment is conducted, let alone before, whether their use was justified in terms of the benefits produced. The only way to guarantee that animals are not used, therefore, is to prohibit their use a priori as a result of a decision that such research is not morally permissible.

In the modern world, too, procedures using animals are criticised for being at best unreliable. The main argument focuses on species differences which we discuss below. Here it is worthwhile briefly mentioning the complaints addressed towards toxicity tests. The LD50, in particular, has come in for a great deal of criticism, and its classical form is not now licensed in Britain. In the first place, it is a very crude measure of toxicity since the results vary according to a variety of factors such as species, diet, general condition of the animals and even the temperature. In addition, except perhaps in the context of an industrial accident or in the case of an unsupervised child or an attempted suicide, the short-term nature of the tests is not an accurate reflection of the long-term exposure humans would be subject to in the case of many substances (Ryder, 1975: 56). In some cases in the classical version (where the experiment is completed when the dosage at which 50 per cent of the animals die is discovered), animals die, not because of toxicity at all but because of the damage that force feeding does to the organs of the body. With relatively harmless substances, it can be appreciated that massive amounts will have to be consumed before the death of the animals ensues.

It is the species differences, above all, which have been focused on by anti-vivisectionists. Various procedures are criticised in this way. One such is the artificial induction of disease or disablement through, for instance, injecting cancer cells or inducing shock and fits, in order to experiment with remedies. Here, it is claimed that the resulting conditions have little in common with naturally-occurring diseases or with the diseases that occur in man (Mayo, 1983). A more common complaint is that various substances can have widely differing effects on different species. Some examples are well known. For example, arsenic is deadly to man but not to sheep; iron-oxide dust is a carcinogen in humans but not in hamsters, mice or guinea pigs; morphine sedates man but stimulates cats; aspirin causes birth defects in rats and mice but not in humans; penicillin is highly toxic to guinea pigs and hamsters but not to humans; chimps are not particularly susceptible to the HIV virus. These species differences, of course, can have dire consequences as, most notably, when the drug thalidomide was marketed as a sedative after extensive and successful animal trials only to be found to cause birth defects when taken by pregnant women. Even when retested on animals, the same result only occurred on certain species of rabbits (Sharpe, 1988: 72–3, 86–92, 105–7). Likewise, the arthritis drug Opren was tested satisfactorily on primates but killed over 60 people before it was withdrawn. Similarly, species differences can hinder medical progress because drugs which are proved harmful to animals may never be made available, or may be delayed, although they are harmless to humans.

Again, few would disagree with the facts here. It is difficult, although by no means impossible, to extrapolate from animals to humans. But no one ever said it was easy. It still does not make it worthless to use animals. For the anti-vivisectionist, the kind of guaranteed results that would justify using animals are not forthcoming. For the pro-vivisectionist, using animals is not perfect but is better than nothing. Their answer to drug disasters such as thalidomide would be two-fold. One, that there is always an element of risk involved in taking a new therapeutic product and if the general public want new drugs they will have to accept that risk. Second, that short of testing such a drug on humans first, the only solutions are not to have the drug at all (an issue we discussed above) or to test it more widely on different animals (which was the lesson many scientists drew from the thalidomide case).[3] The debate then is again not exclusively (or even mainly) about facts but is about the differing perceptions of what should be regarded as unnecessary suffering which are inextricably linked to the moral status of animals.

The development of alternatives to animals in the laboratory offers a way out of this dilemma since it removes the necessity for ethical judgements. Indeed, it is the existence of alternatives – such as *in vitro* tests using tissue cultures, the use of lower organisms and computer models – which has led to dialogue between animal welfare groups and the research community. The anti-vivisection movement is always ready to claim that fewer animals could be used if scientists really made an effort to find out. In some cases this is no doubt true. In addition, as long as animals are regarded as disposable tools, there will be little incentive for scientists to develop alternatives. It should not be forgotten, however, that it is a useful tactic to be able to claim that scientists could use alternatives, since it fuels the image of them as wicked sadists who actually want to inflict pain on animals. For the anti-vivisectionist, any opportunity to use alternatives, irrespective of their value, should be grasped. For many researchers, the best available methods should be adopted, and if that means animals then so be it.

All of this brings us back to the 1986 (Scientific Procedures) Act. The significant point to make in the context of what has been argued above is that the Act, and subsequent regulations made under it, provides little content to the cost–benefit analysis required, or at least the content is not publicly known. Rather, it

is left to the Home Office inspectors and, in certain cases, the
Animal Procedures Committee, to decide what constitutes necessary suffering. It is essentially the inspectorate's morality that
counts here. There is a great need then for a public debate in
Britain (and elsewhere) about the ethics of animal experimentation, and this should be reflected in much more prescriptive
regulations removing the discretion the inspectors currently have
in deciding what procedures should be licensed. As part of the
wider public involvement in animal experimentation decision-
making it would also seem sensible to widen the membership of
the ethical review committees, so that all interests in the community can be more adequately represented.

This chapter has sought to describe and quantify the many
ways in which animals are utilised as laboratory tools and to
examine the extent to which these uses are valid. No other issue
concerning animals has provoked such a ferocious debate, and
animal researchers have taken the brunt of the forceful approach
of the reinvigorated animal protection movement. This is because
the stakes are so high. Unlike animal agriculture, the infliction of
(sometimes severe) suffering is the recognised and undisputed aim
of many procedures and so the purpose of these procedures has
become an increasingly bitter battleground. Even though meat
eating is recognised as being unnecessary in terms of human well-
being, it is easier to continue the practice in the knowledge that
animals are reared and killed humanely. Even though this is
strongly disputed, reforms to modify or abolish factory farming
and to tighten up slaughterhouse regulations do not mean that
meat eating has to stop. An attempt to end the suffering of laboratory animals, though, would mean nothing less than abolition
since suffering is an integral part of many procedures. Yet, it is
claimed that the cost to humans of abolition would be astronom-
ical. It is for this reason that the modern anti-vivisection
movement has homed in on the scientific validity of animal experimentation. By so doing, the debate has polarised even further
because the interpretation of the empirical evidence is deeply
coloured by prior ethical perceptions. Few would deny that
animal experiments are totally ineffective, just as few would claim
that they are absolutely indispensable. But those who advocate
the continual use of animals do so because they hold that it is still
worthwhile to use them even if the human benefit of so doing is

usually limited and only occasionally really valuable. Those, on the other hand, who hold that animals have a higher moral status are not prepared to sanction this.

Notes

1 Interestingly, Singer (1990: 81–2) adopts the argument from marginal cases when discussing animal experimentation although, as we have seen, he is not obliged to do this since he does not recognise the validity of Frey's 'quality of life' argument. One can only surmise that he thought this toned-down version would be more acceptable in the context of a discussion of animal experiments.
2 Incidentally, Sharpe does not mention the polio vaccine, which has virtually wiped out the disease since its introduction in 1950.
3 This was the view, for instance, of Professor Michael Drury, former president of the Royal College of General Practitioners. Quoted in the *Observer*, 17 November 1991.

6

Wildlife conservation

Wildlife conservation is a confused issue. In particular, the motives behind it are so varied that it appeals to a wide constituency from animal welfare and rights advocates to those who emphasise the benefits to humans of biological diversity, and, at the other extreme, those – adopting an ecocentric position – who suggest that the whole of nature has value independently of its value to humans (Lowe, 1983; Garner, 1994). The dominant anthropocentrism explains why the problems facing many wild animals through human exploitation and neglect have generated more public concern and inter-governmental action than those relating to the domesticated species we have examined so far. However, both ecocentric and anthropocentric (or human-centred) approaches to wildlife conservation, and thereby much of the theory and practice of conservation as articulated by some pressure groups as well as public authorities, are difficult to reconcile with the moral theories discussed in relation to companion, farm and laboratory animals.

Conservation and the moral status of animals

Why conserve wild animals? Clearly, there are many answers to this question but a crucial dimension concerns the interests served by conservation. We might want to keep animals around because it serves our interests to do so and the fact that the interests of some animals are promoted as a result is merely an indirect consequence of the furtherance of human interests. According to this view, the natural world has no value in itself but is merely a resource for humans to manage. As N. W. Moore (1987: 257), a British conservationist, explains:

> We should never forget that the objective of conservation is no less than to maintain the living resources of the world so that each generation can use and enjoy them.

An alternative approach to wildlife conservation, and indeed to nature generally, is to argue that we should protect wild animals, and the whole of nature, because they have intrinsic value: value, that is, which is independent of the value that humans apply to them (see Fox, 1995; Leopold, 1949; Naess, 1973).

We should note firstly that the gulf between these two – anthropocentric and ecocentric – approaches is significant. The former holds that wild animals only have extrinsic value. That is, they are valuable insofar as they provide benefits for humans, but when they cease to have value to us, or they are in conflict with a greater source of value for us, then their interests can be sacrificed. By contrast, the ecocentric ethic holds that wild animals have moral standing, that they can be morally harmed directly, and what we do to them should not merely be judged by the benefits to us of a particular course of action.

We need, secondly, to explore the relationship between the ecocentric and anthropocentric approaches to wild animals on the one hand, and, on the other, the various moral theories – the moral orthodoxy, and the challenges to it in particular – we considered in relation to the issues discussed in the preceding chapters. The anthropocentric approach is clearly inconsistent with any of the moral positions which suggest that animals have moral standing or moral worth, since the latter hold that we have direct duties to animals, and that their worth is not reducible to the worth they provide for humans. More complex is the relationship between the ecocentric ethic and the various moral theories we discussed in earlier chapters. Here, there is one main similarity and a number of significant differences.

The similarity is that both the ecocentric ethic and the animal rights/liberation ethic seek to remove humans from the moral pedestal. All sentient beings matter morally. By contrast, ecocentrics seek to extend moral standing beyond the realm of sentiency to incorporate the whole of nature, sentient and non-sentient alike. An alternative, middle-way, 'biocentric' position is to assign moral worth to living parts of nature, thereby including more than those who are sentient but excluding the inanimate objects accorded moral worth by ecocentrics (Taylor, 1986). It might be argued that the ecocentric and biocentric positions are not easy to sustain because it is difficult to see how a non-sentient entity can be morally wronged if it cannot experience hurt. As Singer (1983: 123) points out: 'There is a genuine difficulty in understanding how chopping down a tree can matter *to the tree* if the tree can feel nothing.' An entity can have moral worth but not as much as another entity. Ecocentrics, therefore, are not committed to what might be called biotic egalitarianism, whereby every part of nature is of equivalent value. Preference can still be given to sentiency, so that those with this characteristic have greater moral worth. As Fox (1984: 199) puts it: 'Cows do scream louder than carrots.'

There is a tendency in Green thinking, of both ecocentric and anthropocentric hues, to accord value to whole ecosystems or species rather than the individuals within them. There is a preoccupation with endangered species in national and international wildlife conservation. This is partly for the non-anthropocentric reason that the extinction of a species can alter the balance of an ecosystem. Justifications for wildlife conservation are more often than not, though, coined in terms of the human losses that follow the extinction of a species. We might lose the aesthetic beauty of at least some species, or their economic or medicinal value.

This holism is clearly at odds with the individualistic rights or welfare approaches to animals we have considered in previous chapters. Indeed, ecologists often complain about the lack of ecological sophistication in the animal rights movement (Callicott, 1995). Leopold's classic formulation of the ecocentric position is instructive here (1949: 217). 'A thing is right,' he suggests, 'when it tends to preserve the integrity, stability and beauty of the biotic community. It is wrong when it tends otherwise.' Such a holistic view, of course, can never be acceptable to an advocate of animal rights. For instance, if there is a choice between saving a few members of an endangered species or many more of a common species, an ecocentric might argue that ecological integrity demands the former option (as indeed might an anthropocentric environmentalist concerned about the loss to humans of a particular species). For an animal rights advocate, however, the fact that some animals are members of an endangered species is irrelevant, so in the event of a moral conflict as described above, the choice must be to save the more populous group, since by doing so more individual rights are being protected (Regan, 1984: 359–61).

The theoretical fault lines we have been discussing are hugely important in the political debate about wild animals. They might explain, for instance, why there is relatively little co-operation between conservation groups and the rest of the animal protection movement, in addition to providing the essence of the conflict within the conservation movement itself. Further, the anthropocentric nature of much conservationism explains why it has a much higher public profile (with the possible exception of companion animals) than the other issues relating to animals discussed in this book. In order to illustrate how these theoretical conflicts are played out in practice we will look at the way wild animals are treated in national and international law in addition to the debates surrounding wildlife conservation.

International wildlife treaties

Co-operation between sovereign states in the field of nature conservation is not a new phenomenon. With the widespread incidence of virtually uncontrolled hunting in the nineteenth century, for instance, both hunters and naturalists became concerned about the increasing number of endangered species. It is estimated that in British East Africa some 10,000 animals were shot by hunting parties annually (Boardman, 1981: 144). As a result, seven countries including Britain signed one of the first treaties – the Convention for the Preservation of Animals, Birds and Fish in Africa – in 1900 (Ryder, 1989: 215). In recent years, with the growing threat to the world's flora and fauna and the rise of a greater environmental awareness, a greater urgency has been provoked.

Since the seventeenth century around 350 species and subspecies of animals – including the sea mink and Steller's sea cow – have become extinct, and one authority has estimated that half of the species which are known to have disappeared during the past 2,000 years have been lost since 1900 (Regenstein, 1985: 118). The 'red list' of endangered species, compiled by the World

Conservation Union (on which see below), concludes that mankind is causing extinctions at 50 times the natural rate (*Guardian*, 29 September 2000). Exact figures are difficult to come by, not least because man is aware of only a fraction of the species which have lived, and do live, on the earth. Excluding plants and vegetation, estimates of the total number of living species vary between five and thirty million and yet only about one and a half million have so far been identified (Regenstein, 1985: 119). It is a humbling thought to recognise that many species may have disappeared recently without humans ever realising they existed. Perhaps the most potent symbol of the slaughter was the American passenger pigeon. Once one of the most prolific species in North America with tens of millions existing in the eighteenth and early nineteenth centuries, it was, due to widespread shooting and destruction of habitat, completely wiped out by 1914 when the last one (poignantly named Martha) died in Cincinnati Zoo (Ehrlich, 1990: 238).

Wildlife conservation has taken on an international dimension for obvious reasons. In the first place, animals do not respect national boundaries. Members of an endangered species may exist in a number of countries and effective protection involves united action. In particular, it is impossible effectively to conserve birds at the national level since the vast majority migrate. There is little point in having strong regulations protecting birds in one country if a neighbouring state allows them to be indiscriminately slaughtered when they pass over its territory. Secondly, live animals, and the various products that can be derived from them, form a significant part of international trade. It is much more difficult to protect animals in one country if others do not seek to prevent them being imported. Thirdly, although some animals may only exist in one country, others may have an interest in protecting them, and participation in an inter-governmental organisation is an effective means of offering their assistance.

Lyster (1985: xxii) distinguishes between three types of treaties. Firstly, there are those designed to protect either a single species or a group of species. Here, most notably, is the International Convention for the Regulation of Whaling (ICRW) although treaties also exist to protect seals, polar bears and birds. Secondly, there are regional nature conservation treaties such as the Convention of Nature Protection and Wildlife Preservation in the Western Hemisphere, and thirdly there are the 'big four' wildlife treaties all concluded in the 1970s and all open for most countries to join. These four treaties, which provide 'the centre-piece of international wildlife law', are: the Convention on Wetlands of International Importance Especially as Waterfowl Habitat (known as Ramsar); the Convention Concerning the Protection of the World Cultural and Natural Heritage; the Convention on the Conservation of Migratory Species of Wild Animals (the Bonn Convention); and finally the Convention on International Trade in Endangered Species of Wild Fauna and Flora (CITES).

In addition to these, the earlier emphasis on the protection of individual species, often without reference to habitat and their place within a particular ecosystem, has been largely replaced by the ecologically more credible focus on nature's interconnect-edness and the need to preserve biodiversity. This new sophistication culminated in the Convention on Biological Diversity (CBD) agreed at the UNCED in 1992 which runs in tandem with other, more established, international conservation agreements.

These examples of international co-operation did not occur in a vacuum. They have come about as the result of an increasingly complex network of permanent inter-governmental and non-governmental organisations. Thus, the Council of Europe, the European Union, UNESCO and the UN Environment Programme have all been involved in either initiating, utilising or administer-ing conservation agreements between nations. Mention should also be made of IUCN which, as an organisation containing governments and government agencies as members, as well as pressure groups, has been particularly influential in the conserva-tion field doing much of the groundwork, for instance, which led to the signing of the CITES treaty in 1973 (Boardman, 1981: 88–91).

It is not possible here to consider all these treaties in detail. Instead, three treaties – those concerned with whaling, the trade in endangered species and the CBD – will be examined since these enable us both to identify some of the common characteristics of international agreements and to highlight major conservation issues. Two more general points, though, can be made here. In the first place, mainly as a result of the influence of ecology within the conservation movement, it is now widely accepted that the major threat to most species is not man's deliberate exploitation of animals but the indirect consequence of the destruction of their habitat – usually for agricultural purposes.

Secondly, it is striking how often one comes across anthropocentric justifications in the wording of treaties. Some, such as the whaling convention and the Convention for the Protection of Birds Useful to Agriculture (signed in 1902), were unmistakably set up with economic interests in mind. With others, the motive soon becomes clear. Thus, a treaty to protect birds signed by the USA and Japan in 1972 refers to their 'aesthetic' and 'scientific' qualities whilst the preamble to a bilateral treaty concluded by the USA and the Soviet Union in 1976 states that 'migratory birds are a natural source of great scientific, economic, aesthetic, cultural, educational, recreational and ecological value'. Likewise, the Ramsar treaty explains that wetlands 'constitute a resource of great economic, cultural, scientific and recreational value' whilst the Bonn Convention insists that 'wild animals ... must be conserved for the good of mankind' (Boardman, 1981: 75–6, 180). All of this might be true but there is no mention here of the argument that birds and mammals should be protected because they themselves have an interest in not suffering or not being killed.

Whaling
The hunting of whales dates back to about AD 800 although it did not become a major commercial operation until the sixteenth century. Whales have a large variety of commercial uses – from providing blood for fertilisers to the use of tendons for stringing tennis rackets – although now that alternatives are available for most of their uses they are now hunted mainly for their meat which remains a delicacy in Japan, the leading remaining whaling nation (Allaby, 1986: 146–7). By the present century, it was recognised by those countries involved that there was a need to control the number of whales 'taken' in order to ensure a plentiful supply in the future. After an abortive attempt in the 1930s, interested parties signed, in 1946, the International Convention for the Regulation of Whaling, the purpose of which was 'to provide for the proper conservation of whale stocks, and thus make possible the orderly development of the whaling industry'. This set up a

standing body, the International Whaling Commission (IWC), to regulate the industry by imposing annual quotas determined by calculating the maximum sustainable yield. Once the numbers dipped below this level and threatened the commercial potentiality of a particular species, the IWC could protect it and this did not rule out, as the whaling nations have now discovered, a complete ban on all commercial whaling. In other words, the original justification for protecting whales was irredeemably anthropocentric.

As a device to conserve whales, the IWC has been an abject failure. Not all whaling nations have belonged to it and, although their catch has been comparatively small, it serves as a reminder that at any time a more significant party can withdraw and decide for itself how many whales it should take. In order to encourage the widest possible membership it was therefore necessary, as with most treaties, to introduce a get-out clause whereby as long as parties register their objection to a particular decision within ninety days, they are not bound by it. Secondly, there are doubts as to whether, in the case of whales at least, conservation for commercial purposes can actually succeed. This is because, on self-interested grounds, it is sensible for whaling nations to exploit whale stocks as quickly as possible and then use the income to invest in other projects (Cherfas, 1988: 200–3). The only reason for conserving whale stocks (excluding non-consumptive factors) is if they provide a commodity which is absolutely essential and which cannot be replaced by an alternative. This is not the case for any of the whaling nations (although in the years after the Second World War whale meat was the only cheap source of protein in some countries). Thus, the history of the IWC has shown that species are protected only once stocks of particular whales are virtually exhausted and it is not commercially viable to continue taking them. Thus whalers have moved on from one species to another, aided by technical advances such as the introduction of the explosive harpoon gun in the 1860s which enabled the catching of the faster whales, and the modern factory ship in the 1920s which enabled whalers to hunt further away from land for a longer period of time (Radway Allen, 1980: 11–12). These developments turned whaling from an often dangerous and never one-sided contest, as immortalised in Melville's novel *Moby Dick,* into a form of mechanised slaughter.

The number taken annually rose gradually, reaching a peak of approximately 64,000 in the early 1960s. Of the fourteen 'great' whales, all but the small minke have now been ruthlessly exploited. For instance, the numbers of the blue whale (equivalent in weight to twenty-five full-size elephants and the biggest creature ever to have existed on earth) have dwindled from about 250,000 in 1900 to between 200 and 2,000 today, and yet it was not protected until 1963, by which time it was rarely seen (Brown, 1990). Even though the IWC employs scientists, there is in any case no precise way of determining how many whales in a particular species are left. Rather, the quota system is based on a good deal of guesswork and the decisions made are more to do with political expediency and economic self-interest than genuine conservation.

In 1982 a five-year moratorium on commercial whaling to begin in 1986 was agreed by twenty-five votes to seven and this continues despite the best efforts of Japan to try to buy the support of poorer countries for proposals to resume whaling. Further diminishing the chances of a resumption of whaling, the IWC agreed, in 1993 and 1994, to set up whale sanctuaries in the Indian Ocean and the Antarctic respectively. The moratorium owes more to the dominance of non-whaling nations within the IWC than to the desire of the few remaining whaling nations to conserve whale stocks. The whale had become the focus of the emerging environmental movement's campaign and Western governments, not threatened economically by a ban, have been happy to court public opinion by using their muscle within the IWC. Whales, though, are still taken. Indeed, Japan, the USSR, Norway and Iceland immediately announced objections to the 1982 decision and all but Norway, which sets its own quota for commercial whaling, have only eventually grudgingly accepted the commercial ban mainly because of the ability of the United States to exercise punitive sanctions (Cherfas, 1988: 114). Moreover, the treaty also allows nations to catch whales for scientific purposes independently of the quotas set by the IWC and, despite regular objections from the IWC, most of the whaling nations still use this as a cover for continuing commercial whaling since they are not prohibited from marketing the meat of those whales caught. Thus, despite the moratorium, Cherfas (1988: 118–19) estimates that, between 1985 and 1987, 11,000 whales were slaughtered.

The IWC has in recent years been hijacked by nations who do not stand to lose anything by the introduction of a ban and its original purpose – to maintain the whaling industry – has been lost sight of. Whaling nations are further disadvantaged by the need for a three-quarters majority on key issues. To some extent, no doubt, the moratorium on whaling reflects a feeling that whales have intrinsic value and to catch them with exploding harpoons is cruel. It also reflects competing anthropocentric justifications that whales are majestic creatures and on aesthetic grounds should be protected. One should ask here, perhaps, whether whaling is any more barbaric than many of the practices in intensive farming or the procedures carried out on animals in the name of science that have been described in earlier chapters. The whaling nations have become increasingly impatient with the IWC. Following the Reykjavik meeting in 1991 when the global ban was confirmed for another year, at least one country, Iceland, announced its intention of leaving the organisation and resuming commercial whaling. It has since asked, without success, to rejoin the IWC and has not in fact resumed commercial whaling (*Guardian*, 24 July 2001), although it did resume what it claimed to be scientific whaling in 2003 (*Guardian*, 16 August 2003). With growing evidence that some whale stocks are now sufficiently large, it has become increasingly difficult to justify continuing the moratorium without clearly infringing the provisions of the treaty. One final point that should be emphasised is that whaling would have declined anyway without the moratorium. Indeed, it is arguably the case that whaling is likely to continue for longer, not because it remains economically valuable to the countries involved (it was always a niche cuisine in Japan and only about a third of Japanese have ever eaten it) but because the hostility towards them has turned the issue into one of national pride. If this is the case, then groups such as Greenpeace may inadvertently not have saved the whale but prolonged its agony (Cherfas, 1988: 215–17; Day, 1987: 116).

The trade in endangered species

Many species have become endangered and many animals have suffered because they are valuable trading commodities. Humans have hunted and caught wild animals for their meat, their ivory, their fur and skins and to furnish the exotic pet trade. Whilst the trade in animals is, of course, far from new, it has increased markedly since the 1960s, and is now the third biggest illegal trade after arms and drugs, estimated in the 1990s to be worth between five and ten billion dollars a year (*Guardian*, 26 February 1994). As a recognition of the dwindling nature of many species of flora and fauna, CITES, which Boardman (1981: 94) describes as the 'central focus of world conservation politics', was concluded in Washington in 1973 and came into force in July 1975.

The main part of the treaty, which has now been adopted by over 130 countries, contains the three appendices which consist of lists of species and corresponding levels of protection accorded to them. Appendix I contains those species which are defined as 'endangered': such a status forbids any commercial trade in them and only in 'exceptional circumstances' allows trade for other purposes. Appendix II contains species which are classified as 'threatened' and trade in these is restricted, although commercial trade is still permitted as long as the country of origin accepts that this will not diminish the number of any particular species to a dangerous level. Appendix III includes species which are not in I and II but which are protected by the national law of a particular country. Around 2,500 animals and 35,000 plant species are listed in either Appendix I or II. To trade in these species, permits, issued by member states, are required and they remain protected unless the biannual meeting of the parties votes by a two-thirds majority to remove them. The same procedure is adopted to move a species from one appendix to another or to add an additional species to any of the lists. Nothing, of course, prevents member countries from adopting stricter regulations than those provided by CITES (Cooper, 1987: 171).

The terms of the convention are overseen by a Secretariat, funded by the parties, and based in Switzerland, and are put into effect by national legislation. In what is an unusual clause for an international agreement, each party must allocate a Management Authority to administer the regulations and a Scientific Authority to advise it. In Britain, these two roles are performed by the Department of the Environment, Food and Rural Affairs (DEFRA) and English Nature, along with its Welsh and Scottish counterparts.

There are a number of problems with the treaty. In the first place, many countries are not members and therefore do not require import licences. Some of the seventy countries who are not members (mostly in the Far and Middle East) still trade in endangered species or the products derived from them, such as ivory. Similarly, countries are entitled to declare a reservation against any listed species at the time of joining or any species added to Appendix I or II whilst they are members (Lyster, 1985: 9). Once the reservation is declared (as Japan did in the case of whales), the provisions of the treaty relating to that particular species do not apply. Both these factors aid the smuggling of endangered species since, although an export licence is still required from a member nation or one that has not exempted itself, no import licence is required for entry to a country which either is not a member or has a reservation. This provides an incentive for smugglers who know they only have to be concerned about the route out of one country and not the route into another. By the use of methods such as secret compartments and even carrying contraband concealed on the body, smuggling becomes relatively easy, since hard-pressed customs officers do not have the time to search every load. Added to this are three further problems: some countries do not expend much effort in enforcing the treaty; it is sometimes extremely difficult for customs officers to determine the species being imported; and finally, even when transgressors are caught, the penalties imposed often do not provide an effective deterrent (Carter, 1991). Britain, for one, has been described as an international centre for the illegal wildlife trade as a result of weak laws and the low priority given to wildlife conservation by magistrates (*Guardian*, 9 May 2002).

Clearly then, the treaty is far from perfect and poaching and smuggling remain endemic problems. Many endangered species are affected. The trade in primates (all of whom are listed in either Appendix I or II), for instance, is not only ecologically damaging but also particularly distasteful since mothers are generally shot in the process of capturing their offspring. Those that are caught end up as pets, or in disreputable or ignorant zoos, laboratories (where the demand for primates to use for AIDS research has soared) and even on Spanish beaches making a living for photographers (*Sunday Times*, 12 May 1991).

The major cause of concern in recent years has been the ivory trade. Ivory from both elephants and rhinos is an extremely valuable commodity. As a result, all four species of rhino face extinction. Even though the black rhino, along with the other three, has been a protected species since 1975, its numbers are still declining as a result of poaching. Elephants too have suffered from the demand for ivory. One estimate suggests, for instance, that the number in Africa had fallen from about one and a half million in the early 1980s to about 500,000 by the end of the decade (Jackman, 1989).

The role of CITES here has been inextricably linked with the strategies for protecting elephants and rhinos from poachers and it is important to note a fundamental dispute over strategy that has arisen amongst developing world governments and Western conservationists. On the one hand, there are those who side with a complete ban on the ivory trade and a tough regime to protect African game from poachers. Most of the developed nations favour a total ban and got their way when the black rhino was transferred to Appendix I in 1975 and the African elephant in 1989. This resulted in particular from the slaughter of elephants by poachers in Kenya where, in response, a tough protection policy involving shooting poachers on sight was introduced by President Moi in the late 1980s, and has been replicated elsewhere since (*Guardian*, 7 September 1990; 13 May 2002).

On the other side of the debate are those who suggest that the only way to conserve effectively economically valuable wildlife is a policy of 'sustainable use'. Here, it is argued that the mostly poor rural people who live near African game reserves (and in the vicinity of many areas populated by endangered species) must be allowed to exploit wildlife otherwise they will see conservation as a threat. As a result, not only will they have no incentive to help to protect wildlife, but they may actually join forces with the poachers to extract some benefit for themselves. Sustainable use has been adopted, apparently successfully, by a number of southern African states led by South Africa, Zimbabwe and Botswana. It involves culling a regulated number of elephants each year and distributing the benefits (in terms of the proceeds from meat, hides, ivory, and in some cases from allowing tourists to kill game) amongst the local communities, the best known scheme being the Communal Areas Management Programme for Indigenous Resources (CAMPFIRE) in Zimbabwe (see *Guardian*, 20 May 1997). The problem is that this strategy requires, above all, the reopening of the ivory trade in order that the market price increases. When the elephant was added to Appendix I, the states who practised this strategy exempted themselves and they are now campaigning for a resumption of the trade on a larger scale.

The pressure to adopt a sustainable use strategy has been immense, and it has resulted in a limited resumption of the ivory trade, and the transfer of elephants from Appendix I to Appendix II of the CITES treaty. This was agreed by 76–21 votes of CITES parties in 1997. Namibia, Botswana and Zimbabwe were permitted to resume, in a very limited fashion, marketing ivory. Only a relatively small amount of existing stockpiles can be sold, Japan is to be the sole trading partner and mechanisms must be in place to counter the emergence of a black market. Another limited sale was agreed in 2002 (*Guardian*, 13 November 2002).

The conservation establishment, represented by the WWF and IUCN leadership, has come round to accepting the logic of this sustainable use strategy. Thus, the WWF/IUCN *World Conservation Strategy* document, launched in 1980, argued that endangered species must pay for their own survival which must not be achieved at the expense of Third World living standards. This is reiterated in an updated document *Caring for the Earth: A strategy for sustainable living,* launched in October 1991. This has been far from acceptable to most conservationists, however, and it is significant that the WWF, facing pressure from its broader membership (and from its fear that the general public in the West would be less likely to fund its activities if it thought that elephants were being shot with the WWF's blessing), fell into line with the majority who favoured the ivory trade ban in 1989. The controversy was further illustrated by the resignation, in November 1990, of the CITES secretary general Eugene Lapointe, who was forced out, at least in part, for his vociferous support for Zimbabwe's management scheme in particular and the principle of sustainable use in general.

The issues here are complex and it is difficult to make generalisations about the most effective strategy which may vary from country to country. A number of observations, though, can be made. In the first place, note that we are considering sustainable use as a strategy here, and not in terms of its moral legitimacy (which is examined below). Secondly, there would seem to be a lot to be said for sustainable use as a strategy. African game causes significant problems for the rural communities who live alongside it. The competition between wildlife parks and local communities for land is intense. Kenya, for instance, has the highest population growth in the world and requires an increasingly large agricultural base. In addition, elephants are enormously destructive and can cause serious damage to crops on the periphery of national parks. On these grounds alone, it is hardly surprising that local people acquiesce in the activities of poachers. Added to this are the amazing benefits that can accrue from active participation in poaching, with the sale of a large pair of tusks, for instance, equivalent to ten years' income for African villagers (Ehrlich, 1990: 248).

Nevertheless, as a conservation strategy, sustainable use presents a number of problems. In the first place, the biggest obstacle is that, however well the system is policed, a limited resumption of the ivory trade opens the door to the introduction of illegally poached ivory. Whilst a ban operates, all ivory trade, in those countries that have agreed to it, is forbidden. A resumption raises the problem of distinguishing genuine quotas from illegally poached ivory. Thus, whilst a regulated trade in elephant ivory was in operation between 1985 and 1989 the slaughter of the animals by poachers continued unabated. At least the introduction of a complete ban diminished the market for ivory and therefore made poaching less worthwhile, particularly if the participants risked being killed.

The supporters of sustainable use, of course, argue that poaching occurred during the period of limited trade precisely because the local people were not given enough incentives to stop it. Thus, those countries adopting the strategy have been penalised for the failure of countries such as Kenya who did not. Furthermore, the more successful conservation becomes, the more animals there will be, eventually requiring culling in any case. Why not, therefore, use the ivory from culled animals to benefit local people?

There are a number of responses to all of this. Firstly, it assumes that a total ban could never be made to work. But it is surely not inconceivable that through better enforcement of the regulations, greater security on nature reserves and stronger penalties for poaching, it could be made to work or at least work more effectively. Secondly, although it is no doubt true that greater conservation success will necessitate culling anyway, it could be argued that not only is culling less objectionable morally but it is by far preferable in a conservation sense. This is because culling is a regulated activity whereby old and sick animals can be killed whereas poaching is a haphazard affair which can lead to the removal of healthy animals, thereby diminishing the quality of the herd. Finally, there are other ways of benefiting local people besides enabling them to participate in the profits made from dead animals. In particular, ecotourism is big business in many African countries and there is no reason why the benefits from this could not be spread more widely.

Eco-imperialism As we pointed out earlier, we might want to protect endangered species because we recognise their intrinsic value or even their right to exist. This is certainly one explanation for the opposition towards a strategy which involves a limited amount of sustainable utilisation of such species. Indeed, the attempt to protect African game (symbolised by the CITES ban on the ivory trade), even when this is achieved at the expense of the interests of local indigenous populations, coupled with the authority given to the wardens of some national parks to kill poachers, would seem to represent a victory for animal rights advocates. It is certainly true that mainstream animal welfare and rights views are becoming increasingly influential within the conservation movement, and conflict between groups and individuals emphasising the animal protection approach and those emphasising a human-centred conservationism has been endemic. In Britain, both the LACS and the HSA, for instance, have had run-ins with the RSPB because of the latter's unwillingness to oppose the shooting of grouse on the grounds that wildlife habitats are managed effectively as a result. Likewise, animal protectionists have been critical of the priority given to humans by FoE and, particularly in its earlier days, by Greenpeace. FoE did not, for instance, support the whaling moratorium since it regarded the ethnic rights of Inuit as superior to the protection of whales. Similarly, Greenpeace decided in the 1980s to drop their campaign against the fur trade when it came to their attention that fur provided a crucial source of income for some Canadian and American peoples. This decision so annoyed some Greenpeace activists that, under the leadership of Mark Glover, they split away in 1985 to form the anti-fur group Lynx which held an uncompromising anti-fur position (Ryder, 1989: 219, 234, 236).

We should be careful that we do not simplify the divisions within the conservation movement. In particular, the theory of sustainable use can be seen as both an ideology and a strategy. As an ideology, it serves to emphasise the view that wildlife conservation, as a matter of principle, should never take precedence over the interests of humans so that, in the event of a clash between the interests of wildlife and the interests of humans, the latter should never be sacrificed for the former. As a strategy, on the other hand, it serves to emphasise the view that, whatever the personal views of conservationists, it is recognised that without stressing the human benefits of conservation it is, in practice, unlikely to gain enough support to succeed. Indeed, there is a strong case for saying that the reluctance to adopt a sustainable use strategy amounts to a clear case of double standards which amounts to a kind of 'eco-imperialism'.

Those such as whalers and developing country governments and peoples, stand to gain from the exploitation of endangered species (and, indeed, other species of wild animals to whom the developed nations attach some status), and stand to lose by allowing the protection of such animals to come before development projects which will benefit their populations. Why then should they be expected to sacrifice their interests in favour of the largely anthropocentric interests of the developing world in maintaining the existence of endangered species such as whales and elephants? Moreover, why should they take any notice of the complaints of developed world conservationists and governments about the cruelties inflicted on animals such as whales, when animals are exploited by the millions in factory farms and laboratories in the developed world? What is revealed here is not, then, a conflict between human interests and animal interests. Rather, it is a conflict between *competing human interests*.

Seen as such, the case for allowing poor developing countries to utilise animals, even if they are listed as endangered, becomes much stronger. At the very least, Northern conservationists should demonstrate how local people in the South will benefit from the protection of their country's wildlife. If there is no convincing answer forthcoming, then there would seem to be no justification for preventing the utilisation of endangered species *even if* this results in extinction for some of them. The only way of logically avoiding this conclusion is to argue that the animals should be protected from human exploitation because they have a right to be treated with respect. But once this is accepted, then, as we have seen, nothing would stand in the way of granting this status to other wild and domesticated animals. The choice for Northern conservationists (and governments) is therefore clear. Either accept that there is nothing in principle wrong with killing threatened species (painlessly) even to the point of extinction or accept that the killing of animals for food or in pursuit of scientific progress is morally wrong.

Of course, in practice, wild animals do suffer at the hands of humans, in the same ways and sometimes worse than domesticated species. One can, for instance, criticise the methods used to trap fur-bearing animals or some of the practices involved in animal trading on the grounds that they are inhumane. Whaling too would seem to fit into this category. Leaving aside the more contentious issue as to whether killing a mammal with a brain larger than humans and with an average lifespan of seventy years is morally wrong, the method used to catch whales (a harpoon carrying an explosive charge which is detonated inside the body) is almost certainly inhumane and it is difficult to see how an improved system of killing them could be devised which does not cause suffering to these intelligent sentient creatures.[1] To their credit, the British government has changed its tactics within the IWC to argue, consistently with its position regarding domestic animals, that whaling should not be resumed until a humane way of killing them is found (*Guardian*, 27 May 1991).

Given the suffering inflicted on wild animals, the onus is on trappers, traders and hunters and those who support their activities to show that this suffering is necessary. Since whaling is now more concerned with issues of national pride rather than economic or dietary necessity, the case of the whaling nations is weak (see Regan, 1982: 104–7). The one exception here might be the Alaskan Inuit who do rely on their 'take' of (bowhead) whales much more than the big rich whaling nations, although even their dependence on this catch has declined. The key point, though, is that once we get involved in arguments about what constitutes unnecessary suffering then they apply universally to all animals, irrespective of whether they are part of an endangered species. On these terms, unless we introduce the right to life principle, we would be more justified in painlessly killing an animal from an endangered species than painfully and unnecessarily killing an animal from a species that was common. That this is not the conventional approach is a reflection of, on the one hand, the anthropocentric nature of our approach to animals and, on the other, the way in which the peoples of the developing nations are perceived by the rest of the world. Here, one can answer Richard North's question in the affirmative: 'Isn't it true ... that for most of us, the animals and wildlife of the Third World seem glorious, and their peoples an embarrassment?'(North, 1991).

The Convention on Biological Diversity
Particular international treaties, such as CITES and the ICRW, now operate in tandem with an overarching biodiversity convention. The Convention on Biological Diversity (CBD) was negotiated in a two year period prior to UNCED and, by 1998, had been ratified by 170 states. Like the particular example of the African elephant, biodiversity in general cannot be distinguished from development issues. The vast majority of the world's most species-rich habitat can be found in developing countries. Over half of all the species so far identified, for example, can be found in the tropical rain forests. In the case of climate change negotiations, the North can take action to reduce carbon dioxide emissions whilst seeking the long-term participation of the South. No such luxury is present in the case of biodiversity. If biodiversity is to be protected, the immediate and active involvement of developing countries is required, and the only chance of achieving this is to provide a range of incentives for this involvement.

The need for incentives was recognised in the CBD which confirms sovereignty rights over genetic resources and upholds the principle that developing countries have a legitimate claim to a proportion of any future profits made from the exploitation of biodiversity. Provision was also made for financial aid for the maintenance of biodiversity, to be distributed through the Global Environment Facility. In addition to this, signatories are expected to develop their own national strategies for biodiversity, to provide inventories of biological diversity and to monitor biological resources.

When considering the progress that has been made since the

1992 Earth Summit in Rio, there are some grounds for optimism, tempered by the existence of serious obstacles. Little new funding to enable developing countries to preserve biodiversity has been forthcoming. Crucially, politicians in the United States have been lukewarm about the CBD from the outset. In particular, the sovereignty rights enshrined in it provoked the United States delegation at Rio, heavily lobbied by the biotechnology industry, to refuse to accept the treaty, and although Clinton did sign subsequently, the CBD has not yet been ratified by the US Senate. Having said all this, the general principle of sovereignty rights and a fair exchange for the fruits of biodiversity enshrined in the CBD has facilitated a number of so-called 'bioprospecting' agreements. Here companies – usually pharmaceutical companies – agree to provide a payment, and a small proportion of any future profits, to the biodiversity holders in return for gaining access to potentially valuable resources. There are now at least a dozen such schemes operating world-wide (Tuxhill, 1999: 112). The best known is the first such agreement between the US company Merck and a private biodiversity institute in Costa Rica.

The CBD has also been criticised for its general vagueness, and, in particular, for its lack of timetables and targets. The first round for the reporting of national biodiversity strategies was in January 1998 but less than half of those who signed the CBD met this deadline. The biggest challenge is to integrate concern for biodiversity into general plans for sustainable development and, in turn, ensure that it becomes a key component in a range of policy sectors such as trade, agriculture and forestry. Some progress has been made here but too often short-term economic requirements take precedence. The World Trade Organisation's free trade mission threatens existing environmental measures, particularly in Europe (Purdue, 1995). Likewise, the road away from agricultural intensification has been slow and haphazard. Finally, familiar divisions between the North and South have, so far, militated against the concluding of a global forest convention.

Wildlife protection in Britain

The position of wildlife in Britain reveals similar anomalies to those present on the international stage of wildlife conservation. These arise because there are a variety of motives behind legislation pertaining to wildlife. Prohibiting unnecessary suffering to animals as part of a recognition that individual animals have interests which we have a duty to take into consideration, although it is the dominant theme in the treatment of domesticated animals, played, until recently, relatively little part in the treatment of wild animals. The starting point here is the major anti-cruelty statute in Britain, the Protection of Animals Act 1911. As we saw in Chapter 3, this legislation applied only to 'domestic' and 'captive' animals. The courts generally refused to include wild free-living animals within the Act's remit even when they had, to all intents and purposes, been unable to escape from their assailants (Todd, 1989: 15–18). As a consequence, unless a particular wild animal was covered by other legislation, it was not an offence to gratuitously kick, beat, burn or in other ways torture it.

This particular loophole was partly closed by the 1996 Wild Mammals (Protection) Act, although neither the provisions of this nor the Protection of Animals Act apply to captive animals released for hunting or coursing (Radford, 2001: 213). The anomaly did not come about by accident, however, and it reflects the fact that anthropocentric motives essentially dominate official thinking about wild animals. This can be seen more clearly if we look at other legislation designed to protect wild animals. Here, it becomes apparent that the law protects those species which humans value most and of course these species get better protection than unfavoured wild animals and domesticated animals in farms and laboratories where it is in human interests for them to suffer and/or be killed.

Of all animals, it is birds which have been favoured by legislative action. Since the first legislation in 1869 (the Preservation of Seabirds Act), there has been a constant stream of statutes, dealing with common and endangered species and seeking to protect them for their own sake, culminating in the sections relating to birds in the 1981 Wildlife and Countryside Act (see below) (Robinson, 1989). Also subject to separate legislation have been otters and badgers, both endangered species, the former protected in 1977 under the Conservation of Wild Creatures and Wild Plants Act 1975 and the latter under the Badger Acts of 1973 and 1991. Game birds, seals, salmon, hares and rabbits have also been protected during the breeding season through various statutes

(Cooper, 1987: 131–2). The aim of much of this legislation is to maintain stocks so that humans can continue to exploit them, a classic instance of the anthropocentric emphasis of much legislation relating to wild animals. Finally, mention should also be made of the Endangered Species Act 1976 which implemented Britain's obligations under the CITES convention, thereby establishing in British law the principle that endangered species should have a privileged status.

The major piece of British legislation relating to wild animals in general is the Wildlife and Countryside Act of 1981 which puts into effect the provisions of the Council of Europe Convention on the Conservation of European Wildlife and Natural Habitats (the Berne Convention) which was concluded in 1979 and came into force in 1982. Under the Wildlife and Countryside Act a hierarchy of protection is provided which is complete for some animals at one end of the spectrum and non-existent for those at the other. Thus, although section one states that it is an offence intentionally to kill, injure or take any wild bird (excluding game birds and those that can be shown to have been born in captivity), this only applies to those endangered species, such as birds of prey and some owls, which are listed in schedule one of the Act. Other species, such as crows, house sparrows and feral pigeons, have no protection, although they do have under other legislation. Mammals are treated much the same. Thus, schedule five of the Act prohibits the taking, killing or injuring of endangered species such as the red squirrel, the bat and the common dolphin, but other wild animals not mentioned in the schedule are not covered at all by the legislation (Cooper, 1987: 121–7).

The Wildlife and Countryside Act now runs in tandem with Britain's biodiversity obligations agreed at the Rio Summit. As part of the British government's commitments under the CBD, a biodiversity action plan was drawn up, and published in 1995, after meetings between civil servants and interested groups such as the National Farmers Union (NFU) and the RSPB. This plan, to be funded by conservation groups and government, consists of action plans for 116 key species and 14 types of habitat (*Independent*, 6 June 1997). Of course, any such plan cannot be divorced from other areas of government, relating to land-use planning and agriculture. The existing system of controls over Sites of Special Scientific Interest have proved to be inadequate, and important habitats continue to be damaged by the continuing emphasis on agricultural intensification and the pressure to build on green-field sites.

Blood sports

The discrimination we referred to in the previous section is symbolised by the absence of legislative restrictions on blood sports (or field sports as their adherents prefer them to be called). This is an issue, of course, which has provoked ever increasing political debate but has still failed, at the time of writing, to be resolved either way in England and Wales. In Scotland a ban on fox hunting and hare coursing was introduced in August 2002 and the National Trust and the Forestry Commission, the latter a government body, have banned deer hunting on their land throughout Britain (see Chapter 7). Field, or blood, sports consist of the hunting of foxes and deer, the hunting and coursing of hares, the shooting of game birds and fishing (as a sport rather than a commercial activity). Badgers and otters were also hunted but they are now protected species. We should also mention mink hunts here since they are becoming increasingly common as the animal (which can be found in the wild as a consequence of initial escapes from fur farms) is regarded as a pest. The Burns Report, published in 2000, found that there are about 200 registered packs of hounds in England and Wales which hunt foxes, estimated to kill between 21,000 and 25,000 foxes a year. In addition, there are three registered staghound packs killing about 160 red deer a year, 100 packs of hounds which hunt hares and 20 mink hound packs (*Guardian*, 13 June 2000).

The dominant criteria for wildlife protection preclude any discussion of the case for abolition. Foxes, hares, deer and fish are not endangered and, with the possible exclusion of deer, are not, with the exception of those in the animal protection movement, animals upon whom humans place any great aesthetic value. If, however, we apply the moral theories discussed throughout this book, then it becomes possible to consider the case for blood sports in the same way that we considered the case for animal agriculture and vivisection. That is, at the very least, if blood sports cause animals to suffer, then those who support them have to show that this suffering is justified.

The hunting community argues that hunting a fox is actually equal to or even more humane than other methods of control or other ways in which foxes might naturally die. Leaving aside for a moment the issue of whether any control is necessary, there are serious doubts as to whether hunting is quite as humane as is suggested. Two points here need to be made. In the first place, foxes are not natural prey animals and they catch their own prey by utilising their speed. They are therefore totally unprepared for the stamina required to escape from the hunt. It is faintly ridiculous then to say, as some hunters have alleged, that the fox enjoys the chase or that it is somehow natural, since there are absolutely no grounds for suggesting this to be true. Secondly, although the Masters of Foxhounds Association issues a Code of Conduct which requires that the fox is shot immediately the hounds catch up with it, there is evidence that this does not always happen, the consequence being that the fox is ripped apart by the hounds. Allegations of cruelty by hunts (involving pulling a fox cub out of a hole to be rehunted) were confirmed on one occasion by a video of the Quorn Hunt in Leicestershire, secretly shot by the LACS (*Sunday Times*, 3 November 1991). In addition to this, as the anti-hunting lobby never tires of reporting, fox hunts also on occasions cause enormous suffering to pet animals which they attack and tear apart often on the property of the pet's owner. The report from the committee chaired by Lord Burns – set up by the Labour Government in an attempt to resolve the issue – declared with unmistakeable clarity that 'we are satisfied that this experience [of being hunted] seriously compromises the welfare of the fox' (*Guardian*, 13 June 2000).

Less objectionable, at least superficially, is the hunting of deer (which occurs only in the West Country), since they are natural prey animals and it could be argued that hunting with hounds has merely replaced their now extinct predator – the wolf. However, deer hunts, presumably for entertainment purposes, often choose the fittest animals so that the chase can be prolonged whereas predators would choose sick and injured animals to attack. Not only can the taking of healthy animals be damaging to the survival prospects of the deer population, but it is also unnatural and the evidence suggests it causes immense suffering to fit animals expected to run long distances before they drop (*Guardian*, 22 May 2000). As with the fox, hounds will attack and kill a deer if they reach the animal before it can be shot.

Hare coursing remains particularly controversial although it is far less popular than fox hunting. At coursing events, such as the premier Waterloo Cup held at Altcar, hares are beaten one by one onto a course upon which two greyhounds compete to catch it. The principal aim is to award points for the dexterity of the dogs and this does not necessarily require the killing of the hare, many of whom escape. Leaving aside the fear engendered by the chase, when the hare is caught there is little doubt that it suffers, particularly if the two dogs reach the animal at the same time and begin tearing it apart. In particular, there can be a considerable time between the dogs catching the hare and the arrival of a course steward whose job it is to remove and kill it.

Finally, animal protection groups, with the exception of the Campaign for the Abolition of Angling, have fought shy of criticising angling partly because it is an extremely popular pastime and also because it is much more difficult to establish that fish can suffer. Two RSPCA inquiries in the 1970s – chaired by Lords Medway and Cranbrook respectively – did come out in support of the view that fish can feel pain and, if that is the case, the methods used to catch them, and sometimes the way they are treated once caught, would seem to inflict suffering and require justification, as would the other wildlife casualties injured or killed by anglers' line or lead weights.

Given that suffering is clearly inflicted in blood sports, we need to ask how far it is justified. If the only justification for hunting, shooting and fishing is that it provides entertainment for the participants then, unless we have an almost Cartesian regard for animals, these practices should be banned, particularly as there is an alternative in the form of drag hunting. We do not, though, have such a low regard for animals. Public opinion polls have usually demonstrated considerable opposition to hunting presumably on the grounds that it is regarded as unnecessary. Furthermore, if we accept the entertainment logic for hunting and killing foxes then why not for domesticated animals too? Yet we do not accept this as there are uncontentious laws protecting domestic animals from gratuitous cruelty.

The hunting fraternity recognise that they have to provide more weighty justifications for their 'sport'. The first shot in their armoury is that the fox is a pest, causing immense damage to agriculture by taking poultry and lambs, and therefore needs to be controlled. This argument was also accepted for a long time by the RSPCA until the 1970s when the radicals began to change the Society's direction (see Chapter 2). Realising, perhaps, that the pest argument was not working effectively, blood sports enthusiasts have increasingly (and cleverly) turned their attention to conservation justifications for hunting, fishing and shooting. Thus, it is argued that foxes and deer survive because they and their habitats are protected by farmers who enjoy hunting them. If hunting was banned, foxes would be killed as pests and their habitat destroyed. Anglers, similarly, maintain that they are the best guarantee of unpolluted rivers since they have a vested interest in keeping them clean, just as game bird shooting is justified on the grounds that it provides an economic incentive for preserving habitats which would otherwise disappear.

The hunting community have also employed the economic argument, that abolishing blood sports will have a severe impact on the already impoverished rural economy. Last but not least, the hunting community have, more recently still – under the auspices of the Countryside Alliance – sought to ally hunting with wider countryside concerns thereby claiming that rural communities are persecuted by an urban majority who do not understand their way of life. Hunting, then, should be preserved because to abolish it is to ride roughshod over the rights of minorities, a key principle of a liberal democracy.

What should we make of these arguments? Firstly, the argument that foxes are a pest is clearly exaggerated. Foxes will kill poultry but since most poultry is kept indoors in battery cages, they are hardly likely to be greatly affected. In addition, it is difficult to see why free-range poultry cannot be protected against foxes at night, when the animals are active. There is now strong evidence too that foxes are not a threat to lambs. The impression that they are has probably come about because the remains of dead lambs are found in fox earths, but this does not prove that they killed them as opposed to removing those that had already died. Ironically, it may even be the case that foxes are useful to farmers since the evidence is that foxes prefer to prey on rabbits, voles, carrions, slugs and beetles, all of whom can be extremely destructive to farmers (*BBC Wildlife Magazine*, January 1991:

61). A practical demonstration that hunting is not necessary to control the fox population was that during the ten-month period in 2001, when hunting was suspended because of the foot-and-mouth epidemic, research suggested there was no appreciable rise in fox numbers (*Guardian*, 5 September 2002). The fact that there have been claims that hunts regularly breed foxes to ensure an adequate supply rather undermines the force of the pest control argument (*Observer*, 17 February 2002).

In terms of the conservation justification for hunting, we should make the initial point that the protection of a particular species is not an animal welfare issue. Indeed, if the choice was between the humane slaughter of all foxes, deer and game birds and the continuation of suffering through hunting, then the former would have to be accepted. Leaving that aside (and the inconsistency between the pest and the conservation angle), there would seem to be some logic in the conservation case. It is true that farmers would not necessarily kill foxes as pests. Nevertheless, farmers deprived of hunting would be more likely to destroy fox habitats. But then this would not necessarily involve any greater suffering to individual foxes (and probably far less) than hunting them, bearing in mind that the survival of the species or the reduction in numbers (which would be the consequence of a reduction in suitable breeding sites) are not animal welfare issues. If deer were no longer hunted, there would probably have to be culling. Again, though, the killing of animals by experienced marksmen has to be preferable to the fear and often violence involved in the hunt.

We can apply similar arguments to fishing and shooting. It is undeniably true that pressure from anglers helps to keep rivers clean but the question we have to ask is whether this benefit to fish and other wildlife outweighs the suffering caused by fishing. Certainly, there would seem to be a strong case that this is so. The implications are, though, that if it were found that anglers ceased to have an impact on the condition of rivers, either because, despite their efforts, the condition of rivers deteriorated or because they remained free of pollution in any case, then fishing would not be justified. This serves to emphasise that, given the suffering inflicted, fishing for pleasure alone is not justified even in terms of the moral orthodoxy. Shooting animals is a more complex matter because of the diversity of activities covered by the term. Killing animals instantly and painlessly is not a welfare problem but, particularly given the lack of expertise prevalent in game bird shoots where anyone who pays enough can participate, suffering is inflicted. Given that it is not necessary to shoot at living creatures, there is little justification for it to continue. It probably is true that habitat is preserved as a result of the need to breed and raise game birds but many other wild animals who are a threat to the game (and to the success of the shoot) are, often illegally, killed by gamekeepers as a result.

The economic case for hunting has also been exaggerated. Burns estimated that between 6,000 and 8,000 full-time jobs depend on hunting (significantly less than that claimed by the Countryside Alliance), but only 700 of these result from direct employment by hunts. Job losses, the report continues, would be offset within a 7–10 year period (*Guardian*, 13 June 2000).

Finally, there is the protection of rural minority rights argument. Here, it should be questioned, firstly, how far rural communities do in fact regard hunting as an integral part of rural life. Opinion polls suggest that, whilst support for hunting is stronger in rural areas, opinion is still divided with considerable parts of the rural electorate wanting abolition (Worcester, 1995: 22). The fact that the hunting community can invoke minority rights in support of their activities might be, as Chapter 1 suggested, a reason for rejecting liberalism as an adequate ideological location for animal protection. More to the point, the argument only stands if it is deemed acceptable to do anything one likes to animals on the grounds that we should not intervene in the moral choices of individuals, whether in the minority or majority. Such a position is surely illegitimate. It would justify not legislating to ban, for instance, bear baiting, dog and cock fighting, and yet these are illegal in Britain precisely because there is a consensus that such activities cause unnecessary suffering to animals. The same could be said for hunting.

We have suggested then that there would seem to be a strong case for the banning of at least some blood sports. Remember that the case against them developed above is based on the moral orthodoxy. If one adopts the alternative rights view then all forms of blood sports are clearly illegitimate since to kill some, even if the consequence is to lessen the total amount of harm, violates the rights of individuals (Regan, 1984: 353–6).

The fur trade

Killing animals for their fur is another issue where conservation can come into conflict with animal welfare. Thus, the anthropocentric version of the former can justify conserving fur bearing species on the grounds that extinction would damage the fur trade or that we should not allow such animals to become extinct because they are aesthetically pleasing to us. Animal welfare, on the other hand, is more concerned with the level of suffering involved for individual animals (irrespective of whether or not they are part of an endangered species) and whether or not that suffering is justified. Again, as with blood sports, the rights view would automatically prohibit killing animals for their fur as a violation of their rights.

Seen in animal welfare terms, the case for ending the fur trade would seem to be strong. The level of suffering inflicted on wild-caught animals is intense. The steel jawed (or gin) trap is still widely used throughout the world (although it was banned in Britain over thirty years ago) and animals (including some so-called 'trash' animals who were not the intended victims) may be left in agony for several days until they die, gnaw off a trapped limb and escape, or are put out of their misery when the trapper returns and kills them, either by standing on them until they suffocate or by bludgeoning. Given this, we require a very substantial benefit to accrue from it and yet wearing fur is not necessary, fur being, in the West at least, essentially an item of fashion. Of course, there are economic interests involved but society must ask itself whether, in this case at least (even though we are accepting here that animals have a fairly minimal moral status), the suffering inflicted really does justify the production of an essentially trivial item where alternatives readily exist.

These alternatives, of course, often involve products – such as leather – derived from other animals and defenders of fur are entitled to ask whether it is inconsistent to attack the farming of fur-bearing animals (the method which provided, until its abolition, over 90 per cent of British fur) whilst continuing to accept the farming of other animals for human benefits. There is a case to answer here. It should be noted firstly that those who challenge the moral orthodoxy would reject the farming of any animals and are therefore immune from the inconsistency charge. From the standpoint of the moral orthodoxy it is, I think, valid to say that there are fewer objections to fur farming than to the cruel trapping of wild animals. Here we must apply the same criteria as we did to farm animals in general and ask how much suffering it involves. In terms of slaughter, the killing of fur farm animals by gassing or electrocution raises significant welfare problems. The husbandry of fur-bearing animals raises even more. Minks and Arctic foxes are used to ranging across wide areas in the wild and yet are kept in small wire cages. If one then objects that other farmed animals, such as veal calves and battery hens, are just as much deprived of performing their natural behaviour patterns, then the moral orthodoxy would concur and argue that all such practices should be prohibited. It was these arguments that persuaded the British Labour Government to introduce the Fur Farming Prohibition Order in 2000, which came into force on 1 January 2003, when the last remaining thirteen fur farms in Britain closed down, although the owners were given financial compensation. As a result, Britain has become the first country in the world to ban fur farming.

In Britain, the fur trade has gone into a steep decline, before levelling off in recent years and showing some signs of a modest upturn. Department of Trade and Industry figures revealed that the biggest fur traders in Britain sold only £11 million worth of goods in the first half of 1989 compared to £47 million in 1987 and £80 million in 1984 (*Guardian*, 11 June 1990). Few fur retailers are left. Harrods, for instance, announcing the closure of its famed fur department after 140 years of trading in 1990, reported a 40 per cent drop in sales over eight years. Even Oxfam decided at around the same time to ban the sale of fur in its 800 or so shops. In so far as this reflects public recognition of the cruelties involved, as opposed to, say, a change in fashion or even the onset of milder winters (as the fur trade often claims), then public opinion would seem to be ahead of legislative action for it is perfectly legal to catch most animals for their fur. Certain methods are illegal in some countries. Most notably, the leghold trap has been banned in the EU and over 60 countries, but is still widely used in Eastern Europe, the United States and Canada (Wilkins, 1997: 80–3). The ban in the EU on the import of products derived from animals caught by the leghold trap, however, has been a constant source of political conflict (see Chapter 7).

In other countries, the fur trade has not declined to the same degree. World-wide, some thirty million animals are trapped in the wild for their skins and a further forty million are raised and killed on fur farms (Ryder, 1989: 235). America, in particular, would seem to be particularly guilty of operating the double standards which derive from focusing on anthropocentric conservationism. For, although the US has some of the strongest conservation programmes and legislation in the world, it also catches more animals for their fur than any other country in the world and sales of fur in that country account for about one-third of the world market.

An international ban on the trade of furs, of course, would be the most appropriate mechanism for halting the fur trade, but it is unlikely to happen. CITES does prohibit trade in endangered animals such as the leopard, tiger, jaguar and ocelot, but the fur trappers simply turned to more common species such as the margay and the lynx. Given that the sustainable use strategy of IUCN and the WWF positively encourages the continuation of the fur trade, animal welfare, let alone animal rights, views would seem to have been defeated, at least for the present, internationally if not in Britain.

This chapter has revealed that wildlife conservation is a problematic issue. Some wild animals are protected by a considerable bulk of national and international law and, whilst there is still much to be done to prevent the further killing and suffering of these animals, it is heartening to see that an increasing number of governments support the attempts to keep them alive in their natural habitats. Here, though, lies the problem. For this protection tends to be afforded only to those animals to whom humans attach a value, and this value is equated with the promotion of human interests. It is not generally equated with a recognition that we have duties to animals because they are sentient beings who have an interest in not suffering and even in not being killed.

As a consequence, inconsistencies abound. Thus, those wild animals that humans regard as being more important alive are treated much more favourably than common domesticated animals on farms and in laboratories. Significantly, as a result of the value applied by Western conservationists and the public at large, it tends to be the interests of endangered species in the developing world which are (indirectly) promoted ahead of those of many people in the South. Not only has this proved to be of dubious validity as a strategy, it is also morally repugnant since it involves sacrificing the interests of often very poor native populations without any corresponding sacrifice on the part of the developed world. Of course, it is recognised that in order to 'sell' conservation, it is necessary to stress its value to humans. This, though, is a dangerous strategy since the implication is that once conservation ceases to be of value, then wildlife is dispensable. Now, in many cases, conservation is very much in the interests of humans, but it is not always so and conflict between human and animal interests is inevitable.

Arguably, then, a more enduring basis for conservation is the approach which holds that wild animals should be treated as ends in themselves with interests that must be taken into account. The significant point is that this must apply to all animals whether endangered or not, whether in the developing world or in rich Western nations, and whether useful to humanity or not. The challenges to the moral orthodoxy argue that animal and human interests should be given equal consideration. If one holds this view, then a considerable number of human interests will have to be sacrificed, but the riposte is that justice is very rarely painless.

Notes

1 The oldest whale to be caught was calculated to be 114 years old. For a detailed examination of the capacities of whales see Cherfas, 1988: 15–56.

7
Animal protection and public policy

The preceding four chapters have been concerned primarily with the substantive policy issues relating to the ways animals are treated. The extent of legislative intervention and the moral case for further legal restraints and behavioural alterations have been outlined. Public policy, of course, is not made in a vacuum and is never simply a product of moral principles, however valid one may think them to be. More important is the crucial contribution made by pressure groups. Indeed, without the concerted efforts of those who have perceived a need for greater legislative protection for, and a change in society's attitude towards, animals, there would not be a set of political issues here requiring resolution. These final two chapters are concerned with the strategies employed by the animal protection movement which they hope will lead to the achievement of their objectives.

The animal protection movement provides a useful case study of modern pressure group politics, not least because it contains a broad spectrum of approaches. It is useful to make an initial distinction here between what may be described as mainstream and legal approaches (examined in this chapter) and the variety of activities which can be listed under the heading of direct action (examined in Chapter 8). As this chapter will seek to show, a multiplicity of mainstream and legal strategies are employed and the debates within the animal protection movement about their validity are just as fierce as those involving direct action. In particular, it should be reiterated, as we saw in Chapter 2, that seeking action and legislative change from public authorities, although of central importance, represents only a part of the movement's activities. Groups also undertake or finance research, police the existing law and provide direct assistance to animals in need. In addition, much effort is directed towards changing social attitudes towards animals, both as a means of indirectly influencing government through the power of public opinion and as a means of altering the behaviour of individuals as consumers and as owners of animals.

Arenas for change

There are a number of arenas that the animal protection movement has utilised. The most important are as follows:

1 the consumer;
2 the courts;
3 the sub-national level;
4 the supra-national level;
5 national decision making.

Influencing the consumer

An important way in which animal protection groups can seek to further their objectives is through changing public attitudes towards animals in general and targeting the consumer in particular. Indeed, this would seem, theoretically at least, to be a particularly fruitful dimension of activity. It is important to distinguish here between attempting to influence the behaviour of consumers and attempting to utilise public opinion in order to indirectly influence the government. This latter tactic is common amongst cause groups, particularly those who do not have access to decision makers. The former strategy, whatever its effectiveness, is independent of the actions of government and only requires government help to make consumer choices easier. Put simply, if consumers refused to buy factory farmed meat and eggs (or any animal products at all), cosmetics tested on animals and fur coats, there would be no demand for them and therefore no point in using animals to produce them.

The modern animal protection movement has not been slow to recognise the potential of consumer choice. Most campaigning groups engage in consumer-orientated strategies of one sort or another. Thus, Animal Aid has organised an annual 'Living

Without Cruelty' exhibition held at Kensington Town Hall which promotes vegetarianism, veganism, alternative medicines and cruelty-free cosmetics and household goods. Likewise, a coalition of groups including Animal Aid, CIWF and the Vegetarian Society have mounted an annual 'Meat Out' event in December (to coincide with the Royal Smithfield Show) where awards are presented to those who have made a significant contribution to animal protection that particular year (FARM co-ordinates a similar event in the US called the 'Great American Meat Out'). The BUAV, similarly, has moved towards a consumer-orientated strategy in the last decade or so, launching 'choose cruelty free' and 'health with humanity' campaigns with the aim of promoting a consumer boycott of animal tested products. The RSPCA has taken the consumer-driven strategy one stage further by initiating, in 1994, a 'Freedom Foods' scheme in which the Society validates certain products which meet animal welfare criteria – although they have been regularly criticised for setting the standards too low (*Independent*, 7 April 1995; *Sunday Times*, 11 June 1995).

Perhaps the most effective consumer campaign to date has been the one directed against the fur trade. Lynx, and its successor Respect for Animals, have orchestrated a barrage of hugely effective advertisements on billboards, in newspapers and in the cinema. These included the now legendary poster depicting a woman wearing a fur coat with the words (which did not go down too well with the women's movement): 'It takes up to 40 dumb animals to make a fur coat. But only one to wear it'. Equally impressive was the David Bailey-directed cinema commercial in which blood from a fur coat pours over the audience at a fashion show.

It is difficult to determine the extent to which the animal protection movement has been responsible, but there is no doubt that more and more consumers have used their purchasing power to avoid products which they feel involve the unwarranted use of animals. There are surely, however, limits to this strategy. In the first place, consumers are not usually given enough information with which to make an effective choice. Animal protection groups can, of course, seek to provide this information but have limited resources particularly when compared to the wealth of business concerns using animals. As it is, at the point of sale, consumers (many of whom have limited knowledge of the issues raised in this book and limited time with which to find out) are not told what processes are involved to produce the finished item they are buying. Thus, egg producers do not have to indicate the battery origins of their products, fur manufacturers do not have to label their coats to indicate they derive from animals caught in traps and cosmetic manufacturers do not have to label their products with details of the animal tests carried out, or even indicate that any animal tests have taken place. In addition, there is no doubt that, because of the commercial advantages, some companies are making misleading claims by, for instance, marketing as 'cruelty-free', products where the ingredients, as opposed to the finished product, have been tested on animals. Only legislation or, alternatively, pressure put upon the businesses concerned, would remove these problems but then other tactics become necessary.

No group expects a purely consumer-orientated strategy to be totally effective. Thus, much attention in recent years has been directed at the producers themselves. This is particularly the case with cosmetics where campaigns have sought, with some success, both to publicise which companies still use animals and to persuade them to find alternatives. Indeed, such has been the pressure on manufacturers in Britain and elsewhere that, in June 1989, four major international corporations – Benetton, Avon, Revlon and Faberge – announced they would no longer test their products on animals. Appalled by the implications of this, the Cosmetics, Toiletry and Perfumery Association launched a campaign to defend their members' use of animals (Beauty Without Cruelty resigning from the Association as a result) and the equivalent organisation in America – the Cosmetics, Toiletry and Fragrance Association – mounted a similar defence of animal testing (*Guardian*, 4 August 1990). That cosmetics manufacturers take the campaigns against their use of animals seriously was particularly highlighted by the response of the British branch of L'Oréal who employed a PR firm to put their case to the public and – a clear sign that the campaign was hurting – actually invited Animal Aid to talk to them (*Outrage*, August–September 1990: 5). The campaign culminated in the British government reaching a voluntary agreement whereby cosmetic companies agreed to refrain from conducting any more animal tests on finished cosmetic products or their ingredients in Britain, although such toxicity tests are still conducted elsewhere.

There are doubts, though, about whether the consumer strategy has *any* long-term worth without a parallel campaign for legislative change. For the unpalatable truth probably is that, however intense the campaign to increase the public's knowledge about the products they are faced with, most people, for a variety of reasons – not least that they are not persuaded by the moral arguments – will not be affected enough to change their purchasing habits. Most people still eat factory farmed meat and eggs and buy cosmetics that have been tested on animals. The numbers who do not may have increased, but they still barely represent a dent in the total number of animals used. There is now a greater choice available to those who are convinced that certain practices are wrong but whilst that may be a step towards what the movement is aiming for, it is a very small step. For what is required is not, to mention one instance, a choice between free-range and battery eggs, but no battery eggs at all. Whilst directly seeking to alter public morality is important, such widespread change as that being discussed here requires a direction to be provided by a political elite. Those who are tempted to think otherwise should ask themselves how many people would wear seat belts or crash helmets – an issue, remember, involving self-interest and not the altruism required in the case we are discussing – if it were legal not to do so.

The courts
Another channel open to animal groups is to use the courts. This can be undertaken in order to prosecute particular individuals for cruelty or to seek judicial review of a government decision. In both Britain and America, the courts are used most often to prosecute cruelty to animals cases. The vast majority of cases brought, and convictions obtained, by the RSPCA involve pet animals. This is because cruelty that might be liable to prosecution is obviously much less easy to detect if it takes place on farms or in laboratories, and, in the case of animal experimentation, the regulating authority has been reluctant to prosecute. In addition, the courts have shown themselves reluctant to convict in all but clear-cut cases of gratuitous cruelty and have shied away from the controversial nature of the institutional use of animals.

There are some notable exceptions here. In 1985, for instance, the BUAV took the Royal College of Surgeons to court for causing unnecessary suffering to monkeys at one of its laboratories and although the Royal College successfully appealed against the initial conviction, the case aroused great publicity for the anti-vivisection cause. The second exception occurred in 1989 when one of the biggest egg producers, Daylay Eggs, was fined £800 (and faced considerable bad publicity) after the death of 1,200 chickens in its care (RSPCA Annual Report 1989: 6). Also worth noting, finally, was the successful prosecution of two employees of Huntingdon Life Sciences in 1997, after their cruelty to dogs was revealed by an undercover operation by animal activists (see Chapter 5). In America, too, there have been some high-profile cases involving alleged institutional animal cruelty, most notably the prosecution of Edward Taub for cruelty to monkeys in his laboratory in Maryland (see Chapter 5).

The biggest disadvantage for the RSPCA in its enforcement role is its lack of statutory power. Only the police have the power to arrest a person suspected of cruelty to animals and not even they (let alone RSPCA staff) have the power to search the premises of a suspect since animal cruelty is not considered to be a serious enough offence to warrant this intrusion. This is not the case in America where, in a number of states, humane societies and SPCAs are incorporated as law-enforcement agencies – giving them powers equivalent to the police. These powers differ from state to state but, in many, a humane society or SPCA officer has the power to enter premises and take an animal from its owner without a warrant in addition to making arrests and carrying weapons (Leavitt and Halverson, 1990).

In the United States, the animal protection movement has used the legal system against federal and state public authorities more readily than in Britain, partly because of the political role of the American judiciary as the upholder of the Constitution and partly because of the greater willingness of American individuals and groups to resort to legal action. It is often difficult, however, to get legal standing to represent the interests of animals (Francione, 1995). Constant battles have been fought with federal agencies and animal research interests over the operation of the Animal Welfare Act (Garner, 1998: 214–23). Symbolising the importance of the legal option is the ability of the American animal protection movement to attract the support of the legal profession through organisations such as the Animal Legal Defence Fund, which began in the late 1970s as a study group of concerned lawyers but which has become a legal arm of the animal rights movement consisting of 300 qualified and student members (*Animals Agenda*, July–August 1991: 40–1).[1]

In recent years, the British movement has shown itself more willing to take the legal route. CIWF has been particularly active in this regard, challenging, for example, the export of British animals to Spain, and the use of Coventry airport for the export of veal calves. The BUAV, too, has successfully used judicial review to establish that the Home Office was illegitimately still licensing the oral LD50 test despite the existence of a less severe alternative (Radford, 2001: 165). Similarly, NAVS was granted a judicial review in 1998 to ascertain whether the government was legally entitled to pursue a policy of blanket confidentiality of everything contained in a project licence application, as a result of which the government agreed to drop the policy (*Guardian*, 22 October 1998). Uncaged Campaigns also won a notable victory when they persuaded a court to overturn a decision which prevented the public dissemination of documents critical of xeno-transplantation experiments conducted at HLS. One unsuccessful example was the action taken by a number of animal protection organisations against the government's unwillingness to use Article 36 of the Treaty of Rome to prohibit live exports. Finally, mention should also be made of the LACS which prosecutes hunts which trespass on its land and provides a free legal service to anyone who wants to prosecute hunts for trespassing and damage to property or pets.

One final point worth making here is the potential for improving the welfare of animals through constitutional provisions which the courts must uphold. This has been the goal of the so-called 'Great Ape Project' which seeks to enshrine the rights of the Great Apes. In Germany the rights of animals have been enshrined in the constitution, although the degree to which this is merely a symbolic gesture remains to be seen.

The sub-national level

Influencing decision makers is obviously a key priority for any pressure group and animal protection organisations are no exception. The strategies adopted to achieve this end will obviously depend upon the nature of the political system within which organised groups are operating. In Britain's unitary political system, parliament is sovereign and, as the supreme decision maker, must be the prime target for groups seeking major legislative changes, and the sub-national level of government has relatively little influence on animal protection issues. In a federal system, such as the United States, the influence of sub-national levels of government can be much greater. Animal welfare laws can therefore differ considerably from state to state. For example, there are wide differences in hunting and trapping laws. New Jersey, for instance, has banned the use of the steel-jaw leghold trap, whilst severe restrictions on its use exist in Florida and Rhode Island.

Although local authorities in Britain are subordinate to parliament, they have, as previous chapters have shown, been given a number of powers which animal protection groups can exploit. Local councils can be approached over conditions in pet shops, zoos and slaughterhouses and can be lobbied over their approach towards the treatment of strays and their policy towards nature reserves and dissection in schools. Thus, at least partly due to a campaign by local animal groups, Liverpool City Council became the first local authority to ban dissection in schools (*Outrage*, October–November 1991: 4). In addition, many left-wing Labour councils in the 1980s adopted animal charters which provided for an enlightened approach in their responsibilities towards animals. Most importantly, local animal groups have often successfully petitioned local authorities to ban circuses and hunts on council-owned land. Begun in the early 1980s by the LACS, the latter strategy has proved effective with about 120 councils declaring their opposition to hunting by the early 1990s (LACS Annual Report 1989: 12) although this process was reversed by a court ruling in 1995 that local authorities did not have the right to prohibit hunting on moral grounds alone (*Guardian*, 15 December 1995).

It is possible too for animal advocates to utilise the planning system in order to fight proposals with an animal dimension, for example the building of a new slaughterhouse or animal experimentation facility. Thus, the South Cambridgeshire District Council twice turned down an application from Cambridge

University to build a primate research facility on green belt land, partly on the grounds that it would be a target for animal rights activists and therefore become a public order problem. Animal Aid commissioned a planning expert to report on the proposal, arguing that it ran counter to government green belt policy (*Observer*, 4 November 2001; *Guardian*, 7 February 2002). Again, though, there is a right of appeal to central government on rejected planning applications and in December 2003 the council's decision was overturned after a planning inquiry. However, the whole process had taken a considerable amount of time, had provided valuable publicity for the animal protection movement, and it appears that Cambridge University are not now in a financial position to build the facility anyway.

Another useful target for the LACS is the National Trust (not a governmental body but an obvious target given its extensive land ownership). After fierce lobbying, the National Trust membership voted in 1990 to ban deer (although not fox) hunting and this decision was introduced by the Trust's ruling council in 1997. A government agency which did ban hunting on its land (8,000 acres of prime deer hunting land on Exmoor and the Quantocks in Somerset) was the Forestry Commission in 1997. Finally, the devolution granted to Scotland and Wales by the first Blair government has also had an impact on animal protection. This is less the case with the Welsh Assembly which has no primary legislative powers, but the Scottish parliament and executive has some real influence, as witnessed already by its decision to ban hunting. The Scotland Act 1998 reserves some powers – on scientific procedures on animals, the import and export of endangered species, and xenotransplantation – to the Westminster parliament, which devolves, in theory, every other animal issue (Radford, 2001: 159–60). It should be remembered, though, that, as with the Westminster parliament, animal welfare policy in Scotland will have to conform to relevant EU legislation.

The supra-national level

Increasingly, important decisions affecting animal protection are being taken by supra-national bodies. Inter-governmental forums, such as CITES, the IWC and the CBD, are important arenas for wildlife conservation organisations to work. The growing importance of the international dimension has spawned international animal protection groups such as IUCN, ICBP and the WSPA, the latter being the only animal protection organisation in the world to have consultative status with the United Nations. Of increasing importance is the World Trade Organisation, a supra-national body overseeing international trade, whose free trade mission has important implications for animal welfare. In particular, it has challenged the EU's right to prevent the import of products from non-EU countries on animal welfare grounds. This has been played out particularly in the context of the fur trade and the leghold trap.

As we saw in Chapter 6, the EU decided in 1991 to ban the use of the leghold trap in EU member states, and to ban the import of fur products derived from animals caught by the leghold trap. In 1995, the EU ban was duly introduced but, as a result of challenges through the WTO by those countries – particularly the United States, Canada and Russia – where the leghold trap was legal, the EU advised member states to postpone introducing the import ban. Subsequently, the EU Commission concluded agreements in 1997 with Russia, Canada and the United States to allow the continuation of the import of furs from animals caught in the leghold trap for the time being. The three countries agreed to phase out the traps over a period of years.

In the European context, of course, it is the EU that is the most significant supra-national body (although mention should also be made of the Council of Europe which has produced a number of conventions on animal welfare which, although non-binding unless ratified by member states, are often a precursor for EU action). In recent years the EU has become much more interested in issues of conservation and animal welfare. This has been, in part, a response to the change of climate dealt with elsewhere in this book, but it is also designed to ensure that competition in the single market is not distorted by drastically varying standards across the EU. The importance of EU action derives from the fact that, within the framework of the Treaty of Rome, legislation emanating from the EU supersedes the national laws of the member states. Thus, the potential for standardising laws relating to animals is great.

In general terms, one should distinguish between regulations and directives. The former are powerful instruments in that they take immediate effect in the member states prevailing over any contradictory national laws that exist. The latter require member states to ensure over a period of time that national laws correspond to the objectives laid out in EU legislation. Some animal welfare regulations – such as on the transportation of animals – have been introduced, but directives – on farm animal welfare, the slaughter of animals, animal experimentation and conservation – have been the norm.

European Union institutions are particularly amenable to pressure group influence, with the European Parliament particularly responsive to animal issues. Groups can either seek to influence the approach taken by their national governments in European institutions, work through the federations of national groups (in the case of animal protection the Eurogroup for Animal Welfare), or lobby in Brussels by themselves. British animal protection groups have quickly recognised the importance of the European arena. CIWF, for instance, have lobbied both the British government and European institutions on the conditions in Spanish slaughterhouses. More significantly still, the RSPB was closely involved with the European Commission in the formulation of the EU Directive on the Conservation of Wild Birds, and Zoo Check was partly sponsored by the EU to undertake a study of European zoos which has resulted in a proposed directive to impose uniform standards (Grant, 1989: 90–108; *Mail on Sunday*, 6 November 1988).

The EU obviously presents an opportunity to achieve improvements in animal welfare across Europe, including those Southern European states whose animal welfare records are very poor. The downside is that the EU often has to appeal to the lowest common denominator, so that many Northern European states already have more stringent regulations than those prescribed by the EU. Moreover, enforcement of EU directives is often weak, and relies too much on member states that may have little interest in such enforcement. Finally, the creation of the single market has been detrimental to British animal welfare because animals, or animal products, can be exported to, or imported from, countries whose animal welfare standards are poorer than those in Britain. This arrangement was seen most clearly during the live exports dispute in the mid-1990s, where the British government claimed it had no power to prevent calves being exported from Britain for the veal trade of other EU states, despite the fact that the conditions they would experience were prohibited in Britain. Attempts by the animal protection movement to utilise Article 36 (now Article 30) and prohibit the trade on the grounds of public morality, public policy or the protection of health and life of humans, animals or plants, failed (Radford, 2001: 149–51). A further problem with the EU from an animal welfare perspective is that it is identified above all else with the Common Agricultural Policy (CAP) which has encouraged agricultural intensification by providing subsidies for producers. This reflects the fact that agribusiness interests remain very influential within the EU.

There are signs, however, that animal welfare has begun, and will continue, to be more important within the EU. This is not just because the number of directives, and their stringency, has increased, but also because the general status of animals has changed. In the Treaty of Rome, animals were described as agricultural products, but now, as a result of a clause in the Treaty of Amsterdam which came into force in 1999, their sentiency is recognised and the treaty requires member states 'to pay full regard to the welfare requirements of animals' when formulating EU policy (Radford, 2001: 105–6). Finally, it is important to note that reform to CAP itself is long overdue. Reforms proposed by the Commission and accepted by the Council of Ministers – although in a much diluted form – make subsidies for farmers dependent on the meeting of environmental, food safety and animal welfare standards (*Guardian*, 10 July 2002).

National decision making

Despite these other channels of influence, British pressure groups who seek significant legislative change must gain access to the national level of decision making. Indeed, we can be more specific than that. A group's chances of success depend to a great extent on its ability to gain access to ministers and civil servants in central government. This is because since the advent of strong disciplined political parties at the turn of the century, a government with a majority of seats in the House of Commons can virtually guarantee the passage of its legislation. Given that since 1945 only one election (in February 1974) failed to produce a majority of seats for one or other of the parties, government defeats on the floor of the Commons are extremely rare.

Furthermore, it is increasingly common for parliament to

delegate extensive legislative powers which enable the executive to formulate specific regulations in so-called secondary legislation which are subject to the minimum of parliamentary scrutiny (Radford, 2001: 153–6). Much legislation concerning animals comes into this category. We have seen, for instance, that the Home Secretary has enormous influence under the terms of the 1986 Animals (Scientific Procedures) Act to determine which scientific procedures should be permitted and that the Secretary of State for Agriculture (now DEFRA) was given the power to issue codes of farming practices under the 1968 Agricultural (Miscellaneous Provisions) Act. The Secretary of State for DEFRA also has the power to add to the list of protected species under the Wildlife and Countryside Act and the power to overturn local authority planning decisions on the grounds that they could damage important wildlife habitats. EU directives, too, are often implemented through secondary legislation. Even when back-bench MPs do choose to introduce animal welfare measures through the Private Members Bill procedure, as has traditionally been the case with hunting, they are unlikely to succeed without active government support, or at least acquiescence.

A classic animal-related example of the power of the executive branch of government in Britain was the fate of the dog registration scheme in the early 1990s. The RSPCA was widely congratulated on the force of its public campaign in favour of a dog registration scheme. But despite the expensive excellence of the RSPCA's campaign, backing from expert opinion and support from a wide range of other groups such as the NFU, the Police Federation and the BVA and from MPs on both sides of the House, the Thatcher government opposed the measure, and the implementation of party discipline ensured the bill failed, albeit narrowly (RSPCA, Annual report 1990: 32). Winning the informed public debate, therefore (particularly when the issue, as in this case, is not high on the public's agenda), is not enough if a group has failed to win the argument where it really matters – in Whitehall and the counsels of government. Indeed, paradoxically, the very fact that the RSPCA had the temerity to mount such a successful public campaign against the government's opposition was always likely to increase the determination of ministers and civil servants to defeat the amendment when it was tabled in parliament.

In the United States, by contrast, the separation of powers at the federal level ensures that pressure groups have more points of access. It is therefore as worthwhile for animal protection groups to lobby Congress as it is for them to focus on federal agencies, although the potential for opponents of animal protection to obstruct is ever present (see Garner, 1998: 215–23). In Britain, because of the centralisation of power, it is important that groups gain what Grant (1989: 19–20) calls 'insider status'. Most groups, with the exception of those – such as the ALF – who do not seek to influence policy makers, want to achieve access to government even if they will not admit as much. As Jordan and Richardson (1987: 190) point out: 'Some groups might *want* to be outsiders, as no doubt some motorists might *want* to drive a ten year-old car'. It is easy to see why insider status is regarded so highly. Access to government gives groups an opportunity to influence policy development at the formulation stage, thereby avoiding the difficult and often fruitless task of reacting against government proposals which, by the time the White or even Green Paper has been published, are unlikely to change fundamentally. A general rule about British pressure group activity is that the most successful groups are those who work quietly behind the scenes, eschewing the glare of publicity. Those, on the other hand, who resort to noisy public campaigns have already lost the argument since they would not need to engage in such tactics if the government was listening and granting to them at least something of what they were asking for.

A useful way of describing and explaining decision making is the so-called 'policy network' approach (Marsh and Rhodes, 1992). This model of policy making is built on the, surely correct, assumption that policy making in modern complex liberal democracies is increasingly sectorised, with a distinct network of actors involved in each policy area. The chances of animal protection organisations achieving their goals will therefore be dependent upon the degree to which they are able gain access to and influence these networks. Some networks are regarded as more open than others. At one end of the spectrum is the ideal-type model of a closed, tightly-knit 'policy community' with a small number of key actors, largely in agreement of key areas of policy and intent upon denying access to those who challenge their interests. At the other is the open, dynamic, large 'issue network', where a wide variety of interests with competing interests and demands compete for dominance. (Marsh and Rhodes, 1992: 251).

It is worth making a number of points about the policy network model. Firstly, it is a useful device not least because it can be applied in a comparative sense to policy making in more than one country, since the argument is that all political systems of any complexity will have sectorised policy making and distinct networks of actors whatever their formal institutional structure. Secondly, there is some dispute about the explanatory validity of policy networks. That is, it is not clear to what extent a particular network is an independent variable able to explain policy outcomes, or whether the network is itself a product of factors exogenous to it such as the role of public opinion or the balance of power between interest groups (Dowding, 1995; Marsh and Smith, 2000). Finally, since the implication of the network approach is that policy change is more likely in an issue network than a policy community, it is possible to make broad generalisations about the legitimacy of public policy by reference to these models, with the issue network appearing to be more pluralist, and therefore democratic, than the policy community, which is more elitist in character. This has great relevance to a discussion of the legitimacy of direct action in pursuit of animal protection, an issue to which we return in Chapter 8.

Trying to identify and describe the variety of different policy networks concerned with animal protection policy making is a complex and time-consuming task. Space precludes a detailed analysis of this here but my own previous work has undertaken this task in some detail (Garner, 1998). To summarise the conclusions of my analysis of animal protection decision making in Britain and the United States, it would seem that policy sectorisation is a reality, and that different networks exist in different areas of animal protection policy. The networks centring on farm animal welfare tend to be more akin to the policy community model whereas the animal experimentation networks are more open and dynamic. Most open of all is the hunting network in Britain, where interested parties have access to members of parliament who, in turn, are not constrained by party lines.

The policy network involved with farm animal welfare policy in the United States is probably the best example of a closed policy community, with agribusiness interests dominating the influential agriculture committee in Congress. This helps to explain why there is no federal legislation governing the treatment of animals on farms. In Britain, the classic case of a group permanently incorporated has been the National Farmers' Union. The partnership between government, or more accurately the Ministry of Agriculture, Fisheries and Food, and the NFU was instituted by the 1947 Agriculture Act which initiated a system of guaranteed prices for all major agricultural produce. In the annual review of prices, the NFU was given a statutory right of consultation. By the early 1960s, as Self and Storing (1962: 37) point out, the relationship was 'unique in its range and intensity'. Indeed, it is not an exaggeration to say that the formulation of agricultural policy and the general management of the farming sector was the joint responsibility of government and the NFU (Grant, 1983).

As a result, proponents of animal welfare interests have not found it easy to gain a hearing for their concerns, although they have been more successful than their American counterparts. A classic example of the NFU's influence was that during the formulation of the Wildlife and Countryside Bill in the late 1970s, the published bill excluded statutory regulations that would have obliged farmers to undertake conservation measures. As a result, the excluded conservation groups were left with the forlorn task of seeking parliamentary amendments. No major amendments opposed by the NFU, however, were successful. By contrast, the RSPB – the only conservation group which was consulted before the proposals were aired in public – achieved a great many of its aims at the initial stages and did not need to fight a rearguard action in parliament (Cox and Lowe, 1983).

The network within which farm animal welfare policy is made in Britain has been subject to a great deal of change in recent years. This is mainly to do with the various food scares in the last decade or so which have revealed starkly the dominance of the producer interests in MAFF, and led to fundamental institutional change, with the animal welfare responsibilities of MAFF being hived off in 2001 to a new Department of Environment, Food and Rural Affairs (DEFRA), along with the animal welfare responsibilities of the Home Office (excluding scientific procedures), and those of the old Department of the Environment. What the long term impact of this change on animal welfare policy making will be is difficult to say.

Merely being consulted by government is no guarantee that a pressure group will have influence within a particular policy network. Likewise, it would be wrong to say that it is pointless for pressure groups to seek to lobby individual MPs. Civil servants will usually consult extremely widely, but that does not mean that a particular group's response will be taken account of. There is an ever-present danger that groups can become 'imprisoned' within the executive, forced to go along with proposals that they have serious reservations about since to publicise their opposition too vociferously puts at risk their privileged position and any future influence that they might be able to exert (Grant, 1989: 19–20). Moreover, the influence of groups can be marginalised. A popular device for government here is to create advisory bodies – in terms of animals the Farm Animal Welfare Council (FAWC) and the Animal Procedures Committee (APC) – on which pressure group representatives are invited to participate. These bodies, though, are often regarded by government, not without justification, as pressure groups themselves. Thus, they enable governments to keep groups happy by involving them but at the same time keeping them at a safe enough distance from where the real decisions are made. We saw in Chapter 4, for instance, that governments have regularly ignored recommendations made by the FAWC, and the APC, too, has been highly critical of the Home Office on occasions.

It would be wrong also to say that parliament is entirely impotent and many pressure groups – particularly those who lack direct access to the executive – do spend a good deal of time seeking to influence MPs. The usefulness of this strategy is dependent upon the issue being discussed. If a party line is attached – as with the government's opposition to dog registration – it is unlikely that enough MPs will be willing to break ranks, even if they have reservations about supporting the party line. Where, as is often the case with legislation affecting animals, no party line is applied, MPs will be voting independently and pressure group influence can be crucial. This can be the case when governments are prepared to accept amendments to their own legislation but these are unlikely to alter a bill fundamentally. More important is pressure group involvement in legislative initiatives by backbench MPs.

There are a number of ways for MPs to introduce bills but the most important is the time allocated in the parliamentary timetable (on Fridays) for backbench members of parliament to introduce legislation in the form of Private Members' Bills. The LACS, for instance, have regularly used this procedure, persuading sympathetic MPs to introduce anti-hunting bills and CIWF, likewise, wrote the Pig Husbandry Bill which was introduced by the Conservative MP Richard Body in 1991.

For groups which seek reforming legislation, however, there are limitations to the Private Members' procedure. In the first place, only those MPs who are drawn near the top of the annual ballot of backbenchers stand any chance of successfully steering their bill through parliament. Even those which are introduced early on in the parliamentary year often fail for lack of time since it is relatively easy for opponents (often themselves primed by countervailing pressure groups) to use parliamentary procedure to obstruct their progress. The only way to prevent an MP from 'talking out' a Private Members' Bill he opposes is to force a closure motion and proceed to a vote. The problem is that a closure motion requires the support of at least 100 MPs and it is rare on a Friday, when many are travelling home to their constituencies for the weekend, for there to be that many MPs available. Even if a bill passes all its stages in the Commons, it then faces the same problems from the Lords, who regard Private Members' Bills with less respect than a government bill fulfilling an election pledge. Thus, it was the failure of no less than 16 anti-hunting bills between 1967 and 1977 that led to the recognition by the LACS that their best chance of success was a manifesto commitment by Labour to abolish hunting. As we pointed out earlier, without government help (in the form of allocating more time), or at least acquiescence, then Private Members' Bills are likely to face difficulties. If government opposes a Private Members' Bill, or part of it – as it did with Body's Bill – its chances of success, of course, are all but gone.

Parliament can also be useful as a means of publicising a group's concerns. Introducing bills even if they are not successful is, of course, one method of achieving this. MPs also have a number of other opportunities to raise an issue of importance; tabling parliamentary questions which are answered by ministers either orally or in written form, sponsoring so-called early day motions and initiating adjournment debates. Between 1985 and

1994, MPs asked a total of 2,266 questions relating to animal issues, constituting about 0.5 per cent of the total number of questions asked, a not inconsiderable number given the range of issues concerning MPs (Garner, 1998: 18).

One has to question, however, the usefulness of such procedures, which are not (with the exception of Question Time in the Commons) extensively – if at all – covered by the media. A more promising avenue for pressure groups is the system of all-party select committees. These give groups an opportunity to give evidence which will be utilised by a committee to draw up a published report. The problem here is that, although the members tend to take a less partisan stance, the government is under no obligation to act upon a committee's report either in terms of legislating or even allowing time for the report to be debated on the floor of the Commons. Thus, the Agriculture Committee's report on modern intensive farming methods, although critical of the government's failure to take sufficient account of the earlier Brambell Report, was largely ignored (see Chapter 4). Reports such as these, though, do serve the useful function of keeping an issue on the political agenda, particularly since they are often reported and discussed in the media.

Animal protection and political parties

In the British political system if a group can persuade a political party to include its demands within a manifesto, and that party subsequently secures an overall majority of seats in the Commons, the group is in with an excellent chance of seeing its aims met. Those groups who strive for regular consultation with government try not to take sides in the party political debate for the obvious reason that they are unlikely to be favourably received if an alternative party wins an election. As we pointed out in Chapter 2, an important explanation for the rise of cause groups in recent years has been the lack of congruence between the emerging new issues and the traditional focus on the left/right division over economic policy that the two main parties remain wedded to. Nevertheless, recognising the need to get animal protection on to the political agenda, there have been concerted efforts, beginning in the late 1970s, to persuade the major parties to adopt commitments on animal welfare.

As we saw in Chapter 1, there have been claims that animal protection is an issue associated with the left, that it is 'essential to understand the central importance of connections between capitalism and animal abuse' (Miles and Williams, 1986: 31). On a practical level, empirical evidence suggests that the most ardent supporters of animal protection, in both Britain and the United States, come from left of centre MPs and members of Congress (Garner, 1999). Some elements of the left of the Labour Party have been particularly concerned about animal issues. The identification and representation of a number of exploited groups, including animals, was the rationale behind much of the Labour left's strategy in London during the first half of the 1980s. The animal rights activist Kim Stallwood, in particular, was active in forging alliances with the radical Labour-controlled London boroughs and the GLC (Windeatt, 1985: 181–3). It is no coincidence that many of these authorities – such as Lambeth and Islington – carried quite progressive animal charters and that Tony Banks, one of the leaders of the GLC, has, since becoming an MP, been one of the most active initiators and supporters of legislation protecting animals. In the United States, an interesting link between the labour and civil rights movements and animal protection was provided by the well known activist Henry Spira. Over the years, Spira had, until his untimely death, been active on all three fronts and quite clearly saw the connection. As he pointed out: 'We identify with the powerless and the vulnerable – the victims, all of those dominated, oppressed and exploited' (Spira, 1983: 373; see Singer, 1994).

At the national level in Britain only the Green Party has a programme of policies that would really satisfy the discerning animal advocate. However, MPs who regularly emphasise animal welfare issues – most of whom can be found in the All Party Parliamentary Group for Animal Welfare – can be found on both sides of the Commons.

Of the two main parties, it is undoubtedly Labour which leads on animal issues, sometimes by a large margin. Labour's 1983 election manifesto was probably the most radical the party has ever put before the voters and reflected the dominance of the left at that time. The commitments to animal welfare reforms were no exception. Thus, the party promised to transform the Farm Animal Welfare Council into a standing Royal Commission on animal protection, to review 'urgently' the 1876 Cruelty to Animals Act, to give 'high priority' to finding alternatives to the use of live animals in scientific procedures and to ban all forms of hunting with dogs. Most significant were the sections on animal agriculture where it was stated that the export of live food animals would be banned as would, over a phased period, 'all extreme livestock systems'. 'Extreme', however, was not defined. A further interesting point to note here is that Labour were also committed to leaving the European Community and would thus have had far more flexibility in animal welfare legislation. By 1992, Labour's intentions had been scaled down although the party still promised, unlike the Conservatives, to aid the passage of an anti-hunting bill, to ban the animal testing of beauty aids, to outlaw fur farming and to introduce a dog registration scheme (Craig, 1990: 382; Labour Party, 1992: 22). Again, in 1997, Labour was widely credited with a much stronger set of animal protection proposals than the Conservatives. The 'New Life for Animals' programme committed a Labour government, amongst other things, to a Royal Commission on animal experimentation, a ban on fur farming, a free vote on hunting, and, subject to meeting EU commitments, an end to live exports. (Radford, 2001: 171).

The one issue where there is a very distinct difference between the two main parties is Labour's long-term opposition to hunting. There are clear reasons for Labour's antipathy towards hunting. In the first place, hunting has always been perceived, however justly, as the sport of the wealthy and opposition therefore coincides with Labour's roots as a working-class party. In addition, it is a safe issue in that, as we saw, a large majority are in favour of abolition and even in rural areas, voters are divided on the issue. Labour politicians have long been associated with the LACS. In 1990, for instance, two Labour MPs, the late Eric Heffer and Kevin McNamara, the former Labour Cabinet minister Barbara Castle and the redoubtable animal welfare campaigner and the late Labour peer Lord Houghton, were all vice-presidents of the LACS. More recently, Angela Smith, elected as a Labour MP in 1997, was a former political officer with the LACS. Although abolition was not, until 1979, official party policy, Labour has often debated hunting and been sympathetic to anti-hunting Private Members' Bills. In the immediate post-war period, the

Labour government refused to support anti-hunting measures since (wrongly) it feared an electoral backlash from rural areas. By the 1960s, however, this fear had eased and Wilson's government turned Eric Heffer's bill to abolish hare coursing and deer hunting into a government bill, only for it to run out of time when the election was called in 1970 (LACS Annual Report 1990: 2; Thomas, 1983: 200–2).

The precarious position of the 1974–79 Labour government prevented any further progress but the party outside parliament, now increasingly under the control of the left, published a document, *Living Without Cruelty,* which contained a commitment to abolish all forms of hunting and coursing. Although the report was accepted by the party's National Executive Committee, Callaghan, again invoking the electoral consequences argument, refused to include the abolition of fox hunting in the manifesto, although the party committed itself to 'the banning of hare coursing and stag and deer hunting' in the 1979 manifesto. Recognising that its chances now depended on the election of a Labour government, the LACS contributed £80,000 towards the party's election campaign (Thomas, 1983: 203–5).

By 1983, as we have seen, Labour's manifesto contained an even more radical commitment to outlaw all forms of hunting with dogs which, of course, includes fox hunting. When power was wrested from the left of the party, Labour's commitment to abolish hunting was toned down, so that in the 1992, 1997 and 2001 manifestos, the commitment to make parliamentary time available for an anti-hunting bill was offered (*Guardian*, 8 August 1991). Nevertheless, the prospect of a ban led the Political Animal Lobby, the lobbying arm of IFAW, to make a £1m donation to Labour, the largest single external donation the party has ever received (*Observer*, 1 September 1996). At the time of writing, a bill to abolish hunting and coursing has not yet reached the statute book, but this fact disguises an enormous amount of complex manoeuvring on the issue.

The initial attempt to introduce a ban was made through a Private Members' Bill introduced by the Labour MP Michael Foster. Predictably, this was talked out. Despite Blair's apparent support for a ban, the political threat of the Countryside Alliance led the government to seek a compromise. To this end an inquiry into hunting chaired by Lord Burns was set up in November

1999. The report, published in June 2000, was inconclusive. There then followed a government bill the following month setting out various options, including the creation of a new licensing authority. MPs again voted for a total ban in January 2001, but the Lords voted for the status quo, thus scuppering the bill as the general election intervened. It was not until March 2002 that a further vote was held with MPs given the choice between three options, including the so-called 'middle way' of a licensing system, which had become Blair's preferred solution. MPs again voted for a ban, but the Lords voted for the middle way. A further six-month consultation period was then announced, before another government bill was introduced, this time seeking to balance cruelty with utility. Despite initially supporting this proposal which would have allowed some fox hunting to remain, MPs eventually in June 2003 voted to reinstate a total ban. This bill then passed to the Lords in October 2003 who voted against it in favour of the original licensing option. The Government now has to decide whether to reintroduce the bill into the Commons and, once voted for by MPs again, invoke the Parliament Act to bypass the Lords.

Animal protection campaigns

The classic approach of outsider groups – those lacking access to government – is the public campaign. Insider groups sometimes pursue such campaigns too, although they have to be careful not to alienate the executive by so doing and will only embark on them when they have failed to persuade government directly. Outsider groups, of course, have no choice. Deprived of a direct line to government they must seek to influence government indirectly by mounting campaigns to influence public opinion. If they are successful, governments may be forced to listen to the group's demands and even grant them access to the decision-making arena.

The classic method of the outsider group is the mass demonstration. Thus, for instance, the NAVS has traditionally organised demonstrations to promote the World Day for Laboratory Animals. Although these kinds of events provide a way for activists to meet and let off steam their usefulness is limited. No doubt some new members are recruited and any publicity for the cause should not be scoffed at, but so many of these kinds of events are held for a variety of causes that they are no longer newsworthy unless they involve violence which, of course, can be counter-productive in any case.

A more effective method is the production and widespread distribution of material which provides information and often utilises the emotive nature of the subject. Most groups seek to use graphic images of animal suffering in their publicity which increasingly now includes web-sites and videos as well as literature. One of the problems faced by campaigners against vivisection (in Britain rather more than America) is the difficulty of obtaining information in the first place. Anti-vivisection groups are thus reliant on often illegally obtained evidence, or have to resort to ploughing through the published papers of scientists to find out if and how they use animals in their research. It is for this reason that NAVS in particular has for ten years or so been running an 'Unlock the Labs' campaign designed to secure greater freedom of information on what is being done to animals in the laboratories.

One of the oft-stated criticisms of animal protection groups is that although the material itself is effective, it tends to be distributed to the already converted and therefore has minimum impact. Most major groups, for instance, publish their own journal such as *Animal Life* (RSPCA), *Outrage* (Animal Aid), *The Campaigner* (NAVS), *Agscene* (CIWF) and the *Wildlife Guardian* (LACS). Although these journals are invariably well produced and informative they reach a limited audience. To overcome this difficulty, greater use is now made of mass communication techniques – web-sites, direct mailing, advertisements in the press and cinema and attracting the attention of the news media. Indeed, the tabloid press in particular has shown a great willingness to attack animal experimentation, the classic case occurring in 1975 when the *Sunday People* revealed that ICI were forcing beagle dogs to smoke cigarettes in experiments on the effects of tobacco. The public outcry which resulted forced the Home Secretary to announce publicly that such research on dogs would not be allowed in future (although it is difficult to say whether this promise was kept) (Ryder, 1989: 245).

Whilst, as we saw, Lynx provided the classic example of a campaign directed at the consumer, the RSPCA's campaign over dog registration is a good example of a campaign aimed at influencing government and parliament indirectly through public opinion. The society spent a great deal of money, employing advertising agency Abbott, Mead and Vickers (who came up with the disturbing 'Registration not Extermination' advertisement which featured a pile of dead dogs killed by animal welfare organisations), commissioning an expert analysis of the issue from the London School of Economics, distributing 400,000 mail shots and forging alliances with other interested groups (*The Times*, 5 April 1990; *Guardian* 30 October 1990). Even though they may have won the argument, it is worth reiterating that the RSPCA lost the vote because the government opposed the idea.

Particular attention in campaigning is directed towards the young since it is, correctly, assumed that they are more amenable to persuasion. Thus, most of the major organisations have a youth group, many of whom have their own specially produced magazines. Ingenious methods have been adopted to influence children. The NAVS, for instance, devised AD, a fictional ex-laboratory rabbit, whose cartoon exploits in escaping from the clutches of 'evil vivisectors' was a particularly effective propaganda tool. Most groups, in addition, seek access to educational institutions through specially designed teaching packs and the provision of speakers to give talks in schools and colleges. NAVS ran, for several years a 'Violence Free Science' campaign aimed at stopping the use of live animals in higher education science courses. American animal protection groups place even greater emphasis on influencing young people. The American Anti-Vivisection Society, for instance, created an organisation called Animalearn in 1990 which offers courses on animal rights to secondary students. Such has been the success of these youth campaigns that defenders of the use of animals in science and agriculture have placed more emphasis on countering them (see Chapter 2).

The use of celebrities to promote a group's aims is a particularly useful strategy to attract the young as well as media interest in general. A typical approach is to list those celebrities who are vegetarians, or to use them to front campaigns, as CIWF have done with Joanna Lumley. The anti-fur campaign has often used models. PETA in Britain currently use the pop star Sophie Ellis Bextor as the face of their campaign against fur. Some have used

their celebrity to set up their own animal protection organisations. The TV writer Carla Lane is a good British example of this
whilst the Paris-based Brigitte Bardot Foundation was set up in
1976 and in the United States Doris Day set up her Animal
League for similar purposes.

Increasingly, the role of national organisations is to facilitate
campaigns that have their roots at the local level (see Chapter 2).
CIWF, for instance, had campaigned against live exports for
years, and were instrumental in providing national leadership for
the outpouring of local protest that began at the end of 1994.
Anti-vivisection groups, similarly, publicised widely the allegations against Huntingdon Life Sciences from the mid 1990s, and
have supported and publicised the activities of SHAC, once the
local group was created. These locally driven campaigns have
produced some of the most innovative forms of protest, which has
often gone beyond attempts to influence public opinion and
towards direct action (see Chapter 8).

Strategy

It was mentioned in Chapter 2 that an important classificatory
dimension of the animal protection movement is strategy. Whilst
ideology, or, to be more precise, the distinction between welfare
and rights, is crucially important in explaining the modern animal
protection movement, a more thorough typology should distinguish between ideology and strategy (Garner, 1998: 82–92).
Here, a threefold classification is apparent. Firstly, there are those
who are *animal welfarists in ideology and strategy* in the sense
that they accept the inferior moral status of animals and therefore
can support reformist measures without any qualms of
conscience.

The real conflict occurs over the strategic position adopted by
advocates of animal rights. Those who are *absolutists in strategy
and ideology* argue that there is no animal welfare means to an
animal rights end. According to this view, most associated with
Francione (1996), animal rights advocates should only support
measures which seek the abolition of particular practice involving
animals – such as the abolition of meat eating rather than reforms
to factory farming. Francione's approach was developed as a
critique of what he sees as the failings of the modern animal rights

leadership which he accuses of being 'New Welfarists' in that they are willing to accept a reformist route to an animal rights end. Most, if not all, national animal rights organisations are therefore *philosophical absolutists and strategic pragmatists*.

Expertise, moderation and respectability

Francione's position was, at least partly, developed in response to the first edition of this book. I remain committed to the view that the strategy adopted by animal protection organisations should be informed by the general pressure group literature on the prerequisites for achieving group goals. Firstly, groups are often consulted by government because they can offer expertise, a quality which can be invaluable to decision makers. The issue of animal protection is no exception. Thus, those groups with relevant knowledge are, all things being equal, more likely than not to be consulted by government at one time or another and more likely to have an impact on government proposals. This is at least part of the reason, for instance, for the influence of groups such as FoE, the BVA, the RSPCA and the RSPB, the latter having an acknowledged expertise in bird protection and European Union legislation relating to it. In addition, the WWF is the classic example of an insider group which uses its conservation expertise as a means of gaining access to governments throughout the world. Many animal groups, particularly wildlife groups and those campaigning against vivisection, do employ experts, but they face formidable opposition, most notably in the areas of farming and science. It is not surprising, therefore, that in these areas government tends to take notice of those groups – such as FRAME and UFAW – who can claim equivalent expertise. Indeed, FRAME acted as a principal adviser to the government during the preparation and passage of the Animals (Scientific Procedures) Bill and it has had regular representation on the APC (as has the RSPCA) established by the above legislation to monitor its working and to advise ministers and civil servants in the Home Office (see Chapter 5).

A crucial factor which plays a significant part in a government's attitude towards a group is the extent to which it is united. A group or set of groups involved in the same issue area who are divided, unsure of their objectives and turned in on themselves, are unlikely to be taken seriously by decision makers. Divisions within the animal movement, usually based on the rights/welfare divide, have been prominent on occasions. The corollary to unity is that if access to decision makers is to be achieved, this unity must be based upon the articulation of moderate and realistic aims pursued in a conciliatory and calm fashion. Of course, if one argues, as does Francione, that reforms to the treatment of animals short of abolition are not worth having, then this strategic argument becomes void. For most animal advocates, though, at least some reforms of this kind are worth having. Indeed, unity around a set of achievable aims has been the key to explaining the progress made by the animal protection movement in recent years.

As we saw above, the fact that a group adopts an abolitionist animal rights-based set of objectives does not automatically preclude it from agreeing on a more limited set of immediate aims with which it can unite with other groups. CIWF, for instance, accepts that, although it seeks the long-term objective of universal vegetarianism, immediate priority should be given to campaigning for short-term reforms in modern farming methods. As a result, it has had considerable success in persuading the British government to ban sow stalls and tethers amongst other things. Similarly, one of the reasons for the success of the live exports campaign in getting a sympathetic public and governmental response was its limited and reasonable aims. Thus, the campaign maximised support because it was not asking for the end of meat eating but for an end to the transportation of live animals. This inclusivity was illustrated nicely by a campaign poster which read 'You Don't Have to Stop Eating Meat to Care – Ban Live Exports' (Benton and Redfearn, 1996: 51). In fact, the campaign was well supported not least because it was widened even further by the police decision to invoke the Public Order Act to try to stop the protests. Thus, the protests arguably became as much about civil rights and police powers as they were about animals.

Advocating compromise and achievable goals does not necessarily mean that abolitionist demands cannot be made. Public backing for such a proposal, however, is a crucial element. Thus, animal protection groups, as we saw, have resisted the temptation to compromise on anything short of abolition of hunting, and, given that public opinion has been on their side for some time, they have been right to do so. Unity here was achieved by the creation in 1996 of a formidable alliance between the RSPCA, LACS and IFAW called the Campaign for the Protection of Hunted Animals. Significantly, the abolition of hunting can be justified on the moral orthodoxy grounds that it is a practice that causes unnecessary suffering. The LACS's insistence that the abolitionist goal be maintained was illustrated by the removal of James Barrington as the organisation's executive director as a result of his suggestion that hunting might remain under a licensing system (*Guardian*, 15 December 1995).

The search for unity in the animal movement goes back decades. In the forefront of efforts to create unity in the 1970s and 1980s was the Scottish group Advocates for Animals (formerly the Scottish Society for the Prevention of Vivisection) led by the late Clive Hollands. Although the Society's ultimate aim was, and is, the complete abolition of vivisection, it does not see it as a realistic ambition in the short term. Hollands' strategy, therefore, was to develop alliances between groups for particular purposes. Hollands was a central figure in four major linked initiatives – Animal Welfare Year between August 1976 and August 1977; the creation of consultative bodies concerned with particular areas of animal use; the attempt beginning in the late 1970s to persuade parties to adopt manifesto commitments on animal welfare; and the attempts to influence the content of the Conservative government's legislation on animal experimentation (see Hollands, 1980). All these initiatives were characterised by attempts to forge unity around a 'realistic' programme of reforms. Whilst all of them achieved a modicum of success, all were marred by division.

Animal Welfare Year, a national publicity campaign to highlight animal welfare issues, attracted the support of over sixty animal protection groups, not all of whom would have wholeheartedly agreed with the moderate programme being put forward. The LACS, for instance, participated in the event even though the abolition of hunting was not on the agenda. As a result of the sense of unity engendered by the Year, a number of consultative bodies consisting of representatives from various interested groups were set up, most notably the Committee for the Reform of Animal Experimentation (CRAE), the Farm Animal

Welfare Co-ordinating Executive and the National Joint Equine Welfare Committee. These joint bodies formed the basis for the 'Putting Animals into Politics' campaign led by the General Election Co-ordinating Committee for Animal Protection (GECCAP) which led to the adoption of manifesto commitments on animal welfare by the three main parties.

This proliferation of acronyms may not make compelling reading but it was a sign that the animal protection movement was beginning to come to terms with the nitty-gritty of traditional pressure politics – the need for hard internal bargaining to fashion a plausible and achievable programme with a single voice to express it. The whole enterprise, though, was threatened by the ever-present divisions within the movement. It should be emphasised that the radicals were not the only 'culprits'. Many of the more moderate groups refused to participate in any or some of the initiatives. Thus, the WWF, the RSPB, the UFAW and the PDSA did not take part in Animal Welfare Year or the subsequent attempt to influence political parties. Their reasons for not doing so varied. Partly, no doubt, it was a dislike and fear of associating with the more radical groups. Both the WWF and the RSPB, for instance, thought that involvement might blur their identity – a euphemism for being associated in the public mind with the radical animal rights advocates. Others, such as the PDSA and the UFAW, rather timidly preferred to remain aloof from controversy, choosing to concentrate instead on their 'safe' secondary activities lest their charitable status should be put in jeopardy.[2]

Some at the other end of the ideological spectrum also refused to participate. The NAVS was the major society opposed to Animal Welfare Year stating that the 'aims of Animal Welfare Year are not unfortunately sufficiently radical for the NAVS to give their enthusiastic support'. In addition, although the society was initially a member of CRAE, it withdrew in 1980, again because it was not proving radical enough. Even GECCAP could not confine the radicals. When it was revived for the 1983 election, the LACS, the BUAV and CIWF formed the Animal Protection Alliance which sought stronger commitments from the parties (*The Times*, 3 November 1982).

Major legislation concerning animals introduced by government is rare. Thus, the formulation and enactment of the Animals (Scientific Procedures) Act 1986 provides a useful opportunity to consider the legislative strategies and impact of the animal protection movement (for a fuller account of this see Garner, 1998: ch. 9). Predictably, the movement's response to the legislation was characterised by division. CRAE had been formed in 1975 in order to impress upon the (then Labour) government the need to provide a replacement for the 1876 Cruelty to Animals Act. Dominated by moderates such as Lord Houghton and Clive Hollands (particularly after the NAVS and Richard Ryder had resigned precisely because of its moderate slant), CRAE had quickly gained access to the Home Office providing (largely ignored) written and oral evidence, for instance, to the Home Secretary's Advisory Committee's Enquiry into the LD50 test. Jointly with FRAME and the BVA, CRAE continued to lobby the Conservative government (which had promised in its 1979 manifesto to legislate on animal experimentation) in addition to discussing proposals with scientific interests in the Research Defence Society.

The negotiating position of the CRAE/BVA/FRAME alliance was that the infliction of pain on animals in the laboratory should only be allowed in exceptional circumstances when 'it is judged to be of exceptional importance in meeting the essential needs of man or animals'. Further, the alliance argued that there should be a substantial reduction in the number of animals used, that alternative methods should be developed and used wherever possible and finally that those still using animals should be subject to public scrutiny. The government's White Paper, published in 1983, however, refused to accept the CRAE's pain clause and stated that only when animals were found to be 'suffering severe and enduring pain' must a particular procedure be terminated (Hollands, 1985: 176). As a result of further lobbying involving regular meetings with Home Office officials and David Mellor (the junior minister responsible for the bill), the CRAE alliance achieved some of its aims. In the supplementary White Paper published in 1985 (which corresponded closely to the eventual Act) the government moved a long way on the public accountability question and whilst the 'severe pain' clause remained, CRAE's suggestion of a cost–benefit analysis was taken up (see Chapter 5) (*The Times*, 25 May 1985).

When the government's proposals were first published (in the 1983 White Paper), a number of groups including the BUAV, the NAVS, Animal Aid and the Scottish Anti-Vivisection Society (now Animal Concern) formed the Mobilisation for Laboratory Animals Against the Government's Proposals. Their objection was twofold. In the first place, they were unhappy with the composition of the proposed Animal Procedures Committee which they saw as being dominated by those involved in the use of animals. Secondly, they argued that certain procedures – the Draize and LD50 tests and animal testing for weapons, cosmetics, tobacco, alcohol and in psychological research – ought to be abolished outright since the discretion given to the Home Secretary would leave him susceptible to pressure exerted by scientific and industrial interests. But these alternative proposals were never going to be acceptable (and, incidentally, were strangely irrelevant in anything but a symbolic sense since these procedures accounted for a small proportion of the total – see Chapter 5). In any case, the radicals had already missed the boat since they were not involved in the formulation stage. Indeed, they were not even invited to the press briefing given by David Mellor to launch the revised White Paper in 1985 (Ryder, 1989: 249–54; *The Times*, 17 May 1985). By the time the bill reached parliament, of course, it was unlikely to be changed fundamentally, particularly given Labour's acceptance of the proposals.

The eventual legislation is far from perfect, but was significantly better than nothing. Animal welfare interests are beginning to be more adequately represented on the APC and the Home Office has abolished some procedures and the use of some species (see Chapter 5). Moreover, anti-vivisection groups, originally opposed to the legislation, have used the new legislative structure to raise issues of concern, usually about allegations of malpractice in particular laboratories. The BUAV, if not NAVS, now adopt a much more conciliatory approach, whilst still remaining abolitionist. This resulted from a battle in the early part of the 1990s between the so-called 'traditionalist' and 'modernising' wings of the BUAV. This conflict, which culminated in chaos at an extraordinary general meeting in 1994, was not so much between different moral outlooks – both sides recognised the case for abolition – but between those who wanted to pursue a confrontational, oppositionist strategy and those who wanted to use the legislative framework to further the anti-vivisection cause (*Independent* 7 November 1994). Finally, Hollands' successor as

Director of Advocates for Animals, Les Ward, took the compromise game one step further by helping, in the early 1990s, to set
up the so-called Boyd Group, a meeting of animal advocates and
scientists involved in animal experimentation – most notably
Colin Blakemore – designed to try to reconcile the competing
interests in the debate (*Times Higher*, 28 April 1995).

The animal rights dilemma

What we have said so far, then, is that insider status can allow
pressure groups to have a significant input into the formulation of
public policy. This insider status, however, is largely dependent
upon a group being perceived by government as moderate and
respectable. What is described as moderate and respectable, of
course, will depend upon the climate of the times, but it is clear
that the radical demands of the 'rights' faction of the animal
protection movement are not regarded as acceptable enough for
government to consider granting it consultative status, unless of
course it is also prepared to limit these demands. To be fair, the
Mobilisation alliance did not put forward an absolutist position
(although it was abolitionist), but it was well known that its
limited set of proposals were the absolute minimum it was
prepared to accept and the government was clearly never going to
go even this far.

The animal rights movement therefore faces a dilemma. Either
it engages in negotiation and compromise with government, and
even with those organisations that have a vested interest in the
continuing use of animals, or it seeks to retain moral purity and
concentrates on public campaigning to persuade public opinion to
move sufficiently towards its position, thus forcing government to
respond. This dilemma does not affect animal welfare groups
since they are already working in the mainstream and so are likely
to be consulted by government in any case. What is more, they
find no problem in entering into a dialogue.

There are advantages in the compromise approach. In the first
place, improvements in the way animals are treated become possible in the short term. These reforms are obviously far short of
what is demanded by animal rights activists (and even sometimes
by moderates within the animal protection movement), but they
go some way, however small, towards the eventual aim. It is also

worth speculating that failure to engage in a realistic dialogue with government and other interested parties would result in fewer and weaker animal protection measures. Thus, it should be remembered that it was the success of Animal Welfare Year and the GECCAP campaign in the first place that precipitated the manifesto commitment to reform the law relating to the laboratory use of animals. Seen in this context, standing aloof in principled isolation seems like a futile gesture. As Hollands (1980: 142) warned in 1980:

> To adopt this position and to refuse to comment on impending legislation, other than to say, 'We do not want it', would be burying one's head in the sand. The legislation will not go away merely because the societies do not want it, and the end result would be that the scientists would get the kind of legislation they want, which may last for another hundred years.

A further factor in support of the compromise approach is that the future success of the alternative strategy is by no means assured. Certainly, there have been some successes – in the altering of consumer behaviour, for instance, which has seen a slump in the British fur trade and an expansion in the market for 'cruelty-free' products. Further, the campaigning vigour of many groups may – however imperceptibly – have contributed to the changed climate which has made legislation such as the Animals (Scientific Procedures) Act more likely. On the other hand, there can be no guarantees that such a strategy will succeed even in the long term. What is clear is that, at present, the more radical demands of the animal protection movement are simply not acceptable to government or to the public in general and it is difficult to see public opinion changing in the near future to make them so. Thirdly, it can also be argued that a failure to accept the realities of practical politics is not a neutral act since it can damage the case being put by those who are prepared to negotiate and compromise. It is possible to speculate, for instance, that much more could have been achieved had the animal protection movement put its whole weight behind a stronger, although still realistic, set of proposals when the Animals (Scientific Procedures) Bill was being formulated and debated.

Critics of the approach of the so-called 'new welfarism' described above would raise the objection that insider status is not worth having, given that the interests of humans, as producers and consumers, will always take precedence. One can have some sympathy with this view. The influence of animal users – such as, in Britain, the NFU, the meat wholesalers and retailers, the Research Defence Society, the medical profession and the pharmaceutical companies – is such that they are in a strong position to ensure that their interests prevail in consultations with government and any protection given to animals is essentially peripheral. This is to assume, though, that the animal users have a monopoly of the resources necessary for achieving their objectives. This is not necessarily the case. One crucial resource which the animal protection movement can invoke, for instance, is the mobilisation of public support. This issue is considered in more detail in Chapter 8.

Another potential problem is that if the animal protection movement were to focus on the business of quietly negotiating and compromising, the public campaigns, to alter the social climate and directly confront those economic interests who benefit from the use of animals, would have to be curbed. In turn, this may give the impression that the use of animals for science or for food or whatever is justified as long as these practices are regulated. But then this would require the animal rights movement to sacrifice its entire belief system – that these practices are not justified because they fail to respect the rights of animals. However, this dichotomy – between the moderation and realism required of insider status and the absolutist campaigns to influence public opinion – is somewhat false. Even public campaigns should not be aimed too far ahead of public opinion. As Chapter 5 illustrated, the animal rights movement has had the biggest impact in its campaign against vivisection when it seeks to challenge the validity of using animals in laboratories on practical rather than ethical grounds. There can be no greater praise for this emphasis than the obvious concern displayed by the scientific community who, in recent years, have been forced to respond by mounting their own defensive public campaigns. They recognise that they are up against, as a letter from a number of senior medical figures in the *British Medical Journal* pointed out, 'a vigorous and well-planned campaign by animal rights activists to persuade the public and the media that animal experiments are both cruel *and* unnecessary' (my italics) (*Guardian*, 25 August 1990).

As a final point on the strategy of the animal protection movement it is important to note that the public are alienated by the style as well as the content of animal rights campaigns. Given the nature of the issues, the danger of a smug kind of preaching is ever present. Campaigns against, say, nuclear weapons do not face the same kind of problem because they are not directed at individual behaviour. Even a campaign on an issue such as abortion will only directly affect a small number of people. Animal protection, on the other hand, is an issue that involves virtually everyone directly. Thus, an aggressive, absolutist campaign is directed at everyone who eats meat or uses cosmetics (the vast majority). Some campaigning gives the impression that the aim is to shame people into changing their ways. Now, whilst this may be justified and may, indeed, have the desired effect on some, it is just as likely to threaten others and alienate them from a cause with which they might otherwise identify. For some in the animal rights movement, there is just a hint of a suspicion that this is what such campaigns are about – an expression of moral purity and a deep-seated need both to be different and to belong to a counter-culture, rather than a genuine desire to influence others to adopt a similar lifestyle. That the former is the case for some in the animal protection movement is undoubtedly true, and, as we saw in Chapter 2, the generation of such an attitude may be extremely important in mobilising and retaining activists. To the extent that these attitudes are more deeply rooted, though, it would provide us with both an explanation for the popularity of the animal rights enterprise for those involved and a reason why it is unlikely to succeed.

We have argued in this chapter that the public policy progress made by the animal protection movement has been largely the product of a willingness to play the political game of compromise. By contrast, images of division and an unwillingness of some groups to compromise has hindered the cause. Gaining access to policy networks more often than not requires some recognition of policy continuity, and the need to maximise public support. This does not mean, as we pointed out, that other strategies are pointless, only that immediate reform is unlikely to come about without the recognition that unity around a set of realistic proposals is essential. Equally, there is a limit, in the present social climate, to what governments will regard as acceptable demands from the animal protection movement, and the freedom that outsider status provides for campaigns aimed at radically shifting public opinion towards the animal rights programme is clearly crucial. What we have not considered so far is the view that, given the influence of the opponents of reform and the laborious and perhaps impossible task of converting public opinion, traditional pressure group politics in this instance represents a hopelessly one-sided affair. In recent years, increasing numbers of activists in the animal protection movement have accepted that this is the case and have sought to protect animals directly. The final chapter considers their case.

Notes

1 For the use of the courts by the American animal protection movement see *Times Higher Education Supplement*, 15 September 1989 on the use of the Freedom of Information Act; Cherfas, (1988: 206) on the legal battle to force the US government to enforce the Marine Mammal Protection Act; and Pacheco (1985: 135–47) on the landmark prosecution of Edward Taub.
2 The RSPCA was in fact criticised by the Charity Commissioners for sponsoring a GECCAP advertisement (*The Times*, 18 June 1980).

8

Animal liberation and direct action

In recent years, the use of various forms of direct action has been adopted by sections of the animal protection movement and this final chapter seeks to provide a framework within which a comprehensive examination of the case for taking such action can be undertaken. In the first part, the activities of those who have taken direct action on behalf of animals are described. An attempt is then made to consider how far these activities are justified. Here, a distinction is made between tactical and principled justifications, the latter category distinguishing between the strategic consequences that flow from granting rights to animals on the one hand and the distribution of pressure group influence on the other. The issue of direct action needs to be treated with care. The quite understandable media emphasis on the most extreme forms has tended to give the impression that the only methods employed by the animal protection movement other than traditional lobbying is planting bombs and burning down department stores. Similarly, the association between these extreme methods and the radicalism of animal rights and liberation views has resulted in a simplistic dichotomy between, on the one hand, traditional animal welfare and constitutionalism and, on the other, the equation of animal rights/liberation with violence and illegality. As this chapter will show, neither view is correct, the former because it fails to recognise the subtle nuances of direct action as a group tactic and the latter because it fails to distinguish between ends and means.

Animal liberation strategies

The animal protection movement has adopted a variety of direct action tactics. It is important to delineate these activities since very different moral and tactical conclusions can be drawn from them. In the first place, one can make a distinction between those which are legal and those which are not. Under the former heading can be included protests directly aimed at institutions using animals or selling animal derived products (such as pharmaceutical companies, circuses and furriers), or those financing institutions using animals or carrying animals abroad. Whilst these activities dispense with the usual political channels, they fall short of illegality. Another increasingly common tactic is for individual activists to seek employment in laboratories which carry out scientific procedures on animals. This has provided much important information and publicity for the animal protection movement, most notably, perhaps, when Alex Pacheco's employment in Edward Taub's laboratory (Pacheco, 1985) ultimately led to the latter's prosecution for cruelty to monkeys, and, in Britain, when Zoe Broughton filmed cruelty to dogs by technicians at the HLS laboratory (see Chapter 5). Finally, here, we can include direct action aimed at disrupting hunts and shoots. Again, by itself, there is nothing illegal about this (although some hunt harassment laws exist in the United States), but more often than not other laws – from trespassing to obstruction and even assault – are broken in the process.

The more controversial activities are those which involve deliberately breaking the law. Again we need to be careful to distinguish between three different types of law breaking. Firstly, there is the classic form of non-violent civil disobedience involving sit-ins and vigils. This tactic was used, for instance, in the occupation of the NIH headquarters in 1984 by about 100 activists (including Tom Regan) attempting, ultimately successfully, to end the funding of Gennerali's infamous head injury experiments at the University of Pennsylvania (Blum, 1994: 117–21). Also included in this category is the common tactic of breaking into laboratories (causing the minimum of damage) in order to gather information and release the animals, and the attempts to prevent the export of live animals by sitting in front of transporters. Secondly, there are those actions which set out deliberately to cause damage to property. Thus, laboratory break-ins are often accompanied by widespread destruction of equipment. In addition to this is the smaller-scale damage caused to butchers, meat wholesalers and furriers through the breaking of windows, the use of super glue on locks, the destruction of vehicles and the paint spraying of fur coats.

Finally, there are the much more serious actions which involve threats to human life and safety. Thus, in recent years, activists have attempted to damage the economic interests of companies by claiming to have adulterated their products, fire bombs have been planted in department stores which sell furs and individual scientists have been targeted with car bombs. On top of this are intimidatory phone calls and letters, often directed at the families of those who are involved in the animal use industry. Particularly worthy of mention is the campaign against the HLS laboratory, which has included the intimidation of staff including a physical attack on the managing director and nuisance and threatening phone calls (*Guardian*, 12 February 2001). Although there is some dispute about this, I concur with those, such as Singer (1985a), who claim that only these attacks on people constitute violence. Indeed, the violence that has been used by sections of the animal protection movement amounts to terrorism, defined by Clutterbuck (1986: 20) as 'the use or threat of violence against small numbers to put large numbers in fear'.

The use of direct action as a tactic by the animal protection movement began with the formation of the HSA in 1964. As the LACS, under the leadership of Raymond Rowley, moved towards a less confrontational stance, a number of activists broke away to focus on the use of non-violent direct action which, given the legislative inactivity, they perceived as the most effective way of protecting hunted animals. Now based in Nottingham, the HSA remains extremely active in the field during the hunting season using a variety of sophisticated methods – from distracting hounds through the use of horns or scent to scaring away the potential victim of the hunt. It is not surprising that hunting became the first target for direct action since its public nature and the accessibility to activists makes it an easier option than factory farms or animal laboratories (Hall, 1984: 42–5; Thomas, 1983: 104–14).

Also engaging in non-violent, although often illegal, direct action are a number of environmental groups. The anti-whaling direct action of Greenpeace – whereby activists in small inflatable motorboats attempted to put themselves between whalers and their catch – became a symbol of environmental awareness in the 1970s and 1980s. Less well known is the Sea Shepherd Conservation Society which was founded in 1977 by Paul Watson, who had been expelled from Greenpeace for his advocacy of tougher methods. His organisation has since been responsible for attacking pirate whaling ships and, in one particularly notable incident, for causing considerable damage to a whale processing station in Iceland. Another offshoot of Greenpeace is the London-based Environmental Investigation Agency, which, since its formation in 1984, has specialised in infiltrating the black-market trade in wild animals. Finally, mention should be made of the radical American environmental group Earth First!, which, founded in 1980, specialises in sabotaging the equipment used by the companies intent on exploiting the natural environment (Allaby, 1986: 210–14; Dobson, 1991: 224–32).

Most synonymous with direct action, of course, is the ALF, versions of which, in addition to Britain, now exist in many countries including the USA, Australia, New Zealand, Germany, France, Italy, Spain, Poland, Sweden, South Africa and Canada. The British ALF was formed in 1976 although its origins lie in a breakaway faction of the HSA dating back to the 1960s. Led by Ronnie Lee and Cliff Goodman, a group of activists became disillusioned with the law-abiding activities of the HSA and, in 1972, formed the Band of Mercy (a name ironically borrowed from the RSPCA's law-abiding youth organisation in the nineteenth century). This group began by damaging the property of hunt participants and supporters but quickly moved on to other targets. Following his release in 1976 from a prison sentence imposed after he was caught breaking into an animal breeding centre at Bicester, Lee formed the ALF, initially a group of about thirty (Henshaw, 1989: 12–20).[1]

In Britain, it was not until the 1980s that direct action began to take a more serious turn both in terms of the number of illegal acts committed and also in the growing use of violence. In 1984 the police, recognising its seriousness, set up the Animal Rights National Index to co-ordinate their response and by the end of the decade most of the leading members of the ALF (including Ronnie Lee) were still behind bars or had served prison sentences (Henshaw, 1989: 102–3, 173–84). The first glimpse of the changing nature of direct action came in 1982 when letter bombs were sent to the four major party leaders. 1984 brought the first attempt to contaminate products when a number of activists claimed to have poisoned Mars Bars (although this was a hoax) and this was followed in later years by similar claims involving L'Oréal products and the soft drink Lucozade (Henshaw, 1989: 63–6; *Guardian*, 14 April 1990, 14 November 1991). From 1983, in addition, there was a spate of department store fires all over the country as a result of activists planting incendiary devices in fur departments. It should be said that the aim was to cause smoke and fire which would set off sprinkler systems, thus damaging the fur stock, but several stores were completely or partially destroyed by fire (Henshaw, 1989: 102–13; *The Times*, 21 December 1988, 24 February 1989). The use of high explosive which severely damaged the Senate House at Bristol University in February 1989 represented a further disturbing escalation of the campaign and the final step towards fully-fledged terrorism occurred in 1990 when, in the space of two weeks, cars belonging to Margaret Baskerville (a veterinary surgeon working at the Porton Down chemical research establishment) and Max Headley (a Bristol University psychologist) were blown up by animal rights activists. Although neither target was hurt, this was more by chance than design and in the latter case a thirteen-month-old baby was injured by the blast (*Guardian*, 1 August 1989, 12 June 1990). It should be noted that the ALF did not take responsibility for many of these actions which were claimed by previously unheard of groups such as the Animal Rights Militia, the Animal Abused Society, the Animal Defence League and the Justice Department. Indeed, the ALF has always proclaimed that it is non-violent in the sense that it does not target individuals or put the safety of the public at risk. Others have claimed that the ALF was really behind all of these actions, simply adopting different identities in order to avoid public odium (Henshaw, 1989: 57, 91, 121). In a sense, such disputes are pointless since they assume that the ALF is a hierarchical organisation with a centralised authority structure. This is not so. Activists operate in autonomous cells and choose their own targets and methods. These may then be reported to the ALF press officer (a position held by Ronnie Lee before his conviction and now undertaken by Robin Webb) who presumably can then decide whether or not to claim them. All that we can say is that there are some activists who are willing to use violence and there is little that the leading members of the ALF can do to stop them, even if they wanted to.

There have been genuine splits on the issue of violence. In 1980, some activists broke away from the ALF to form so-called Animal Liberation Leagues, although by the mid-1980s these had largely disbanded due to widespread arrests. The Leagues were characterised by their choice of targets – usually large animal laboratories – their sophisticated tactics (the use of expensive video cameras, for example, was widespread) and the stress that was put on publicity as opposed to damaging property and rescuing animals. The media – including national news programmes – were often willing to use the evidence collected and it was a raid by the South Eastern Animal Liberation League in 1984 which resulted in the prosecution of the Royal College of Surgeons (Henshaw, 1989: 84–8, 78–84).

There have been accusations from within the animal protection movement that some of the more violent actions have been the work of *agents provocateurs* (Ryder, 1989: 281; *The Times*, 2 December 1982). We simply do not know if these claims are true or not. It is certainly the case, though, that there have been instances where opponents of the animal rights movement have tried to frame activists. One hunt supporter, to give one example, was jailed for nine months for placing a home-made bomb under his own vehicle before claiming it was the work of animal activists (*Wildlife Guardian*, Winter 1990–1: 5).

It should be pointed out that direct action represents a very small part of the animal protection movement's tactics and actions which have actually put people's safety at risk constitute only a small proportion of the total amount of direct action. To put matters into perspective, not one person has been killed as a result of direct action by the animal protection movement. Indeed, animal rights activists have had to endure considerable violence themselves particularly at the hands of hunters and their supporters as well as 'heavies' employed by circuses (*Guardian*, 12 October 1989, 12 November 1991). Worse still, a number of activists have been killed, including Claudia Ross, an American conservationist, murdered by an unknown assailant, and the photographer Fernando Pereira who died in 1985 when the Greenpeace ship *Rainbow Warrior* was sunk by the French secret service in Auckland Harbour (Ryder, 1989: 282–4). Other deaths have been the 18-year-old activist Mike Hill in 1991 (who was killed when, in trying to jump off the back of a hunter's pick-up truck, he was dragged underneath), 15-year-old Tom Worby killed on a demonstration, and, most significantly of all, Jill Phipps, killed by falling under a livestock transporter trying to load veal calves on to a flight at Coventry airport in 1995 during the height of the live exports protests. Mention should also be made of Barry Horne, serving an 18-year jail sentence for arson (one of a number of draconian sentences given to animal liberationists) who died after his fourth hunger strike in 2001 designed to highlight the Labour government's reneging on a promise to set up a Royal Commission on animal experimentation. Whilst the use of violence by animal activists is not justified merely by reference to their opponents' behaviour, it is only fair to recognise that it is not a one-sided affair. Indeed, one would almost expect violence to be more prevalent amongst the users of animals since they have more to lose (in economic terms at least) than their opponents have to gain by preventing this use.

The ALF claims about 2,500 activists, although police estimates put the hard-core number at around 250, of whom only about fifty were prepared to use explosives and incendiaries (Monagham, 1997: 112). Another indicator of sympathy for the ALF comes from the ALF Supporters' Group which provides financial aid to help pay the legal costs of activists and to provide books and educational material for those convicted of offences and may also, although this is only speculation, provide help for the purchase of materials used in animal liberation activities. No membership figures are available, although Henshaw (1989: 133) estimates that (in the late 1980s) about 2,000 contributed money or other resources to the ALF.

Despite the fact that relatively small numbers are involved in participating in and financially supporting direct action, the cumulative effect of their activities has been considerable. It has been claimed, for instance, that annually between November 1982 and 1986, 2,000 separate actions caused £6 million worth of damage, and there is no evidence that things have slackened in subsequent years (Ryder, 1989: 280). In 1999, for instance, official figures revealed 1,200 reports of animal rights attacks in Britain causing an estimated £2.6m damage to property (*Guardian*, 17 January 2001). The press are an unreliable source simply because whereas in the early days animal liberation actions were newsworthy they have now ceased to be so and relatively small-scale attacks on butchers and fast-food outlets now tend to go unreported. Indeed, the use of more and more extreme and larger-scale actions may well have been a product of the declining media interest in the more minor acts of damage to property.[2] There have been fewer incidents in the United States partly because it is possible to obtain far more information on laboratory animal use without having to break into laboratory premises. The first American ALF laboratory raid was in 1979 and between then and 1990 the American ALF was responsible for at least seventy-five major actions, freeing over 3,000 animals and causing more than $4 million of damage including, most notably, the break-in at the head injury laboratory at Pennsylvania University (*Village Voice*, 6 March 1990).

Since the early 1990s there has been a change of strategy by British animal liberationists. Rather than random and diffuse acts against a variety of, often small-scale, users of animals, direct action is now more often than not targeted at concerted campaigns against larger targets. The classic example here is the direct action targeted against the HLS company. The campaign of harassment of staff and shareholders was so intense that the Home Secretary introduced new powers to criminalise protests outside the houses of targets, and to increase the penalties for sending hate mail (*Guardian*, 22 February 2001). HLS itself won a court injunction in April 2003 preventing animal rights activists from approaching within 50 yards of employees' homes and permitting only one demonstration every 30 days in an exclusion zone outside the company's two sites (*Guardian*, 17 April 2003).

Whatever the sympathy expressed in private for those who use violence in pursuit of animal liberation, it is universally condemned in public by all of the mainstream groups including, most significantly, by those who advocate a rights view. Not surprisingly, the animal welfare part of the movement is opposed to all but the most benign forms of direct action. More difficult to gauge is the attitude to direct action of animal rights groups.

Here, there is considerable variation, albeit often of tone rather than substance. A surprising number of the groups which have arisen in the last twenty years or so have remained totally immune from the issue of direct action. Thus, despite their ultimate desire to abolish zoos (Zoo Check), factory farming (CIWF) or the fur trade (Lynx and now Respect for Animals), these organisations have, at various times, condemned law breaking, remaining aloof from those activists willing to adopt such tactics. The LACS, too, has remained stubbornly isolated from the debate about direct action, leaving the HSA to focus on disrupting hunts, a strategy that is necessitated by the possibility of legislative influence.

Animal Aid is constitutionally committed to lawful campaigning and is publicly very hostile to the ALF. Commenting on the Bristol car bomb, for instance, it declared itself to be 'sick of this tiny bunch of half-witted pseudo-terrorists undermining all the vital work being done by ourselves and many others', and whilst its then director, Mark Gold, said that he would not wish to 'condemn the rescue of animals from farms or laboratories', he was bitterly opposed to the ALF, describing its journal *Arkangel* as 'a nasty little magazine' (*Outrage*, August–September 1990: 13). At an Animal Aid Council meeting in 1990, a resolution was passed urging members not to contribute to the ALF Supporters' Group and Gold wrote to Animal Aid contacts asking for their help in ensuring that local animal rights groups adopted a similar policy (*Arkangel*, 4, 1991: 1).

The attitude of the anti-vivisection groups is more ambiguous. From the beginning to the mid-1980s, the BUAV was regarded as the Sinn Féin of the animal rights movement, refusing to condemn the activities of the ALF, allegedly using material gained from illegal acts and even providing the ALF with office space. Indeed, the BUAV was the one mainstream organisation that supporters of the ALF focused on primarily because of its ripeness for takeover in the 1970s (see Chapter 2). Although there were disputes about the use of violence, it is clear that the BUAV wholeheartedly supported direct action in this period (Henshaw, 1989: 159–64). In recent years, however, it has become detached from the activities of the ALF, preferring to concentrate on the kind of mainstream campaigning that was described in the previous chapter. The NAVS, although condemning the more violent activities, still regards break-ins in a favourable light, regularly publicising them and the information they provide. It has always, though, kept the ALF at arm's length and is often defensive when questioned about its attitude towards direct action (see below).

The effectiveness of direct action

Leaving aside, for the moment, the issue of whether or not violent and/or illegal direct action is, in principle, justified, it is appropriate initially to consider to what extent such activity is tactically effective. On this issue, opinions within the animal protection movement are divided. Certainly there are strong grounds for suggesting that at least some types of direct action are extremely useful whilst it is undoubtedly true that other, more extreme, versions risk alienating public opinion.

Above all on the benefit side, the classic ALF tactic of breaking into laboratories and the undercover work of activists disguised as employees has provided a great deal of the material used in anti-vivisection campaigns. For obvious reasons, animal experimenters are unwilling to allow general access to their places of work. This is not primarily because they feel guilty about the work they do (although some might) but because, probably correctly, they feel that the public (particularly when information is filtered through the popular press) would be swayed by the emotion of the issue, consequently overestimating the degree of animal suffering involved and underestimating the potential human benefits that might accrue from such work. As a result, written and visual documentation of what goes on in laboratories is, particularly in Britain, difficult to come by. The published papers of scientists can be consulted, but only a tiny proportion of the animal work done is written up in this form and obviously any maltreatment of animals is not going to be revealed. So, the vast majority of the cases we have mentioned in previous chapters – the cruelty to non-human primates which led to the prosecution of Taub and the closing down of the Pennsylvania head injury laboratory (in America), the removal of Felberg's licence and the HLS allegations (in Britain) to name but four, which have provided enormous propaganda coups for the animal protection movement – would simply not have occurred without direct action.

In addition to the information gathering produced by break-ins, advocates also point to the fact that animals are usually 'liberated' in raids on laboratories (and, to a lesser extent, factory farms), and rescued from possible pain and suffering and almost certain eventual death. The animal research community often claim that this is irresponsible either because the rescued (or stolen, depending on your point of view) animals are incapable of survival in the wild or because they would make unsuitable pets. Whether or not this is true (and information on their destinations is of course clouded in secrecy), since the animals may have suffered and would almost certainly have died in the laboratory anyway, it is unlikely that their treatment will be any worse in the hands of the animal liberators. Certainly, we have no reason to believe that the animals taken are not generally treated with care and responsibility. Indeed, whatever else may be said about the activists involved, it is faintly ridiculous, given their beliefs and the lengths to which they are prepared to go to follow them, to suggest that they would do otherwise.

As we shall see below, the major criticism of the kind of destructive direct action we have described is that it is likely to alienate public opinion. It should be noted here that, for many direct actionists, this misses the point. Indeed, the very reason why many resort to direct action is their (often understandable) frustration at the failure of traditional pressure group activity to produce results. Rather, the alternative strategy is aimed at directly damaging the economic interests of those who use animals. Leaving aside the question of whether they are right to argue that fundamental change can never come about through the normal political channels, it is without doubt true that the activities of the ALF do cost their victims financially.

Every laboratory break-in requires (sometimes extensive) repairs, extra security, the purchase of more animals and higher insurance premiums. Ironically, as a result of the threat, many animal research establishments have turned into fortresses with video surveillance and barbed wire protecting windowless buildings. The prison-like environment often created is a gift to the animal protection movement since it fuels the impression, which anti-vivisectionists want to give, that researchers have something to hide, and aids the comparison, often made by the radicals, with the concentration camps of history, with the animals playing the role of the Jews and the researchers their Nazi guards. Likewise, the property of every butcher, furrier and meat trader attacked has to be repaired and more effectively defended. Finally, the adulteration, or threats of adulteration, of supermarket products has cost companies a great deal of money. It is estimated, for instance, that the manufacturers of Mars Bars lost £6 million as a result of the hoax in 1984 (Henshaw, 1989: 10). It is not just the financial cost that is relevant here but also the non-economic impact of attacks on the victims. One could quite forgive a scientist, for instance, for deciding to stop using animals as a result of the continual threat of attack, or a butcher or furrier for throwing in the towel after yet another window has been broken or lock super glued. There is no evidence that substantial numbers have done so, but one can see the possibility that they might.

There is no doubt, however, that direct action has its disadvantages, the importance of which varies with different types of activity. It is possible, firstly, to exaggerate the positive benefits of direct action. Those individual animals that are 'rescued' from laboratories obviously benefit, but this only involves a tiny proportion of the laboratory animal stock. Similarly, hunt saboteurs cannot be everywhere at once and foxes are still hunted and killed in large numbers. There *has* been a significant decline in the fur trade, but this has come about due to the lack of demand for fur (itself partly to do with a successful traditional pressure group campaign) rather than attacks on the suppliers. It is probably true that some retailers have stopped selling furs because of attacks, or the threat of them, from animal rights activists, but it is surely implausible to suggest that so many outlets would have closed had selling furs remained a profitable business with people still wanting to buy them in large quantities. Similarly, the number of scientific procedures using animals has fallen over the past twenty years or so but this has not come about primarily as a result of ALF attacks but as the consequence of a number of interrelated factors involving financial restrictions, the greater use of alternatives and public opposition (again precipitated by lawful campaigning) to some forms of animal testing.

The point is then that direct attacks on the users of animals are unlikely (unless they reach hitherto unparalleled levels) to lead to the achievement of desired objectives without corresponding legislative initiatives and alterations in consumer behaviour of the type referred to in the previous chapter. This would not be a problem if it could be said with some certainty that direct action does not hinder attempts to influence public opinion and public authorities. The major criticism from sections of the animal protection movement, however, is that this is precisely what it does. The media emphasis on the extreme forms of direct action, it is argued, discredits the whole of the movement since the more moderate groups are tarred with the same brush. In addition, attention is diverted away from the issues on to the nature of the activities themselves – their threat to public safety and what can be done to stop them.

In assessing the strategic validity of direct action, we need to distinguish between different varieties of direct action. There is little doubt that violence directed against people or which threatens their safety is not popular. That does not mean, however, that other forms of direct action are regarded in the same light. Indeed, laboratory break-ins and undercover work, for instance, receive remarkably few criticisms. Not only have the groups who are dubious about the moral and tactical validity of this form of direct action benefited from the information provided, but the media too have quite happily used it without passing critical comment on the way it was obtained. Even these non-violent, direct action strategies are problematic though. As a result of laboratory raids scientists have increasingly hidden behind their windowless buildings refusing, for fear of attack, to discuss their work in public. Thus, there is precious little dialogue between the scientific community and the animal protection movement. For many radical activists, of course, this is a good thing. An alternative view is that, in a world where science still has enormous public prestige, such a dialogue is essential if governments are going to listen to proposals for reform. In addition, although it is obviously important, and quite correct, to distinguish between violent and non-violent versions of direct action, these subtle nuances may well be lost on a public not widely versed in the intricacies of the issues. In this context, it may well be wise for the animal protection movement to remain as law abiding as possible since to be associated with violence in any form can be extremely dangerous.

This is to assume, of course, that the use of terrorist tactics is counter-productive. Superficially, at least, the impact has been mixed. On the positive side, it could be argued that it serves a

useful function for the moderate groups, enabling them to claim
that if some of their objectives are not met there is the likelihood
of an escalation of direct action (Hollands, 1980: 153; Ryder,
1989: 279, 284). Such a ploy obviously depends upon these
groups being able to distinguish themselves from the direct
actionists. The RSPCA has clearly been able to do this, but the
more radical animal rights groups have been less successful and
their leaders are often put on the defensive when asked to
condemn direct action or to confirm that they have used material
gained from illegal acts.

It is possible to claim, in addition, that even though the positive results of direct action have been limited, it has not had
much of a negative impact. It has not, as we have seen,
prevented the general rise in membership and donations to the
animal protection movement in general. Similarly, the planting
of incendiary devices in department stores selling furs did not
appear to hinder the law-abiding anti-fur campaign. Of course,
the validity of this argument probably depends upon the level of
activity. An escalation of violence against people may well
change public opinion dramatically. In this sense, the animal
protection movement has been very lucky that no one has been
killed as a result of direct action (and it should be noted that
the objective of some of it *has* been to cause death or serious
injury). Had one fireman died in the course of fighting a
department store blaze or had the child who was the innocent
victim of a bomb aimed at the Bristol University scientist been
killed, there could have been a reaction which would have
severely damaged the animal protection cause. This leads to the
rather paradoxical conclusion that the terrorist tactics of animal
rights activists have not had much of a negative impact because
they have failed to achieve their objectives. The question to ask
is – Can the movement on behalf of animals risk the consequences of terrorist 'successes' in the future?

Political obligations and animal rights

The rest of this chapter is concerned with the extent to which
illegal direct action is justified as a matter of principle. This is a
hugely complex question which involves the relationship between
three factors: the moral status of animals; the nature of the illegal

activity; and the nature of the political system within which this activity takes place.

In this section, we deal with the relationship between holding a philosophical conviction that animals have rights and the practical defence of these rights. Here, I think, the implications are profound. It is no accident that the use of direct action in defence of animals has burgeoned at precisely the moment when a concerted philosophical attempt to justify granting rights to them has occurred. Indeed, activists regularly justify breaking the law on the grounds that they are obeying a higher moral law which must take precedence (Henshaw, 1989: 83–4).

By granting rights, we build protective fences around individuals in order to prevent their most important interests from being sacrificed except in the most exceptional circumstances. They cannot, for instance, be legislated away even if the decision to infringe rights is arrived at through the use of democratic mechanisms. The infringement of some rights is, in any case, not compatible with democracy. Thus, the right to vote, free speech and freedom of association are essential prerequisites of a society in which democratic norms operate. Other rights, and in particular the right to life, are not essential elements of a democratic system although they may obviously be regarded as desirable for other reasons. A society based on act-utilitarian principles, for instance, would not guarantee a right to life and yet Bentham and his disciple, James Mill, put forward the classic defence of democracy on utilitarian grounds (Barker, 1937).

Clearly, then, if we grant rights to animals these rights are infringed on a daily basis and the nature of the political system in which this occurs has no bearing upon this fact. In particular, we cannot say that infringing the rights of animals can be excused or treated less seriously in some way just because the decision to allow these rights to be violated was arrived at through democratic procedures. The implications of this for the necessity of direct action are clear. Whether this justifies the extreme forms of violent action that we have described in this chapter is a moot point. To risk killing innocents as a by-product of the campaign against those involved directly with the use of animals, for instance, would not seem to be justified on the grounds that equally important rights risk being violated in the process. The case of those involved directly with the exploitation of animals, though, is a different matter entirely since, by violating the rights of animals, they lose the protection afforded to them by the very same rights. Thus, if my life is seriously threatened I have the right to defend myself even if this means infringing the right to life of the person doing the threatening. Crucially, in addition, if an individual whose rights are being violated cannot defend themselves then any third party who is aware of this should not stand idly by but is entitled, and indeed required, to intervene to stop the rights violation. Thus, as Regan points out (1984: 249), his respect principle 'imposes the prima facie duty to assist those who are the victims of injustice at the hands of others'.

Many, no doubt, would disagree with these conclusions but it is important to recognise why they would do so. There is nothing controversial about the way in which they are derived from the granting of rights to animals. What is open to question is whether animals do indeed have rights in the first place – and particularly the right to life. To see that this is so it is useful to substitute humans for animals as the recipients of rights in the above arguments. If we do, it quickly becomes apparent that the conclusions are not unreasonable. Indeed, the gross violation of the most significant interests of individuals involved does not have a parallel in the modern Western world and we would have to look to the most despicable regimes of the past, or some of those existing today in certain parts of the world, to find an adequate comparison. The one exception perhaps is that of abortion and it is significant to recognise the similarities between the arguments of the animal rightists and the anti-abortionists. Both claim that their cause is based on a higher moral law and elements within both camps have resorted to violent direct action (attacks on abortion clinics have been particularly prevalent in the United States) which they believe is justified in order to protect fundamental rights. Without wanting to enter into a detailed comparison here, it might just be noted that more animals suffer and die at the hands of humans than do human foetuses (assuming they *can* suffer) and it is, at the very least, open to debate that a healthy adult animal is a more worthy candidate for moral concern.

Given the strong case for what would be regarded as extreme forms of direct action in defence of animal rights it is something of an anti-climax, albeit an understandable one, that Regan himself fails to draw the revolutionary conclusions that appear logically to follow from his philosophical arguments. Rather than support direct action enthusiastically, Regan, like many of the leading exponents of animal rights, is very cautious. He does not say anything concrete about strategy in his major work, but in other places he has extolled the virtues of Gandhian principles of non-violent civil disobedience (indeed it was Gandhi's writings which converted Regan to the animal rights cause in the first place). Thus, Regan does not oppose breaking into laboratories in order to gain information and free animals (and it would be strange if he did oppose this since he regards animals as persons who cannot be regarded as property which can be stolen), but causing damage to property and threatening violence towards those who exploit animals is illegitimate (Regan, 1984: 24–5, 174–8). One is reminded here of Brian Barry's rather unkind comment on John Rawls' similarly limited conception of civil disobedience. Thus, Regan's support for very mild forms of illegal direct action is, in the face of what he regards as such fundamental injustices, 'reminiscent of the horrible little girl in the "Just William" stories whose all-purpose threat was "If you don't do it I'll scream and scream until I make myself sick"' (Barry, 1973: 153).

To be fair to Regan and others, though, their opposition to more extreme versions of direct action is not based on a moral argument so much as a tactical objection that such action is likely to be counterproductive and, as we have seen, they are probably correct (Regan, 1984: 182). Nevertheless, for someone who objects so much to utilitarianism, it is odd that Regan adopts precisely this approach on tactical grounds – that direct action should be undertaken only in so far as it is likely to produce overall desirable consequences. Certainly, it is likely that many of those who use direct action against animal exploiters do so not primarily because they believe that in the long run it will produce beneficial consequences for animals in general, but because they regard it as morally correct to intervene whenever possible if this helps particular animals *whatever* the long-term consequences. On the rights view, of course, they would seem to be justified.

Democracy, pressure groups and the distribution of political influence

Imagine that animals do not have rights, or that we are wrong to draw the conclusion that at least certain forms of illegal direct action are justified as a consequence of granting rights to them. Is there still a case for breaking the law? Here, it is commonly assumed that this depends upon the way in which a decision we are considering disobeying has been made. More precisely, it is argued that a decision made by democratic means – by, that is, a majority verdict after free and open debate – is in some way more legitimate than a decision taken in another way and therefore we are more obliged to obey it. As Peter Singer (1974) convincingly shows, this assumption stems from the equal role assigned to individuals in democratic decision making and the consequent 'fair compromise' between competing demands that results. In such a system, disobeying the law is illegitimate because it represents an attempt to gain more influence than is due thereby undermining this balance, whereas a decision reached without a fair compromise would not have the same legitimacy.

Disobeying the law would still be justified in a fair compromise system, Singer argues, but only (if we exclude disobedience on the grounds of a deeply held moral conviction) if there is no other way of getting a fair hearing for a particular case. Thus a democratic decision may have been taken but it may not have been taken with all the relevant views and facts being available (Singer, 1974: 72–83). There are obvious problems in determining when a particular case has not had a proper hearing, not least because there is always a tendency for those whose case has been rejected to assume automatically that if only the public had heard the full story they would have adopted an alternative point of view. Nevertheless, there would seem to be a case for some direct action by the animal protection movement on these grounds. In particular, as we have indicated before, the use of animals in scientific procedures is a notoriously secretive business and there is a strong case for saying that the anti-vivisectionist case is not heard properly as long as the public is not allowed to see and read about what goes on in laboratories. Similarly, those environmental groups who use direct action to reveal the often illegal activities of whalers or fishermen or ivory traders are, despite the fact that they might break the law themselves in the process, behaving consistently with democratic principles by revealing information to the public which may affect future decisions.

By no means all forms of direct action used by the animal protection movement, though, are justified by the need to present a fair case. There is a considerable difference between actions that help a group to persuade the majority to adopt its point of view and those that seek to prevent, through coercion and intimidation, a majority decision being carried out. Clearly, a central purpose of the ALF and other associated individuals is to do precisely this. Put simply, in the context of animal experimentation, then, there is a case in a democracy for breaking into laboratories in order to provide written and visual documentation of animal use which would not otherwise be made available to the public. On the other hand, it is illegitimate in a democracy to damage laboratories, intimidate employees and take animals from them.

It is obviously the case that a 'pure' fair compromise system can only operate effectively within a small-scale community where everyone is directly and equally involved in decision making. Singer (1974: 13–15), for instance, illustrates the principle by reference to the decision making structure of a small Oxford college. No modern complex society comes close to meeting the criteria for a direct democracy in practice and it is doubtful if any of them ever could. As a consequence, we can only talk of approximations towards political equality. In such societies, elections obviously provide an important means by which the views of individuals are represented in the decision making arena. There are, though, obvious problems with elections as a tool of representation. In the first place, they are only held intermittently and, in Britain at least, the electoral mechanism rarely ensures that the governing party is elected with a majority of the votes cast. Even if it were, it is by no means clear what the electorate want their government to do since each party puts forward a multiplicity of policy proposals in their manifesto and the voters are limited to choosing between a small number of alternative programmes all of which may exclude a policy commitment desired by a large number of the electorate (Singer, 1974: 112–20).

Because of this, political scientists have increasingly recognised that it is the system of group politics which holds the key to the question of political power. The importance of groups was first recognised by Bentley (1967) and his analysis was built upon by Truman (1951). Groups representing every conceivable interest and cause exist to lobby decision making bodies continually on a more or less permanent basis and it is this pressure, rather than the individual choices made by voters in elections, which, above all else, determines policy outputs. It is an analysis of group politics, then, which will tell us how far any particular decision or decisions made, including those involving animal protection, approximate towards the fair compromise ideal and thus the point at which it is legitimate to prevent or obstruct the carrying out of such decisions. Such a point would seem to be reached when a particular interest or set of interests exercises *undue* influence in the policy making process in the sense that its influence is not warranted by the support for its demands within the wider society. In this situation, rather than enhancing democracy, the pressure group system actually undermines the already limited impact of elections. Determining the extent to which undue influence is exercised by those groups who use animals is a huge task and one that is well beyond the scope of this book. What we can do, however, is to chart the course which such an analysis would follow.

The starting point for any analysis of pressure group politics is the so-called pluralist approach.[3] Pluralists argue that in liberal democracies the outputs of government are a reflection of the distribution of influence amongst groups and since there is no one dominant interest or set of interests these outputs remain responsive to the demands of society. Thus, the defining characteristic of a democracy is not majority rule but rule by minorities whereby a multiplicity of interests compete for the ear of government, thereby ensuring that power remains diffuse and fragmented (Dahl, 1956: 133–7). It is clear, of course, that, in reality, some groups have more resources than others and as a result are more influential, but this does not necessarily undermine the pluralist theory. Pluralists are not saying that groups have influence exactly in proportion to the numbers they represent but that there are no predominant classes, interests or groups whose preferences prevail in all issue areas at all times. Minorities rule rather than a minority class or elite group.

government with great authority. Sectional groups are always likely to have an advantage here since, by definition, the potential membership of cause groups is the whole of society, and consumers, a particular target of the animal protection movement, are notoriously difficult to mobilise. In addition, as Mancur Olson (1965) emphasised, sectional groups can offer inducements in order to attract members (see Chapter 2). For one thing, they pursue the self-interest of members but many private benefits – such as pension and insurance schemes – are also often available.

It is also undoubtedly true that some interests exercise influence in a second, less obtrusive way, as a result of their structural position in the economy. This has been most notably emphasised in the work of the American political scientist Charles Lindblom (1977). Lindblom argues that business interests hold a privileged position in capitalist societies deriving from their control over production, investment and employment decisions – decisions which are vital for everyone in society. Thus, government action is constrained by the need to retain the confidence of the business community (secured by not threatening their interests) since their chances of retaining power depend largely upon the state of the economy. This is particularly the case with multinational concerns that have the option of moving their operations to another country.

Clearly, much of this is applicable to those interests who benefit from the use of animals. Virtually all users of animals – from circuses to hunters – emphasise at some point in their defence that there would be economic consequences if their practices were curtailed or banned. The biggest effect would obviously centre on animal agriculture and experimentation. Even though there is a moral case for reforms to the system of factory farming and meat eating is unnecessary in dietary terms, the meat industry is important economically. Farming by itself employs very few but there are a whole range of other industries – concerned with agricultural chemicals (itself represented by the Agricultural Chemicals Association and the British Agrochemical Association), animal slaughter, animal by-products, meat packing and transporting, meat wholesaling and retailing to name but a few – who have a vested interest in the continuation of animal agriculture as a competitive concern. Thus, even reforms to animal agriculture, let alone its complete abolition, have their costs in terms of more expensive products which would be unpopular domestically and disadvantageous for export markets.

Similarly, as Robert Sharpe (1988: 59–65) has convincingly shown, in health terms we do not need so many drugs, many of which are either trivial or are replicas of those already existing. In addition, it is clearly not in the interests of drugs companies (nor the meat, dairy, tobacco, and alcohol industries for that matter) for governments to emphasise that the modern killer diseases are to a large extent preventable since the demand for their products (developed by using animals) would decline as would the consumption of products which are major causes of heart disease and cancer. Likewise, any reduction in the demand for drugs would have a knock-on effect on the contract laboratories that do most of the animal-based work and the breeders who supply the animals. But in terms of the economy the pharmaceutical companies (and the other related industries) are important. In 1983, for example, the twenty-five leading drug companies reported sales of a staggering US$35 billion. Significantly, the economic importance of the pharmaceutical industry was recognised in the 1983 White Paper introducing the government's proposed alternative to the 1876 Cruelty to Animals Act. 'The United Kingdom', it pointed out:

> has a large pharmaceutical industry which makes a large contribution to our balance of payments and employs 67,500 people. In devising new controls it is very important not to put industry at risk unnecessarily. (Sharpe, 1988: 122)

The implications of this unequal influence, if that is what it is, should be clear. As Peter Singer (1974: 123–4) points out, if groups:

> should find themselves faced with a law which they opposed, but was passed because of the disproportional influence of other groups, they cannot be urged to obey on the grounds that the pressure group system is a fair compromise.

Does this, then, justify breaking the law in pursuit of the protection of animals? Well, in order to answer the question in the affirmative we would have to show not only – as we have sought to do – that those groups which represent the interests of those who benefit from using animals *do* exercise influence but also that this influence is exercised so as to frustrate the democratic will. In general, it would seem that, in the context of animal protection at least, this is not the case.

Thus, even though the resources available to animal user groups are formidable, we should not neglect to consider the importance of public support which is available to all groups however rich or well organised they are. The analysis provided by Lindblom does show that groups who have important economic sanctions are valued by governments and the role of powerful vested industries that rely on the exploitation of animals is certainly worthy of more extensive study than can be provided here. A cursory glance reveals, however, that the economic benefits such groups provide are of value to society in general and there is little reason, in terms of the use of animals at least, to suspect that this does not meet with general approval. As Jordan and Richardson (1987: 81) point out, 'it is the essential point of the phenomenon that no conflict is recognised between what is "good for General Motors" and "good for the country"'. Unless we can show, then, that there is a fairly widespread desire for the economic benefits derived from the utili-sation of animals to take second place in the light of an awareness that what is done to animals is morally wrong, it cannot be said that undue influence is exercised by animal user groups. It may be that the public's desire for good health is being frustrated by the activities of powerful vested interests led by the pharmaceutical industry, but it *is* this desire and not their desire for the welfare of animals that is foremost here.

Given that we have placed great emphasis on the resource of public opinion, attitudes and values, there is another dimension to this argument which ought to be mentioned. Pluralists have often been criticised for deriving their conclusions from a decision making based methodology. It has been argued that this neglects the way in which power can be exercised in more subtle ways. In particular, the ability of powerful forces to exercise ideo-logical control whereby their interests become widely accepted through the moulding of people's wants is seen by some as crucial (Lukes, 1974: 21–5). Indeed, Lindblom (1977: 202) himself argues that another dimension of their privileged position is that 'businessmen achieve an indoctrination of citizens so that citizens' volitions serve not their own interests but the interests of businessmen'.

This would seem to be particularly relevant to the issue of animal use, since there is no doubt that the meat and pharmaceutical industries engage in a continual effort to convince people that eating meat and having a wide range of drugs available is both morally correct and materially advantageous. Both have the advantage of being able to promote their products in a favourable light whilst, in Britain at least, animal protection groups, even if they had the income to compete, are prevented from advertising on television. The images created by the promotion of meat products inevitably seek to disguise the sometimes grim realities of factory farming. Children are obviously a prime target. As Mason and Singer (1990: 109) explain, the meat and poultry industries in America 'sponsor colouring books and other materials for children that show farm animals in anthropomorphic, comic book fantasies. There is no hint, of course, of feed additives, stress, crowding or debeaking'. As a consequence, there is little pressure – except from the counterculture represented by the animal protection movement – for fundamental change.

It would be unwise to underestimate advertising as a means of shaping people's interests, but the problem with this kind of approach is that we can only speculate that if the public was aware of the issues in all their complexity (assuming they are not already), then it would then want reforms in the way animals are treated. But we simply cannot know if this is true. Indeed, there is a strong case for saying that it *is* in people's real interests to continue supporting the exploitation of animals because economic benefits do accrue from it. In addition, we should not neglect the considerable income at the disposal of the animal protection movement which, as we have illustrated in earlier chapters, has had an impact on the way in which people think about the way humans treat animals.

This chapter has considered the use of direct action by elements of the animal protection movement. We saw that although damage to property is a common direct action strategy, unpremeditated violence, or the threat of it, has played a relatively small role. In assessing direct action, a distinction was made between its usefulness as a strategy and the extent to which it is morally and politically justified. In moral terms, the granting of rights to animals leads to the conclusion that direct action in their defence is not only permissible but also a moral duty, although whether this justifies some of the more extreme actions involving violence is an open question. In political terms, it was argued that a system of decision making that allows for what Singer calls a 'fair compromise' between competing interests does place constraints on disobeying the law. In reality, however, modern industrial societies can only provide mechanisms that approximate to this ideal of political equality. In the system of pressure group politics, powerful economic interests who benefit from using animals have considerable resources which seriously disadvantage the campaign for change. Although further research into the role of the key animal exploiters is needed, a preliminary examination would suggest that the animal protection movement can make considerable progress through the mobilisation of public opinion. That is not to say that such a task will be easy nor ultimately successful, but it does mean that participation in mainstream pressure group politics is still worthwhile.

Notes

1 Henshaw has written the only book-length study of the ALF and I have benefited from the information provided. It is not, it should be added, a particularly good book. Unduly repetitive, it is a journalistic account rather than a scholarly work. More seriously, the author is extremely hostile to the direct actionists and some of his factual assertions are disputed by activists. Clearly, the book does not adequately distinguish between the various parts of the animal protection movement (he describes Singer, for instance, as an advocate of rights) and the overall impression given, although not intentionally, is that animal rights are synonymous with violent direct action.
2 Ironically, the publicity value of the department store fires just before Christmas in 1988 was severely reduced by the Lockerbie disaster which occurred the following day. (See *The Times*, 21, 22 December 1988.)
3 There is no one definitive pluralist account, but the approach is particularly associated with Robert Dahl (1956). For a concise review of the literature see Jordan and Richardson (1987).

Conclusion

That humans exploit animals is indisputable. Of greater import is the extent to which this exploitation is justified. Here, the challenge to the prevailing moral orthodoxy – which stipulates that humans are entitled to kill, torture and cage animals providing that significant benefits accrue – has had a profound philosophical and political impact. In philosophical terms, the sustained attempt by Regan, Singer and others to set out a rational case for granting animals a higher moral status has revolutionised the teaching of applied ethics. More importantly, it has struck a chord with a new generation of activists who have used these ideas to radicalise the dormant animal protection movement which now provides an unprecedented threat to those who have a vested interest in continuing to exploit animals.

The philosophical challenge of animal rights

As Chapter 1 sought to show, the orthodox position that humans have a superior moral status to animals is surprisingly fragile. The challenge to it comes in two main forms. The weaker version associated with Singer demands that we consider interests equally and since animals have an interest in avoiding pain and suffering there is no reason for giving preferential treatment to a human's interest in avoiding pain and suffering. Singer's approach differs in two main respects from the stronger version associated with Regan and others. In the first place, by emphasising sentiency as the key criterion for moral standing, Singer has difficulty objecting to the painless killing of animals whilst Regan wants to claim that animals, like humans, are 'subjects-of-a-life' who can be harmed in similar ways to humans by death. Secondly, as a utilitarian, Singer has to calculate the overall consequences of an act in terms of its satisfaction of preferences before it can be morally judged, whereas Regan puts forward a deontological rights-based theory which explicitly prohibits such a cost–benefit analysis.

Chapters 3 to 6 revealed that the granting of a higher moral status to animals has considerable consequences for the ways in which they are currently treated. The rights view in particular prohibits (as immoral practices) circuses, most zoos, dolphinaria, and – the twin bastions of animal exploitation – the rearing and slaughtering of animals for food and their use for experimental purposes. Only the keeping of companion animals (under certain circumstances), the euthanasia of irreversibly sick and suffering animals and some conservation strategies (not including those which involve culling some in order to save the many or those which aim to preserve stocks to facilitate continued 'harvesting') escape from immediate moral condemnation.

The application of Singer's equal consideration theory is not so clear-cut although it is potentially as radical. In particular, it would seem that painlessly killing an animal for food, or for use in the laboratory, cannot be an issue of moral concern for a theory based upon sentiency. Furthermore, even though pain and suffering are to be considered as morally important and do occur in both of the above practices, this does not provide for a cast-iron rejection of them. In the first place, it is not inconceivable in principle that animal agriculture could be reformed so that pain and suffering are minimised to such an extent that they become morally acceptable, although Singer is right to say that this is extremely unlikely to happen. Secondly, the infliction of even substantial suffering, is not, on its own, sufficient to rule out an activity on utilitarian grounds. Rather, it is the *total* amount of benefits and costs produced by an act that has to be considered and it can be argued that, in the cases of both animal agriculture and animal experimentation, considerable benefits do result. Singer's utilitarianism, of course, is non-speciesist and so, although it adopts the traditional consequentialist approach, human and animal pain and suffering are to count equally. As we saw in Chapter 5, this would make it justifiable to use humans in the laboratory if by so doing the interests of other humans and animals are maximised. The fact that humans are not used in this way rules out the present use of animals as illegitimate because it is speciesist.

The political challenge of animal rights

These ideas, of course, have played a major part in the revitalisation and radicalisation of the animal protection movement in the last two decades. As Chapter 2 documented, this revitalisation is evident in terms of the number of new groups that have recently arisen, the reported increase in membership of most groups and, as a cause and effect of these, the emergence of an attentive public, more prepared to be vegetarian, to buy only cruelty-free products and to oppose activities such as hunting. This revitalisation has been inextricably linked with the growing radicalisation of the animal protection movement. Many of the new groups are rights-based, advocating the abolition of animal agriculture and experimentation on the grounds that they are immoral. No utilitarian calculation here but a straightforward application of inviolable rights so that, whatever the beneficial consequences, infringement of them is forbidden.

Inevitably, this new radicalism has come into conflict with the old welfare-based ideology and there has been considerable infighting within the animal protection movement as a result. In Britain, this has centred on the RSPCA as the radicals have sought to gain control, thereby capitalising on its wealth and respectability. The fact that the RSPCA is now much more active and radical (although not yet converted to a rights position) is a testament to the effectiveness of this challenge and a potent symbol of the changing face of animal protection. Another is the emergence of grassroots activism, something which has been frowned upon in the past as a result of the inherent elitism of animal welfarism. Armed with a sense of moral outrage and the slogans derived from animal rights philosophy, activists have taken to the streets as never before, demanding change from government and those actively involved in the exploitation of animals.

This brings us to strategy. Chapter 7 warned us against assuming that the absolutist objectives of animal rights groups automatically translate into an absolutist, all or nothing strategy whereby no compromises are acceptable. Thus, we found that

Clive Hollands and Advocates for Animals (then the Scottish Society for the Prevention of Vivisection), despite their commitment to animal rights and the complete abolition of vivisection, led the attempt (within CRAE) to influence the content of the government's proposals to reform the 1876 Cruelty to Animals Act. Indeed, such was their inclination to negotiate with politicians, civil servants and representatives of the users of animals, that insider status was granted, a relatively rare feat for a cause group. Similarly, CIWF have recognised the need to adopt a step-by-step approach and have sought (with some success) to lessen the suffering of farm animals here and now whilst not losing sight of their long-term abolitionist objective. It is clear, though, that these are the exceptions. For the bulk of the animal rights movement, the long-term abolitionist objective is at the forefront of the campaign. As a result, animal rights groups remain outsiders, suspicious of the deradicalising effect of the executive policy making process and not invited inside because of their unwillingness to play by the unwritten rules of the game.

The reforming potential of the moral orthodoxy

There may be a strong case for granting a higher moral status to animals but it should be said that no country in the world has conceded this case by adopting a non-speciesist approach to legislation. Thus, the achievements of the animal protection movement so far (with the exception of some conservation developments) have all come within the confines of the moral orthodoxy. Stricter regulations on factory farming and animal experimentation have been implemented or considered in a number of countries, but the assumption that humans are entitled to exploit animals when it benefits them to do so has not been seriously questioned by public authorities. It is therefore not surprising that attention has focused on those areas of animal use – cosmetics testing, the fur trade, hunting, dog fighting, circuses, dissection in the classroom and so on – where the necessity of inflicting suffering on animals can be more effectively challenged.

There are those who suggest that a liberal animal rights agenda is not the most appropriate ideological location for animal protection, and we should look elsewhere, to socialist and feminist accounts in particular, to genuinely improve the position of animals. Others, and most notably Francione (1995; 1996), suggest that unless we dispense with the property status of animals, and accord legal and moral rights to them, there is little hope of improving the position of animals. That is, animal welfare does not work because the most trivial human interests will always justify sacrificing the most fundamental interests of animals. Francione, therefore, is very critical of those he describes as 'New Welfarists', who accept the validity of a piecemeal reformist strategy gradually increasing the protection afforded to animals within the dominant discourse.

The whole tenor of this book is designed to dispute the redundancy of a reformist approach to improving the position of animals, and to promote, in particular, the utility of the concept of unnecessary suffering. I argued in Chapter 1 that the property status of animals, whilst inimical to the achievement of animal rights, is not inconsistent with reforms designed to improve the welfare of animals. The moral orthodoxy is very imprecise since the notion of unnecessary suffering is extremely difficult to define precisely. But this provides an opportunity for reformers gradually to extend the range of activities that humans regard as unnecessary. Such an approach is much more likely to succeed than one which postulates that animals should be protected, irrespective of the human benefits that will be forfeited as a result. This point, of course, has not been lost on sections of the animal protection movement. The classic example of this approach in action has been the modern anti-vivisection campaign described in Chapter 5. Even though anti-vivisection groups think that it is morally wrong to use animals as laboratory subjects, whatever the benefits, they have taken a conscious decision to concentrate on disputing both the necessity and very existence of those benefits. Thus, cosmetic testing, the production of 'me too' drugs, and the search for cures for diseases which are largely preventable, have been attacked as unnecessary even if animal use has proved useful. In addition, it has been claimed that animal experimentation is, in any case, of little utility (and can be counterproductive). This twin-pronged attack has proved very effective, changing consumer behaviour and putting the research community on the defensive.

All this is not to say that the philosophical and political challenge to the moral orthodoxy has had little effect. On the contrary, as it becomes more widely recognised that animals not only are sentient but also have considerable mental capacities then it will become increasingly difficult to deny them greater consideration. For many people, the point at which inflicting suffering on animals becomes unnecessary has moved to encompass more and more uses to which they have been put. Thirty years ago, for instance, the use of animals for testing cosmetics, or the use of their fur for making coats, was condemned by only a small minority. Now, both practices are widely frowned upon. There are hardly any fur retailers (in Britain) left and the British government has ended the testing of cosmetics on animals. As the radical challenge continues, it is possible to envisage the unnecessary suffering line shifting further as greater awareness of the ability of animals to suffer and the inessential nature of many of the human benefits becomes more apparent.

The advantage, then, of focusing on the flexibility provided by the moral orthodoxy is that, by working within society's widely accepted norms, the chances of persuading the public and decision makers of the need for reform are enhanced. Much was made by Francione of my assertion, in the first edition of this book, that it is difficult to think of legislation improving the welfare of animals that has seriously damaged the interests of the animal users (quoted in Francione, 1996: 137), thus demonstrating, for him, that animal welfare does not work. Two points need to be made in response to this. Firstly, the usefulness of the notion of unnecessary suffering is that, not only does it avoid the need to get involved with contentious philosophical debates about the moral status of animals, but it also, by definition, minimises the conflict between human and animal interests because we are only concerned with ending the suffering that is deemed to serve no significant human interests. In reality, of course, the notion of unnecessary suffering is inherently subjective and is not merely about establishing the accuracy of empirical data. Francione (2000), for instance, wants to argue that virtually all uses of animals are unnecessary, but this position is open to debate, and relies upon us accepting the accuracy of his empirical data and his interpretation of what should be deemed unnecessary.

The second response is to suggest that, since the first edition of this book was written, the prospects for animal welfare, at least in Britain, have improved, and there is some evidence that the dominance of economic interests, particularly in agricultural policy, has begun to wane. Yes, it is true that the number of animals used in scientific procedures has increased in Britain, after many years of decline, and that the genetic engineering of animals raises all kinds of moral issues – although it is debatable how far they fundamentally alter the treatment of animals. On the other hand, as we have seen throughout this book, the election of a Labour government in 1997 has coincided with some beneficial outcomes for animals (Ryder, 2000). The list of achievements includes the banning of puppy farms, a ban on the testing of alcohol, tobacco and cosmetic products on animals, the ban on sow stalls and tethers, tighter controls on live exports, a ban on deer hunting on Forestry Commission land, and a ban on fur farming. Moreover, a ban on fox and deer hunting and hare coursing is tantalisingly close. More significant still, there are signs that at the EU level, concern for animal welfare is growing, and that the position of agribusiness is weakening. Thus, the status of animals has changed in the EU treaty, and agreement has been reached to ban battery cages, the veal crate, and sow stalls and tethers. Arguably more significant still, the Commission has suggested far-reaching reforms to the CAP that would radically shift the agenda from agricultural intensification towards environmental protection and animal welfare.

Throughout the world, of course, the attention given to animal welfare varies. For example, whilst the rights of animals have been enshrined in the German constitution, Francione is right to point out that less has been achieved for animals in the United States than in most of Europe. No federal legislation exists to regulate the raising of animals for food and extremely intensive systems remain largely unchallenged. Likewise, although there is extensive federal legislation concerned with animal experimentation, there is little political control over what is done to animals in the laboratory, as opposed to their general living environment. There are various reasons for this, none of which relate to the fact that animals are regarded as the property of humans. First is the very genuine economic and political clout of the animal use industry. What is lacking too, from the perspective of animal protection, is sustained and intense public support for animal welfare, let alone more radical reforms. There is also, finally, a very strong ideological bias in the United States in favour of moral freedom and technological advance, both of which work against the well-being of animals. Despite these constraints, the fact that claims of concern about animal welfare are now commonplace in the United States represents encouraging progress from a time when the very existence of moral worth for animals was questioned by so many.

Slaughterhouses made of glass

Without doubt the biggest obstacle to improving the welfare of animals is the economic benefits that derive from their use. As we saw in Chapter 8, the meat and pharmaceutical industries are given a privileged status by government not just because of their lobbying prowess but also because of their structural position in the economy. Along with other economic interests, they make crucial decisions which will affect any government's prospects for re-election and so they have to be treated with kid gloves. In these circumstances, decision makers are not likely to accede to the fundamental demands of the animal protection movement and this of course is why the absolutist animal rights groups are kept at arm's length. It is significant to note that the only place where the economic interests of humans have been seriously damaged by the protection of animals is in the developing world where native people, whose livelihoods are threatened by the attempt to save endangered species, are often powerless in the face of Western conservationists and their own governments eager to rake in the income from tourism. As Chapter 6 pointed out, the West exhibits a remarkable degree of hypocrisy by continuing to deny these people the opportunity to benefit from the utilisation of animals (endangered or not), whilst it continues to benefit itself from the exploitation of many domesticated species.

For many, economic benefits are not an obstacle to reform but the very reason why reform should not be implemented. They are the last defence of those who want to maintain the status quo. As Passmore (1974: 191) points out:

> the spectacle of an unemployed man or an old-aged pensioner faced by rising prices is at least as pitiable as the spectacle of an oil-soaked mutton bird. Arguments which direct attention to economic costs are not necessarily specious.

Such an assertion is morally dubious even if one accepts the moral orthodoxy, but the animal protection movement should not ignore the reality that animal exploitation does result in economic gain. Arguments about economic costs are often about the equity of competition between states. Greater protection for animals in one country will put it at an economic disadvantage if other countries do not follow suit. If, for example, one country bans battery cages for hens, its egg industry is put at a serious disadvantage when it has to compete with egg producers in other countries who are not similarly restricted. Likewise, stricter regulations on the production of drugs (limited perhaps only to those which are regarded as necessary) would have serious repercussions in terms of loss of export markets, the relocation of multinational companies and, of course, unemployment. One solution to this problem is to standardise practices internationally. At present there is no world-wide convention on animal welfare (as distinct from those concerned with wildlife conservation) and it is utopian to expect one to emerge in the near future. Nevertheless, there is certainly a great deal of scope for the European Union to impose uniform standards and, as we have seen, it is beginning to take animal welfare more seriously.

Many animal protection groups, on the other hand, regard the moral imperatives as so important that reform must, if necessary, override economic interests. To achieve reform here, though, it is necessary to compete with the powerful economic interests who, as we indicated, are given a privileged position by government. Not surprisingly, some radicals, despairing at the slow process of legislative reform and what they see as a biased system of pressure group politics, have embarked on a campaign of economic sabotage. In moral terms, the granting of rights to animals does justify direct action irrespective of the nature of the decision making mechanism and only tactical judgements as to its utility are relevant. In political terms, however, it was suggested that direct action which aims at preventing people from engaging in practices which are lawful is only justified if the decision to make them lawful occurred as a result of the exercise of undue influence. Whilst it would be true to say that those interests who benefit from the exploitation of animals are extremely powerful, their influence is not illegitimate because there is little evidence that the public in general would support stricter animal welfare laws (let alone the abolition of animal agriculture or experimentation) if that meant considerable economic sacrifice (which, at least in the short term, it might well do).

The consequence of this analysis is that the animal protection movement must continue to direct its attention towards public opinion, since only when people's attitudes towards animals change, and this is reflected in their consumer and voting behaviour, will the greater protection for animals, desired by the movement which campaigns on their behalf, become a realistic proposition. Such a task will not be easy but there are hopeful signs, not the least of which is the growth of the animal protection movement itself.

More abstractly, it is possible to detect a widespread, albeit underlying, unease about the treatment of animals which remains to be exploited. As Serpell (1986: 150–9) and others have demonstrated, this unease is indicated by the use of a whole set of devices in order to disguise the truth. The exploitation of animals is largely concealed from the public gaze. Factory-farmed and laboratory animals are kept in unmarked and impenetrable buildings so as not to arouse suspicion and slaughterhouses are situated away from centres of population, the sanitised end product on the supermarket shelf bearing little resemblance to the living, breathing animal that existed at the beginning of the process.[1] Even the terminology used to describe the various uses of animals is centred on concealing their true nature; the screams of laboratory animals become 'vocalisations', sea creatures are 'harvested' rather than killed, calf meat becomes veal and pig meat pork.

The animal protection movement has sought to undermine this subterfuge both by revealing, in all its glory, what is done to animals and by challenging the right of humans to do it. Many still look away when confronted, others persist in putting the interests of their own species first whatever the consequences to non-humans. The major obstacle remains economic self-interest, a powerful motivator. As Michael Fox (1983: 312), though, points out: 'In the final analysis surely the greater concern is poverty, not of the pocket, but of the spirit'. In this respect, unlike the animals, we have the privilege of choice.

Note

1 The title of this section was derived from a question posed by Tom
  Regan (1987: 67), 'How would we fare psychologically if the walls of
  slaughterhouses were made of glass? What would we feel and do if we
  saw the death of so-called "food animals"?'.

Bibliography

Adams, C. (1990) *The Sexual Politics of Meat: A Feminist Vegetarian Critical Theory*, New York: Continuum.

Adams, C. (1994) *Neither Man Nor Beast: Feminism and the Defence of Animals*, New York: Continuum.

Allaby, M. (1986) *Green Facts*, London: Hamlyn.

Animal Welfare Institute (1985) *Beyond the Laboratory Door*, Washington D.C.: AWI.

APC (2002) *Report of the Animal Procedures Committee for 2002.*

Bachrach, P. (1969) *The Theory of Democratic Elitism*, London: Little Brown.

Bachrach, P. and Baratz, M. (1962) 'The two faces of power', *American Political Science Review*, 56.

Ball, A. and Millard, F. (1986) *Pressure Politics in Industrial Societies*, Basingstoke: Macmillan.

Barker, E. (ed.) (1937) *James Mill's Essay on Government*, Cambridge: Cambridge University Press.

Barry, B. (1973) *The Liberal Theory of Justice*, Oxford: Oxford University Press.

Barry, B. (1989) *Theories of Justice*, Hemel Hempstead: Harvester-Wheatsheaf.

Barry, B. (1995) *Justice as Impartiality*, Oxford: Clarendon Press.

Bateson, P. (1986) 'When to experiment on animals', *New Scientist*, February.

Beattie, G. (1990) 'Throwing a badger to the pit bulls', *Guardian*, 17 May.

Benson, J. (1978) 'Duty and the beast', *Philosophy*, 53.

Bentham, J. (1948) *An Introduction to the Principles of Morals and Legislation*, New York: Hafner Press.

Bentley, A. (1967) *The Process of Government*, Cambridge, Mass: Harvard University Press.

Benton, T. (1993) *Natural Relations: Ecology, Social Justice and Animal Rights*, London: Verso.

Benton, T. and Redfearn, R. (1996) 'The politics of animal rights: where is the left', *New Left Review*, 215.

Blackman, D., Humphreys, P. and Todd, P. (eds) (1989) *Animal Welfare and the Law*, Cambridge: Cambridge University Press.

Boardman, R. (1981) *International Organisations and the Conservation of Nature*, London: Macmillan.

Bomberg, E. (1998) *Green Parties and Politics in the European Union*, London: Routledge.

Broom, D. (1989) 'Overview of British animal welfare', in Blackman et al., *Animal Welfare and the Law*.

Brophy, B. (1965) 'The rights of animals', *Sunday Times*, 10 October.

Brophy, B. (1979) 'The Darwinist's dilemma', in Paterson and Ryder, *Animals' Rights*.

Brown, P. (1990) 'Weeping and whaling', *Guardian*, 13 July.

Browne, A. (2002) 'Ten weeks to live', *Guardian*, 10 March.

Bryant, J. (1990) *Fettered Kingdoms*, Winchester: Fox Press.

Callicott, J. (1995) 'Animal liberation: a triangular affair', in R. Elliot (ed.), *Environmental Ethics*, Oxford: Oxford University Press.

Carruthers, P. (1992) *The Animals Issue*, Cambridge: Cambridge University Press.

Carter, P. (1991) 'Bartered babies', *BBC Wildlife Magazine*, April 1991.

Cavalieri, P. and Singer, P. (eds) *The Great Ape Project: Equality Beyond Humanity*, London: Fourth Estate.

Cherfas, J. (1988) *The Hunting of the Whale*, London: The Bodley Head.

Clark, S. (1984) *The Moral Status of Animals*, Oxford: Clarendon Press.

Clarke, P. and Linzey, A. (1990) *Political Theory and Animal Rights*, London: Pluto Press.

Clutterbuck, R. (ed.) *The Future of Political Violence*, Basingstoke: Macmillan.

Cooper, M. (1987) *An Introduction to Animal Law*, London: Academic Press.

Cotgrove, S. and Duff, A. (1980) 'Environmentalism, middle class radicalism and politics', *Sociological Review*, 28.

Cox, G. and Lowe, P. (1983) 'Countryside politics: goodbye to goodwill', *Political Quarterly*, 54.

Craig, F. (1990) *British General Election Manifestos 1959–87*, Aldershot: Gower.

Dahl, R. (1956) *Preface to Democratic Theory*, Chicago: University of Chicago Press.

Davies, E. (1989) 'Environmental health legislation affecting the welfare of animals', in Blackman, et al., *Animal Welfare and the Law*.

Dawkins, M. (1980) *Animal Suffering: The Science of Animal Welfare*, London: Chapman and Hall.

Day, D. (1987) *The Whale War*, London: Routledge and Kegan Paul.

DeGrazia, D. (1996) *Taking Animals Seriously: Mental Life and Moral Status*, Cambridge: Cambridge University Press.

DeGrazia, D. (2002) *Animal Rights: A Very Short Introduction*, Oxford: Oxford University Press.

Descartes, R. (1912) 'Discourse V', in J. Veitch (ed.) *Rene Descartes: A Discourse on Method*, London: Dent.

Dobson, A. (ed.) (2000) *The Green Reader* (3rd edn), London: Unwin Hyman.

Dobson, A. (2000) *Green Political Thought* (3rd edn), London: Unwin Hyman.

Donovan, J. and Adams, C. (eds) (1996) *Beyond Animal Rights: A Feminist Caring Ethic for the Treatment of Animals*, New York: Continuum.

Dowding, K. (1995) 'Model or metaphor? A critical review of the policy network approach', *Political Studies*, 63.

Dworkin, R. (1977) *Taking Rights Seriously*, London: Duckworth.

Ehrlich, P. and A. (1990) 'Extinction', in Regan and Singer, *Animal Rights*.

Evans, E. (1987; first published 1906) *The Criminal Prosecution and Capital Punishment of Animals*, London: Faber and Faber.

FAWC (1982) *Report on the Welfare of Poultry at the Time of Slaughter*.

FAWC (1984) *Report on the Welfare of Livestock (Read Meat Animals) at the Time of Slaughter*.

Finsen, L. and S. (1994) *The Animal Rights Movement in America: From Compassion to Respect*, New York: Twayne.

Fox, M. (1983) 'Philosophy, ecology, animal welfare and the "rights" question', in Miller and Williams, *Ethics and Animals*.

Fox, W. (1984) 'Deep ecology: a new philosophy of our times', *The Ecologist*, 14, 5.

Fox, W. (1995) *Towards a Transpersonal Ecology: Developing New Foundations for Environmentalism*, Totnes: Resurgence.

Francione, G. (1995) *Animals, Property and the Law*, Philadelphia: Temple University Press.

Francione, G. (1996) *Rain Without Thunder: The Ideology of the Animal Rights Movement*, Philadelphia: Temple University Press.

Francione, G. (2000) *Introduction to Animal Rights: Your Child or the Dog*, Philadelphia: Temple University Press.

Fraser, A. and Broom, D. (1990) *Farm Animal Behaviour and Welfare*, London: Balliere Tindall.

French, R. (1975) *Antivivisection and Medical Science in Victorian Society*, Princeton: Princeton University Press.

Frey, R. (1980) *Interests and Rights: The Case Against Animals*, Oxford: Oxford University Press.

Frey, R. (1983) *Rights, Killing and Suffering*, Oxford: Clarendon Press.

Frey, R. (1987) 'Autonomy and the value of animal life', *Monist*, 70.

Frey, R. (2002) 'Ethics, animals and scientific inquiry', in Gluck, J. et al., *Applied Ethics*.

Garner, R. (1994) 'Wildlife conservation and the moral status of animals', *Environmental Politics*, 3, 1.

Garner, R. (1998) *Political Animals: Animal Protection Politics in Britain and the United States*, Basingstoke: Macmillan.

Garner, R. (1999) 'Animal protection and legislators in Britain and the United States', *Journal of Legislative Studies*, 5, 2.

Garner, R. (2000) *Environmental Politics* (2nd edn), Basingstoke: Macmillan.

Garner, R. (2002) 'Political ideology and the legal status of animals', *Animal Law*, 8.

Garner, R. (2003) 'Animals, politics and justice: Rawlsian liberalism and the plight of non-humans', *Environmental Politics*, 12, 2.

Garner, R. (forthcoming) *The Political Theory of Animal Rights*, Manchester: Manchester University Press.

Gilligan, C. (1982) *In a Different Voice*, Cambridge, Mass.: Harvard University Press.

Gluck, J., DiPasquale, T. and Orlans, F. B. (2002) *Applied Ethics in Animal Research*, Indiana: Purdue University Press.

Godlovitch, S., Godlovitch, R. and Harris, J. (eds) (1973) *Animals, Men and Morals*, New York: Taplinger.

Grant, W. (1983) 'The National Farmers Union: the classic case of incorporation', in D. Marsh (ed.), *Pressure Politics*, London: Junction.

Grant, W. (1989) *Pressure Groups, Politics and Democracy in Britain*, Hemel Hempstead: Philip Allan.

Gray, J. (1987) 'The ethics and politics of animal experimentation', in H. Beloff and A. Colman (eds), *Psychological Survey*, Leicester: Leicester University Press.

Greanville, P. and Moss, D. (1985) 'The emerging face of the movement', *Animals' Agenda*, March–April: 36.

Griffin, D. (1992) *Animal Minds*, Chicago: University of Chicago Press.

Hall, R. (1984) *Voiceless Victims*, London: Wildwood House.

Harrison, R. (1964) *Animal Machines*, London: Vincent Stuart.

Henshaw, D. (1989) *Animal Warfare: The Story of the Animal Liberation Front*, London: Fontana.

HMSO (1965) *Report of the Technical Committee to Enquire in the Welfare of Animals kept under Intensive Livestock Husbandry Systems (the Brambell Report)*, Cmnd. 2836.

HMSO (1965a) *Report of the Departmental Committee on Experiments on Animals (the Littlewood Report)*, Cmnd. 2641.

HMSO (2003) *Statistics of Scientific Procedures on Living Animals 2002*, Cmnd. 5886.

Hollands, C. (1980) *Compassion is the Bugler*, Edinburgh: McDonald.

Hollands, C. (1985) 'Animal rights in the political arena', in Singer, *In Defence*.

House of Lords (2002) *Select Committee on Animals in Scientific Procedures*, Vol. 1. Report 16 July.

Humphreys, P. (1989) 'Transport of animals and their welfare', in Blackman et al., *Animal Welfare and the Law*.

Inglehart, R. (1977) *The Silent Revolution: Changing Values and Political Styles Among Western Publics*, Princeton: Princeton University Press.

Jackman, B. (1989) 'Slaughter that shames mankind', *Sunday Times*, 8 October.

Jackson, C. (1989) 'Europe and animal welfare', in Blackman, et al., *Animal Welfare and the Law*.

Jamieson, D. (1985) 'Against zoos', in Singer, *In Defence*.

Jasper J. and Nelkin, D. (1992) *The Animal Rights Crusade: The Growth of a Moral Protest*, New York: Free Press.

Johnson, E. (1983) 'Life, death and animals', in Miller and Williams, *Ethics and Animals*.

Johnson, W. (1990) *The Rose Tinted Menagerie*, London: Blackwell.

Jordan, B. (1987) 'Science grows and beauty dwindles' in McKenna, W., Travers, W. and Wray, J. (eds), *Beyond the Bars*, Wellingborough: Thorsons.

Jordan, G. and Richardson, J. (1987) *Government and Pressure Groups in Britain*, Oxford: Oxford University Press.

Jordan, G. and Maloney, W. (1997) *The Protest Business*, Manchester: Manchester University Press.

Kant, I. (1965) *Metaphysics of Morals*, New York: Bobbs Merrill.

Keane, H. (1998) *Animal Rights: Political and Social Change in Britain Since 1800*, London: Reaktion.

Kheel, M. (1996) 'The liberation of nature: a circular affair', in Donovan and Adams, *Beyond Animal Rights*.

Labour Party (1992) *It's Time to get Britain Working Again*, London.

Leahy, M. (1991) *Against Liberation: Putting Animals into Perspective*, London: Routledge.

Leavitt, E. and Halverson, D. (1985) 'Animal protective organizations and law enforcement agencies', in Animal Welfare Institute, *Animals and Their Legal Rights*.

Leopold, A. (1949) *A Sand County Almanac*, Oxford: Oxford University Press.

Lindblom, C. (1977) *Politics and Markets*, New York: Basic Books.

Linzey, A. (1976) *Animal Rights: A Christian Assessment of Man's Treatment of Animals*, London: SCM Press.

Linzey, A. (1987) *Christianity and the Rights of Animals*, New York: Crossroad.

Locke, J. (1988) *Two Treatises of Government*, Cambridge: Cambridge University Press.

Lowe, P. (1983) 'Values and institutions in the history of British nature conservation', in A. Warren and F. Goldsmith (eds), *Conservation in Perspective*, Chichester: Wiley.

Lowe, P. and Goyder, J. (1983) *Environmental Groups in Politics*, London: Allen & Unwin.

Lukes, S. (1974) *Power: A Radical View*, London: Macmillan.

Lyster, S. (1985) *International Wildlife Law*, Cambridge: Grotius.

MacDonald, M. (1994) *Caught in the Act: The Feldberg Investigation*, Oxford: Jon Carpenter.

Maehle, A. and Trohler, U. (1987) 'Animal experimentation', in Rupke, *Vivisection*.

Magel, C. (1989) *Keyguide to Information Sources in Animal Rights*, Jefferson, N.C.: McFarland.

Marsh, D. and Rhodes, R. (1992) *Policy Networks in British Government*, Oxford: Clarendon Press.

Marsh, D. and Smith, M. (2000) 'Understanding policy networks: towards a dialectical approach', *Political Studies*, 48.

Mason, J. and Singer, P. (1990) *Animal Factories*, New York: Harmony Books.

Mayo, D. (1983) 'Against a scientific justification of animal experiments', in Miller and Williams, *Ethics and Animals*.

McCloskey, H. (1979) 'Moral Rights and Animals', *Inquiry*, 22.

McCloskey, H. (1987) 'The moral case for experimentation on animals', *Monist*, 70, 87.

McKeown, T. (1979) *The Role of Medicine*, Oxford: Oxford University Press.

Midgley, M. (1979) *Beast and Man*, London, Methuen.

Midgley, M. (1983) *Animals and Why They Matter*, Harmondsworth: Penguin.

Miles, S. and Williams, P. (1986) 'Political animals', *Marxism Today*, April.

Miller, H. and Williams W. (1983) *Ethics and Animals*, Clifton, N.J.: Humana Press.

Monagham, R. (1997) 'Animal rights and violent protest', *Terrorism and Political Violence*, 9, 4.

Moore, N. (1987) *The Bird of Time: The Science and Politics of Nature*

Conservation, Cambridge: Cambridge University Press.

Moore Lapper, F. (1971) *Diet for a Small Planet*, London: Ballantine.

Morton, D. (1989) 'The Animals (Scientific Procedures) Act 1986', in D. Blackman, et al., *Animal Welfare*.

Naess (1973) 'The shallow and the deep, long range ecology movement. A summary', *Inquiry*, 16.

Narveson, J. (1987) 'On a Case for Animal Rights', *Monist*, 70.

Nelson, J. A. (1985) 'Recent studies in animal ethics', *American Philosophical Quarterly*, 22, 85.

North, R. (1982) 'Fur flies among the animal lovers', *The Times*, 25 January.

North, R. (1991) 'The way ahead for a crowded planet', *Sunday Times*, 30 June.

Nozick, R. (1974) *Anarchy, State and Utopia*, Oxford: Basil Blackwell.

Olson, M. (1965) *The Logic of Collective Action*, Cambridge, Mass.: Harvard University Press.

Orlans, F. B. (1993) *In the Name of Science: Issues in Responsible Animal Experimentation*, New York: Oxford University Press.

Orlans, F. B. (2002) 'Ethical themes of national regulations governing animal experiments: an international perspective', in Gluck et al., *Appled Ethics*.

Pacheco, A. (1985) 'The Silver Springs' monkeys', in Singer, *In Defence*.

Passmore, J. (1974) *Man's Responsibility for Nature*, London: Duckworth.

Paterson, D. and Ryder, R. (eds) (1979) *Animals' Rights: A Symposium*, Fontwell: Centaur Press.

Paton, W. (1984) *Man and Mice*, Oxford: Oxford University Press.

Pluhar, E. (1995) *Beyond Prejudice: The Moral Significance of Human and Nonhuman Animals*, Durham: Duke University Press.

Porritt, J. and Winner, D. (1988) *The Coming of the Greens*, London: Fontana.

Purdue, D. (1995) 'Hegemonic trips: world trade, intellectual property and biodiversity', *Environmental Politics*, 4, 1.

Rachels, J. (1983) 'Do animals have a right to life?', in Miller and Williams, *Ethics and Animals*.

Rachels, J. (1990) *Created From Animals*, Oxford: Oxford University Press.

Radford, M. (2001) *Animal Welfare Law in Britain*, Oxford: Oxford University Press.

Radway Allen, K. (1980) *Conservation and Management of Whales*, London: Butterworth-Heinemann.

Rawls, J. (1972) *A Theory of Justice*, Oxford: Oxford University Press.

Regan, T. (1975) 'The moral basis of vegetarianism', *Canadian Journal of Philosophy*, 5.

Regan, T. (1982) *All that Dwell Therein*, Berkely: University of California Press.

Regan, T. (1984) *The Case for Animal Rights*, London: Routledge.

Regan, T. (1987) *The Struggle for Animal Rights*, Clark's Summit, PA: International Society for Animal Rights.

Regan, T. (1991) *The Thee Generation: Reflections on the Coming Revolution*, Philadelphia: Temple University Press.

Regan, T. and Singer, P. (1976; 2nd edn 1990) *Animal Rights and Human Obligations*, Englewood Cliffs, NJ: Prentice Hall.

Reitman, J. (1992) *Stolen for Profit*, New York: Pharos.

Regenstein, L. (1985) 'Animal rights, endangered species and human survival', in Singer, *In Defence*.

Rifkin, J. (1992) *Beyond Beef: The Rise and Fall of the Cattle Culture*, Harmondsworth: Penguin.

Ritvo, H. (1987) *The Animal Estate*, Cambridge, Mass.: Harvard University Press.

Robinson, P. (1989) 'The law concerning the protection of wild birds', in Blackman et al., *Animal Welfare and the Law*.

Rodd, R. (1990) *Biology, Ethics and Animals*, Oxford: Clarendon Press.

Rollin, B. (1981) *Animal Rights and Human Morality*, New York: Prometheus.

Rollin, B. (1983) 'The legal and moral bases of animal rights', in Miller and Williams, *Ethics and Animals*.

Rollin, B. (1995) *The Frankenstein Syndrome*, Cambridge: Cambridge University Press.

Rollin, B. (1989) *The Unheeded Cry: Animal Consciousness, Animal Pain and Science*, Oxford: Oxford University Press.

Rosenberger, J. (1990) 'Animal rites', *Village Voice*, 6 March.

Rowan, A. (1989) 'The development of the animal protection movement', *Journal of NIH Research*, November–December 1989.

Rowan, A. (1990) 'Aspects of the sociology and politics of the animal protection movement', *Proceedings of the Fifth Anniversary Conference*, Tufts Center for Animals and Public Policy, March.

Rowlands, M. (1998) *Animal Rights: A Philosophical Defence*, Basingstoke: Macmillan.

Rowlands, M. (2002) *Animals Like Us*, London: Verso.

Rupke, N. (ed.) (1987) *Vivisection in Historical Perspective*, London: Routledge.

Russell, W. and Burch, R. (1959) *The Principles of Humane Experimental Technique*, London: Metheun.

Ryder, R. (1975) *Victims of Science*, London: Davis-Poynter.

Ryder, R. (1989) *Animal Revolution: Changing Attitudes Towards Speciesism*, Oxford: Basil Blackwell.

Ryder, R. (2000) 'Cultures of cruelty', *Guardian*, 1 March.

Salt, H. (1980) *Animals' Rights Considered in Relation to Social Progress* (originally published in 1892) London: Fontwell.

Sapontzis, S. (1987) *Morals, Reason, and Animals*, Philadelphia: Temple University Press.

Scruton, R. (2000) *Animal Rights and Wrongs*, London: Metro.

Self, P. and Storing, H. (1962) *The State and the Farmer*, London: Allen and Unwin.

Serpell, J. (1986) *In the Company of Animals*, Oxford: Oxford University Press.

Sharpe, R. (1988) *The Cruel Deception: The Use of Animals in Medical Research*, Wellingborough: Thorsons.

Shuster, S. (1978) 'The anti-vivisectionists – a critique', *New Scientist*, 12 January 1978.

Singer, P. (1974) *Democracy and Disobedience*, Oxford: Oxford University Press.

Singer, P. (1979) 'Killing humans and killing animals', *Inquiry*, 22.

Singer, P. (1983) *The Expanding Circle: Ethics and Sociobiology*, Oxford: Oxford University Press.

Singer, P. (ed.) (1985) *In Defence of Animals*, Oxford: Blackwell.

Singer, P. (1985a) 'Animal rights and wrongs', *Times Higher Education Supplement*, 29 March.

Singer, P. (1985b) 'Ten years of animal liberation', *New York Review of Books*, 17 January.

Singer, P. (1990) *Animal Liberation* (2nd edn), London: Cape.

Singer, P. (1998) *Ethics into Action: Henry Spira and the Animal Rights Movement*, Lanham, MD: Rowman and Littlefield.

Spencer, C. (1995) *The Heretic's Feast: A History of Vegetarianism*, Hanover: University Press of New England.

Spira, H. (1983) 'Fighting for animal rights', in Miller and Williams, *Ethics and Animals*.

Stevenson, P. (1994) *A Far Cry From Noah*, London: Green Print.

Sweeney, N. (1990) *Animals and Cruelty and Law*, Bristol: Alibi.

Taylor, P. W. (1986) *Respect for Nature: A Theory of Environmental Ethics*, Princeton: Princeton University Press

Tester, K. (1991) *Animals and Society: The Humanity of Animal Rights*, London: Routledge

Thomas, R. (1983) *The Politics of Hunting*, Aldershot: Gower.

Truman, D. (1951) *The Governmental Process*, New York: Knopf.

Todd, P. (1989) 'The Protection of Animals Acts 1911–64', in Blackman et al., *Animal Welfare and the Law*.

Townsend, A. (1976) 'Radical vegetarians', *Australasian Journal of Philosophy*, 57.

Turner, E. (1964) *All Heaven in a Rage*, London: Centaur.

Tuxill, J. (1999) 'Appreciating the Benefits of Plant Biodiversity', in L. Brown, C. Flavin and H. French (eds), *State of the World 1999*, New York: Norton.

Walker, C. and Cannon, G. (1984) *The Food Scandal*, London: Century.

Webster, J. (1994) *Animal Welfare: A Cool Eye Towards Eden*, Oxford: Blackwell.

Wilkins, D. (1997) *Animal Welfare in Europe*, London: Kluwer Law International.

Windeatt, P. (1985) 'They clearly now see the link', in Singer, *In Defence*.

Wise, S. (2000) *Rattling the Cage: Toward Legal Rights to Animals*, Cambridge, Mass.: Perseus Books.

Worcester, B. (1995) 'Scenting dissent', *New Statesman and Society*, 21 April.

Younge, G. (2000) 'Back in the hunt', *Guardian*, 4 October.

Index